CHINESE FAMILY AND KINSHIP

CHINESE FAMILY AND KINSHIP

HUGH D. R. BAKER

Columbia University Press   New York   1979

306.20951
B167
C.2

Published in 1979 in the United States of America
by Columbia University Press

Library of Congress Cataloging in Publication Data

Baker, Hugh D   R
  Chinese family and kinship.

  Bibliography: p.
  Includes index.
  1.   Family—China—History.   2.   Kinship—China—
History.   I.   Title.
HQ684.A15   1979   301.42′0951   78-26724
ISBN   0-231-04768-1

Printed in Great Britain by A. Wheaton & Co. Ltd., Exeter

To my parents
B R B (JP) and Fairy
with love and gratitude

Contents

viii CONTENTS

Table of Figures

Table of Maps

Preface

Kinship was not the only principle of social organization in traditional China, of course, but it was important enough to merit treatment as a full topic in its own right, and I have made no attempt to stray into other fields in this book. For the most part I talk in terms of 'traditional' China, which is a convenient shorthand for 'pre-twentieth century' China. For this reason I have used the past tense in all but the final chapter, sections of which pick up on the titles of previous chapters for ease of reference and comparison with the present.

Much of tradition is still evident in contemporary society, and especially so in Chinese communities outside the People's Republic. Tradition no more stopped dead in 1900 or 1911 than did modernity begin in 1912 or 1949. So, in trying to assess kinship in action I have been able to indulge unrepentantly in chronological sleight-of-hand, using twentieth-century field-work studies to illustrate features of the traditional scene, and using history to back up analysis of more recent times. This is not ideal, but material must be sought where it can be found.

Out of this has emerged, I hope, a clear picture of the family and its place in Chinese society. It is only a *general* picture, however, a basic account of the stock of kinship principles from which the Chinese could draw. I have dealt with rural China, barely mentioning the city, and I have not attempted to point the differences between areas of China or between the various Chinese sub-cultures. Nor have I gone into much detail on the 'mechanics' of family life—ceremonial, division of labour, child-rearing, day-to-day living, and so on. For such details the reader may go to the many sources quoted in the book. I have used quotations freely: first, to show my debt to the ideas of others; and second, as a means of introducing all the major English-language writings on the Chinese family to the attention of the reader new to this field. The quotations in many cases serve to advance the argument of the text; they are not merely for confirmation of points already made.

Despite the constant reference to other writings, this is my own idiosyncratic view of Chinese kinship. I am perhaps open to the criticism, for instance, that I have given too much space to discussion of the lineage: but it seems to me that the lineage brings most sharply into focus the major features of the system. Ancestor worship, too, occupies no small part of the book: again, I feel that the light it throws on kinship organization warrants such attention. It is my hope that with this book as a basis the reader may more readily understand the complexities of detail which he will meet as he goes on to look more deeply into the subject.

I have held mainly to English-language sources but, where Chinese sources have been used, the translations are my own unless otherwise stated. Chinese terms have been kept to a minimum. Romanization is in the official Chinese *Pinyin* system, except where another form is in conventional use (e.g. Mao Tse Tung). And of course I have not interfered with the romanizations used in direct quotations from other authors.

I should like to record my gratitude to Dr James L. Watson and Mrs Rubie S. Watson for their comments on four of the chapters; and to Mr Dick Wilson, editor of the *China Quarterly*, for his advice on Chapter 8. The late Professor Maurice Freedman read and criticized some of the early chapters. No-one working in the field of Chinese kinship can be out of his debt, myself least of all, for I owe gratitude for his teaching, his guidance, and his friendship too.

School of Oriental & African Studies   H.D.R.B.
University of London.
October 1977.

I

The Composition of the Family

The following quotations from different works on China are apparently contradictory, though all are talking of the family in the twentieth century:

> The Kwock and Cheung families are very nearly of equal size, having an estimated 500 to 750 members each, while the smallest unit is Choy with about 200 to 300 members.[1]

> The average size of 5.21 persons per family may be taken as representative.[2]

> The family multiplies as the children grow up and marry. It is not uncommon for the joint household to consist of four or five generations.[3]

Clearly the authors of these statements were using the word 'family' in different ways. But why the confusion? How big was the family?

The confusion seems to have arisen largely through the Chinese belief in an 'ideal family'. The ideal family consisted of some five generations living together as one unit, sharing one common purse and one common stove, and under one family head. The Chinese called this the 'five generation family' or 'five generations co-residing'.

Unfortunately, some Western observers seem to have accepted the ideal as the actual. Indeed, it is not unlikely that many Chinese people also were beguiled by their own culture into seeing the ideal where in fact it little existed: for the truth is that the five generation family was a rarity and was by no means the most common form of the Chinese family.

But this family form is a useful model to bear in mind, for if we accept the ideal form as having been the ultimate aim of all family growth, then instead of looking at the various types of family as unconnected forms which happen to have existed in Chinese society, we may see them all as points in one development cycle. That is, instead of having a number of different family types to describe, we have one family model which was realised to a greater or lesser extent by all Chinese families.

SIMPLE, STEM AND EXTENDED FAMILIES

The family was founded by the marriage of a man and woman, and enlarged by the children to which they gave birth, or which they adopted. In this, often called the *simple* (or *nuclear* or *conjugal*) *family* we recognize precisely the ingredients which make up our own families in the West. At its smallest it consisted of two people, a man and his wife. It expanded according to the fertility of the couple, or perhaps according to their ability to adopt children. It might further expand by the addition of one or more concubines and their children.

But the simple family is only the first point in the cycle. Differences from the Western family begin to show most clearly when we look at what happened to the children on marriage. While some when they married moved out from the parental home to set up new homes of their own and thus to establish new simple families, this was by no means always the case. Daughters, it is true, almost invariably did leave the parental home on marriage, but sons often brought their wives into the family and continued to live with their parents rather than set up new households and new families elsewhere.

The most common instances of this type of family were where an only son brought his wife into the family, and where only one son amongst several did so. When the son and his wife produced children, there was then a three generation family. But of course this kind of family, often called the *stem family*, was limited in duration—sooner or later the parents would die off, leaving behind a simple family once more, composed this time of their son, his wife and children. A variant of this type was found where the parents might live in rotation with the families of their sons, creating a series of temporary stem families.

Between them the simple family and the stem family accounted for a very high percentage of Chinese families. But what if more than one son married and brought wives into the family? Then quite a different kind of group began to emerge. While by definition the simple family and the stem family were bound to be of small size and to prohibit growth, a family which was to grow and follow the road to the ideal must discourage its sons from setting up separate families elsewhere. They must all bring their wives home to the family, and their sons in turn must do the same.

Once a family burst the barrier to expansion which the simple and stem family pattern constituted, there were all manner of possible permutations of size and generation depth which it could attain. It might go on expanding until the death of the parents, when the sons might decide to split the estate and set up separate families. The sons might, on the other hand, continue to stay together after the death of their parents. In some cases fertility in the group might be low, or mortality high, and keep family size down despite its not losing any sons through division of the estate. In others the family might be huge after only three generations or so. All these variants in which in one generation more than one married son was part of the group we can conveniently parcel up in the term *extended family*—and the ultimate extended family was the ideal family.

The simple family was a common factor in each of the other two types, so that either of them might be broken down into component simple families. There was a progression from simple family to ideal family, and a newly married couple was potentially the germ of any of the three types.

POVERTY AND FAMILY SIZE LIMITATION

As we shall see later, the birth of a son was of the greatest importance to a family, not only in order to provide for the parents in their old age, but also in connection with ancestor worship. A daughter being of no help in either direction her birth was not a matter of such joy or importance.

All families, therefore, did their utmost either to beget a son or, if that were impossible, to adopt one. Ideally a family would have more than one son, thus both multiplying the blessings and insuring against accident. The common expression of good wishes 'May you have a hundred sons and a thousand grandsons' may have exaggerated the issue [sic] but it faithfully represented Chinese feelings about the importance of male descendants.

The following quotations are fairly cautious versions of what might be found in almost any description of rural China in the past two centuries:

> It seems safe to conclude that the imperial countryside was 'overpopulated', in the sense that the total amount of cultivated land was not sufficient to give the average peasant adequate means of livelihood.[4]

> The economic forces tending to pauperize the farmer are clear. The extent and seriousness of indebtedness varies throughout the country. In numerous places the owner tends to lose possession of his land to the money lender and, at best, to become a tenant on his own farm. The tenant sells most of his crop immediately after harvest to pay his debts and is almost at once in need of further loans.[5]

For a poor family struggling for survival in such conditions there can have been little hope of raising a large number of sons, and many perhaps would count themselves fortunate if they could raise even one.

It is immediately obvious, then, that wealth or the lack of it was most important in determining family size. The ideal family could not be achieved by the majority for the simple reason that they could not support sufficient children to begin the necessary expansion.

The factors limiting family size were numerous. Some of them, such as a high infant death-rate and a high rate of general mortality, were the direct consequences of under-nourishment, over-work, inability to afford medical care, and other conditions attendant upon poverty. It may even have been that there was a connection between poverty and infertility, so that fewer live children were born to poor parents. In the 1930s it was found that:

> The mortality in childhood and early adult life is exceedingly high, higher than that in every country listed except India . . .

The terrific mortality of the early years of life in China and India is brought out dramatically by the survival figures. In these countries less than 60 per cent of the persons born alive survive the tenth year, while at age 10 in England and Wales and the United States about 90 per cent, and in New Zealand about 95 per cent of those born are still living. One-half of the people born in India scarcely attain their majority and one-half of those born in China die before they are 28 years of age.[6]

Other factors might be called 'indirect consequences' of poverty, in that they were not the physical results of poverty itself, but rather the social results of what Chinese custom dictated should be done in conditions of poverty. Infanticide, for instance, may be called an indirect consequence of poverty, as opposed to the direct consequence represented by, say, the death of a child from malnutrition. Among indirect consequences we can point to the killing, abandonment, selling and out-adoption of children, non-marriage, late marriage, and birth control.

A poor couple who had produced as many children as they could support—perhaps just the one son—might practise total abstention from sexual intercourse in order to guard against further pregnancies. This method of birth control was certainly common among older couples:

Husbands and wives sleep in the same room as long as their sons are not married. After the latter's marriage, some parents continue to sleep in the same room; others do not. After the birth of a grandchild, it is definitely more desirable for the older couple to live in different rooms; it would be considered disgraceful for the older woman to become pregnant after such an event.[7]

Abortion as a form of birth control is reported by some writers.

Despite these practices (and we do not know how common they were) many children were born into families which could not support them. Infanticide was one method of dealing with the problem. It was probably not as widespread or frequently practised a custom as has commonly been supposed, but there is no doubt that it did go on, particularly with regard to girl babies:

Li Tsung-hsi, *chin-shih* of 1847 and governor-general of Kiangsu and Anhwei in the mid-1860s, said of his native Shansi:

I have learned of the prevalence of female infanticide in all parts of Shansi, but particularly in such southern counties as P'ing-ting, Yü-tz'u, etc. The first female birth may sometimes be salvaged with effort, but the subsequent births are usually drowned. There are even those who drown every female baby without keeping any . . .

The poor regarded the practice as an almost legitimate means of maintaining their minimal standard of living and, in any case, as a dire economic necessity.[8]

Drowning was the most common form of infanticide, but there were others, such as smothering and burying alive. Estimates of the extent of the practice vary considerably:

Authorities such as Dr. Dudgeon, Dr. Lockhart, Prof. Giles, Bishop Moule, Dr. Martin and Dr. G. E. Morrison believe it is not more practised than in Europe. On the other hand, Sir J. Barrow stated that in Peking alone 24 infants daily were thrown out to die and were collected by carts at night; Mr. Douglas asserts that in Fukien 20 per cent of the female infants were destroyed; Mr. Michie stated that it was of very common occurrence among the poor; missionaries in Kuangtung have said that in certain districts only one out of three females is allowed to live; parents in those parts are obliged to go to other places to purchase wives for their sons. Places specially mentioned in connection with the crime are Canton, Foochow, Hinghua, Amoy, Tsung-ming, Ningpo, Hankow and Kiangsi province.[9]

Abandoning of children was also resorted to, often with a real hope that they would be saved from death and given a home:

At the prefectural city of Ch'ao Chau, near Swatow, the author saw, outside the walls of the city, a basket hanging against a wall, looking from a distance something like a cradle. A piece of matting was fastened above it, forming a sort of pent-roof to shelter it from the rain and sun. In this basket, is put any baby whom its parents do not care to preserve, and should any charitable person be so disposed, he, or she, may lift out the forsaken infant and take it home. Failing such rescue, the child ultimately meets the fate of so many of the inhabitants of babydom in China.[10]

Babies were often abandoned on the doorsteps of wealthy families or large businesses, inviting the charity of the inmates. In more recent years banks in Hong Kong have been much favoured in this respect. Orphanages did exist, but they tended to come into active life only in response to pressing initiatives of influential men or hard times:

> The effectiveness of orphanages in lessening the incidence of female infanticide varied from place to place and from time to time. An orphanage adequately provided with funds in nineteenth-century Hsiao-Kan county in Hupei was said to have saved the lives of some ten thousand female babies within the first three years of its founding.[11]

Children could be sold. There was a ready market for girls to act as servants, concubines and prostitutes, but parents had first to raise them to an age when they could be useful, and this they could not necessarily afford to do. One nineteenth-century account goes so far as to give the established prices in Peking, so common was the practice:

> At the present day a young girl of ten or twelve is worth, at Peking, from thirty to fifty taels, and young women commonly fetch from two hundred and fifty to three hundred taels. Poverty is the prime cause of the full markets; and especially in times of famine, drought, and pestilence, it is common for men who at other times would shrink with abhorrence from the deed, to sell their wives and daughters to the highest bidders. Gambling is also responsible for much of the poverty which produces this state of things; and in all large towns there are recognized brokers who deal in these human wares.[12]

It was generally understood that a girl sold to be a servant would eventually be found a husband and allowed to marry out of servitude at the expense of her masters. Girls sold as servants were:

> handed over by a poor family against a customary indemnity in money to a well-to-do family who will feed, clothe and house the child until she is of marriageable age, when a husband will be found for her. In return, she works in the household. Her position, however, is better than that of a mere household servant. She eats at the family table and is considered something between a servant and a modest member of the family. Her parents are supposed by custom to be allowed to visit her from time to time, in order to be at ease in their hearts as to the child's fate.
>
> This custom, which prevails in South China, seems to have given rise to a certain amount of abuse . . .[13]

Boys too were sold as servants, though this was much more rare. Once purchased, the boy was likely to remain with his masters throughout his life. He would probably be found a wife by them, but, in contrast to the case of female servants, marriage did not release him from his position. Instead it was likely that his sons also would remain as servants in the same household. A kind of hereditary retainership was thus set up, to be broken sooner or later by manumission or the failure of the fortunes of the master house. The treatment of servants was in general good, relations between master and servant frequently being quite informal and unhampered by social barriers of avoidance or non-communication. Reluctant as parents might have been to part with their children, there was often a better life ahead of the sold than of the sellers.

Infanticide, abandonment and selling were most often practised in the case of daughters. Sons might fall victim to one or another of these methods of family limitation, but they were more likely to be adopted out of the family which could not support them. With high child mortality rates the heirless were common, and adoption necessarily played a most important role. Ideally it was confined to transactions between close agnatically related kin—that is to say, the most favoured kind of adoption was where a man adopted the son of his brother—but in practice regard for the ideal was probably less than nice. An adopted son lost all rights in his natal family in return for full rights in his family of adoption. As with selling, there was a good chance that the son would profit by the move.

The children raised by a family might reasonably expect marriage as their eventual lot. In the case of a girl in particular, it seems that recognition by the parents of the obligation to marry off their daughter was implicit in their raising her to adulthood. The concept of 'spinster' might be said to be alien to traditional Chinese society—indeed there is no separate term for it in Chinese, the usual translation being not 'unmarried woman' but 'girl not yet married', a significant distinction. That the Chinese system of ancestor worship failed to cater for deceased unmarried females is a related fact which need not surprise us. But for very exceptional circumstances, then, grown daughters were invariably married off. A report of a field-study made in the 1930s tells us that in a village of the Yangtze Plain:

> The sex ratio which results [from female infanticide] actually makes it difficult for poorer boys to get a mate. If we take 16 as the lower age limit for marriage, we find that there are 128 marriageable men, or 25 per cent of the total, who are still single. On the other hand there are only 29 women above 16, or 8 per cent of the total, who are unmarried. Not a single woman above 25 is a spinster. But there are still 43 bachelors above 25.[14]

Sons might be raised and not later married. Thus, a poor family which had with difficulty managed to procure a wife for its eldest son might be incapable of financing the wedding of a second son or, indeed, of supporting another wife if it did. In such cases the unmarried sons might continue to live with the family, or they might leave to seek better fortune elsewhere. Under the traditional inheritance pattern a man's estate was divided more or less equally between all his sons. If an already barely economic estate had to be divided in this way, then clearly the shares would be viable for none of the sons. Non-marriage of all but the eldest son, however, meant that it was probably unnecessary to divide the estate, since the third generation must in any case re-unite the shares in one parcel. With the traditional Chinese view of the family as a long-term continuing entity, one may interpret the marrying of only one son as a paring down of the family to a slender thread which had both a chance of survival and the best hope of revival of family fortunes.

Poverty could also delay the marriage of sons while the necessary wealth was gradually built up. The longer the delay the greater the limiting effect on the family, not only because of the more imminent death of the parents, but also because of the reduced reproductive span of the couple whose marriage was delayed, and because of the pile-up effect on younger sons, who were expected to wait their turn for marriage.

Naturally enough the majority of Chinese families were poor and, if poverty implied inability to expand the family, it follows that the simple and stem forms of the family must have been the most common in China. But what of wealthy families? Were they necessarily different in form? We are led on to a series of considerations which are not all economic.

PRO AND CON THE EXTENDED FAMILY

There were both idealistic and practical reasons for advocating the extended family.

On the idealistic side it may be pointed out that the family was seen as the basic unit of society. From at least as early as the fifth century B.C. (that is, about the time of Confucius) there had existed a list of the important relationships by which man's life should be ordered, and family relationships always figured large in this list. In the *Doctrine of the Mean* (*Zhong-yong*), a work traditionally held to have been written by the grandson of Confucius, appears the following:

> There are five universally applicable principles . . . that of the relationship between ruler and minister, that of father and son, of husband and wife, of elder and younger brother, and of friend and friend.

Mencius, another philosopher of the same period, comments:

> There should be affection between father and son, righteous sense of duty between ruler and minister, division of function

between man and wife, stratification between old and young, and good faith between friends.

The list of relationships most commonly found in more modern works is:

1. Ruler/minister
2. Father/son
3. Elder brother/younger brother
4. Husband/wife
5. Friend/friend

Now these Five Human Relationships (*wu-lun*) were arranged in order of priority, and with the exception of the last one were all superior/inferior relationships too; and so they were intended to give guidance as to the correct weight to be put on any relationship. Properly observed there could be no conflict or friction within Chinese society or within the family group, for every member of the family and of society was held tightly in check by the duty and obedience which he owed to another. Properly observed there could be no conflict, because there was no area of human intercourse not covered explicitly or implicitly by one or another of the five clauses.

The order of those priorities dealing with the family was such that the group could continue to grow indefinitely without friction arising between any of its members. Indeed, if the duties and respect required of each member were to be properly observed, then the group *must* continue to grow indefinitely, for it would not be possible to carry out one's duty of service to one's parents, for instance, if one were not living with them.

From the point of view of Confucian political philosophers there was much to be said for the extended family. As the acknowledged basis of Chinese society the family was in any case very important; and it would clearly be socially advantageous if its stability, conservatism, and mutual responsibility could be spread wider through the expanding of the group. From the viewpoint of the individual in society, membership of such an expanded family enabled him to realise an ideal of human relationships which satisfied both his own desire for tangible stability and also the culturally implanted yearning for just such an extended kin group.

We have records showing that 'five generations co-residing' families existed and were applauded at least as far back as the Tang dynasty, over a thousand years ago. But the vehicle which transmitted knowledge of the ideal and which bore the doctrinal influences which made its attainment possible was the written word, and literacy and education were largely confined to the wealthy. So we must expect that even in this idealistic sphere wealth was of some importance.

The practical reasons for advocating the extended family were mainly economic ones.

Again the tradition of equal inheritance between sons must be considered. Whereas in the West great families contrived to preserve whole their estates by a system of primogeniture which prevented younger sons from inheriting land, the Chinese system worked to ensure the rapid breakdown of estates. A large estate divided between x number of sons might yield x number of viable units, but the chances of those x estates eventually dividing up among the succeeding generation into yet more still viable units were less good—unless more land were added each generation (or unless only one son per generation was born) the original estate was reduced to multiple uneconomic parcels in a short space of years.

Let us suppose a comfortably off family of father, mother, three married sons, their wives and children, and let us endow them with a house and an estate of three rice-fields, the fields being of equal size though separated from each other by an hour's walk. Now, on the death of the father, the three sons decide to divide the estate. Since no two fields are ever considered to be of exactly equivalent yield, the three rice-fields will each be divided into three portions—the sons have immediately lost a certain amount of land, for physical divisions must be driven through the fields. Worse, where one plough and one piece of each farm tool were sufficient before, now three of each are required—there is a capital outlay involved. Again, where before it had been perfectly reasonable to walk a few miles to work in one of the fields, now each son is faced with the prospect of a long hike with a heavy plough to work on only a very tiny patch of land at the end of it. And what about the house? That perhaps cannot be divided. One of them must agree either to have the house and take less land than the others, or buy their shares in the house from them, or they must all sell the house and divide the money (or they must try to live together harmoniously despite the economic separation). But with the capital outlay involved in setting up new households and the small size of the share of each son, none of them is able to make a livelihood from his inheritance. An extreme example, perhaps, but hopefully illustrative of the effects of the equal inheritance system.

But the extended family was a case where the estate was not divided, where land and property remained whole, and where the income from them was used for the benefit of the total group:

> In the peasant household all sons who could work went to these markets to seek employment, and no distinction was made between the eldest or youngest son working out of the village. Because the land was to be divided equally between the sons, the eldest was not favored as would have been the case if the inheritance dictated the land revert to him. The sons gave their wages to the household head, who pooled it with the income earned from the harvest.[15]

Land was the basis of family wealth and the most important form of property in traditional China. It had symbolic as well as economic value, and families would relinquish their holdings only when there was no other option for survival left to them:

> Mortgages were more common than sales and were redeemable at any period after the original mortgage so that land need not pass outside the clan for ever. . . . A sixty year old mortgage . . . which was discovered in the land registers when succession was being determined, was honoured by the mortgagees, though grudgingly, the real point at issue being the *amount* of compensation and not the return of the land, as no figure was stated in the original entry.[16]

Let us look at our example family again. The three sons decide that they will not divide the estate, but will carry on as before their father's death, and live and budget as one unit. They are not faced with any extra capital expenditure on house purchase or farming equipment; they do not lose precious land through dividing bunds; at the very busy planting and harvest times they are a sufficiently large labour force that they do not need to hire outside help in order to get the work done; they find that with help from the wives and children just two of them are capable of running the farming side of the estate while sparing the third, who is then able to go to the nearby market town to work in or perhaps open a shop, and so they can diversify and increase the income of the group; they are able to support the education of the brightest of the youngest generation; and so on:

> The group of which Lin Shang-yung was the *chia-chang* [family head] consisted of forty-two persons. In the oldest generation only Lin himself survived. In the second generation the marriage of each of his three sons had led to the formation of as many *fang* [conjugal families]. The first of these had twenty-two members: in addition to the father and mother it included five sons and two daughters, the wife and seven children of the first son, and the wife and four children of the second. The second *fang*—twelve persons in all—consisted of a father, a mother, four sons, four daughters, and the wife and child of the first son. In the third *fang*, with the father and mother there were five young children. The Lin *chia* [family] had established four households, each associated with a part of the estate. There were the buildings and fields that had been obtained (and later expanded) by Shang-yung when he separated from his brother. In an adjoining village . . . the *chia* owned a rice mill, and in yet another nearby settlement it operated a shop selling fertilizers and animal feed. About twenty-five miles to the south, additional land and buildings had been purchased. In the management of all these holdings, a common budget was maintained. Funds and goods were transferred as needed, and expenditure by the manager of a given enterprise was scrutinized by other group members.[17]

With all these economic advantages goes the political advantage of being a large united group vis-à-vis the rest of society—they are much less vulnerable to intimidatory pressures of all kinds.

Both ideally and practically the extended family seems to have immense advantages. Given sufficient wealth to sustain the group, it seems the obvious form for a Chinese family to have taken. Indeed:

> I would suggest that the tendency to diversify was also found

among the peasantry, but was less obvious. Peasants were prone to marry at a later age and have fewer children survive to maturity, so that in many cases available labour must have been absorbed in the cultivation of family lands. Among the very poor, with little or no land, the effort was to obtain minimal subsistence by any means available. But given a land base of some sort, the hope of economic advancement through diversification might enable the poor to rationalize their desire for many sons.[18]

Yet the incidence of extended families was apparently not high even among the comparatively wealthy. We must now look at the divisive as well as the cohesive features involved.

In a nutshell these divisive features could mostly be summed up in popular phrases such as 'human nature' or 'personality clash'. We have already talked a little of the Five Human Relationships and have hinted at their importance for society and family. The more broadly social aspect will be taken up again in a later chapter, but for now let us isolate from the five the three which deal specifically with the family, namely the father/son, elder brother/younger brother, and husband/wife relationships. Each of these is to be taken at face value primarily, but each also may be extended to include a wider group. Thus the father/son relationship may be taken to include the mother/son, father/unmarried daughter and mother/unmarried daughter relationships, while further extension governs the relationship between senior and junior generations. The elder brother/younger brother relationship holds good for the various permutations of brother/unmarried sister, and may be extended to cover the relationship between age and youth, or elder and younger. The husband/wife relationship extends of course to husband/concubine, but also shows the proper relationship of the two sexes.

Remember that all these three relationships are ones of superiority/inferiority, and that they are listed in order of priority. Therefore the pecking-order which results from this is:

1. Generation
2. Age
3. Sex.

Theoretically, then, any one person should know precisely where he stands in the family by referring to this order: there is a watertight chain of relationships which makes clear to whom each owes respect and obedience. We can illustrate this point with a diagrammatic representation of our example family of father, mother, three married sons and their unmarried children, as in Figure 1:

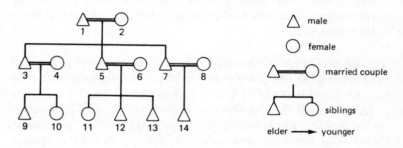

Figure 1. Generation–Age–Sex Hierarchy

Everyone owes obedience to the father (1) because he is superior in Generation, Age and Sex. Everyone but the father owes obedience to the mother (2) because she is senior in Generation and Age. The eldest son's wife (4) owes obedience to her father-in-law and mother-in-law because of Generation and Age, and her allegiance to her husband is only a secondary concern because it is founded on the less important Sex superiority. The youngest son (7) owes obedience to his elder brothers' wives, his elder brothers, his mother and father. The youngest grandson (14) has to obey all the others. The unmarried girls (10) and (11) are only temporary members of the group, because they must eventually be married out of it.

Now, there is a structural conflict involved in this model, because while Generation is clearly superior to Age, it is not the case that Age is clearly superior to Sex. That is to say, (7) can easily see that he owes obedience to (1) and (2) and to (3) and (5), but he may well feel that he is superior to (4) and (6) on Sex grounds, and that these should override the Age consideration. Especially might this be true where (4) and (6) could be wives or concubines considerably younger than himself, though their Age ranking is in accordance with their husbands' not their own ages.

Thus, the heavy emphasis on male superiority in Chinese society already makes for some conflict in this theoretical model.

Let us see what other tensions are built into it. The father/son relationship was so heavily bolstered by ancestor worship, by the legal system, and by the great weight of public opinion that it should have been the least fragile of the bonds dealt with in the *wu-lun*:

> The relationship between father and child has none of the warmth and freedom existing between mother and child. The father's attitude is dignified, even remote; his authority is unquestioned and he expects submissiveness from his sons. . . . When the son is an infant, the father may on rare occasions play with him or take him out. When the boy is old enough to help in the fields, father and son walk together and work together quite often. But by the time the boy reaches the age of fifteen, the father assumes a more dignified attitude toward him and is frequently severe. The son feels uncomfortable with his father and prefers to work with other men in the fields. When father and son do work together, they have nothing to say, and even at home they speak only when there is business to discuss. At street gatherings or in places of amusement, they mutually avoid each other.[19]

Paternal authority was strong. But for this very reason conflict in the later years of the father's life became possible. Used to command and physical superiority, he had to face the fact that his sons would come to dominate the sphere of physical activity, and that they would be less and less willing to accept his judgement as he got older. Mature sons might well respond to an authoritarian father by demanding immediate division of the family estate. The father would be left some land for his own maintenance, but the family as such would be dead. Our example family would have become four separate units, as in Figure 2.

But supposing that the authority of the father and the loyalty of the other members of the family remain strong, then there is a good chance that the group will hold together at least until his death, and even until the death of the mother, should she survive him.

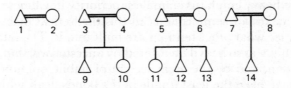

Figure 2. Family Division

If we now kill off the father and mother from our original undivided family, as in Figure 3, we expose several rich sources of conflict in the group. The deaths have removed from the family the first of the priority relationships, namely the Generation one. That is to say, the weightiest of the unifying factors has gone. So the unifying burden falls on the Age and Sex relationships within the now senior generation. We have already indicated that there is a lack of clear priority between these two; but we might here enlarge further on the difficulties at this stage in family development.

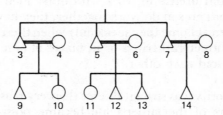

Figure 3. Second Generation Family

To continue to function as a unit there must be co-operation of a high order between the three brothers and their wives. What keeps the brothers together? Natural affection? Well, possibly, but there is often great rivalry and even dislike between Chinese brothers. This rivalry is perhaps exacerbated by a structural paradox: the brothers are economic equals under the inheritance system, but not equals in that the Age relationship gives precedence to the oldest, so that younger brothers may have less control over the joint estate than their shares warrant, this giving rise to resentment and conflict.

If not natural affection, then the elder brother/younger brother relationship of superiority/inferiority must take the strain. But what if youngest brother (7) gets on better with elder brother (5) than with elder brother (3), and will not do as (3) tells him? And what if (3) is stupid and makes wrong decisions on behalf of the family, while (5) and (7) are much brighter and could run things more efficiently? And what if (5) is wilful and insists on not doing as (3) tells him? On the economic side, what if (5) is lazy and does less than his share of the work? What if (7) is extremely hard-working and does more than his share? What if (3) in his role as family head should apportion the income unfairly to each of the three major sections of the family?

The answer to all these questions is that break-up of the group with division of the family property into three seems the most sensible way out of the difficulties. Particularly in the case of economic conflict is fission likely. Since the combined work of the group is improving or maintaining the status and wealth of the family, then we can say that it is much against the economic interests of (3) and (7) to continue to work hard to 'carry' a lazy (5) and his large family, especially as (5) always continues to own potentially one-third of the entire estate. If the estate is divided early, then not only do (3) and (7) work hard for their own immediate benefits, but they also stop improving an estate for the eventual partial benefit of non-contributing (5).

But again, let us say that the brothers do get on well and are able to live together in harmony. Still there are their wives to consider. A wife's only tie with her husband's family is through him, and her future is intimately bound up with his and with her sons'. A wife may be expected, then, to see her husband's interests as paramount in importance, and she may well lack much of the feeling for group unity which her husband and his brothers have.

In this she is perhaps bolstered by control of private funds to which neither her in-laws nor even her husband have access. These funds originally came to her as wedding gifts, and she may guard them as a physical token of the potential and desirable independence of the family composed of herself, her husband and her children:

It is customary and expected that the wife should surrender the 'se-koi' [private money] to her husband when they form their own family unit, even if her finances had previously remained completely independent. Thus, when I would ask men about their wives' money they would claim not to know the total sum involved; but many would add: 'When the family divides I'll find out'. The wife is encouraged to part with her 'private' wealth by the domestic climate preceding partition, which . . . [is] . . . characterized by the unity of husband and wife as they fight for their interests, and those of their children.[20]

Each of the wives of the brothers is likely to be equally narrow-horizoned, and moreover these wives are only very distantly connected to each other through two links of affinity, so that potential conflict between the brothers often might take the form of real conflict between the wives. The presence of children as a cause of friction needs hardly to be spelt out. Hen-pecked husbands are by no means unknown in Chinese society, and the extra strain on the family imposed by such a flouting of the priorities is almost certain to bring about conflict.

Of course, as the next generations come to maturity, the problems become even more acute, for added to the divisive factors already detailed is the lessening degree of relationship between the constituent members of the family. (3), (5) and (7) are full brothers, but (9), (12) and (14) are only first cousins. The Chinese recognised a large body of kin, and tended to stress closeness of relationship by, for example, calling these cousins 'elder brother' or 'younger brother'; but they were still concerned with degree of relationship, and the kinship terminology allowed for the precise distinction between 'brother' and 'cousin' to be made when necessary.

The extended family, then, was wide open to fission, and was in fact a very difficult group to hold together. In a sociological novel one family head:

had wished to maintain the family in an integral unity. The end he desired was considered by all the local world an eminently laudable and virtuous goal. But the internal conflict between the brothers, between the cousins and between the wives of the younger generation had made family life difficult on the scale he envisioned. Strife and complaint were too much for him and he could not help but let the family divide.[21]

Disguised as economic reasons often, the main cause of conflict was the human factor—people just could not get on together. Furthermore, personalities tended to befog the clear structure of family authority, attacking the basis of unity of the family group.

At this point it must be noted that for the sake of clarity we have been taking only very simple instances of family development. There were all kinds of complicating factors which could change the picture. Domestic architecture, for example, varied from area to area of China, and this could have a considerable bearing on forms of residential organization. In parts of Kwangtung province, houses consisted of one single room with a kitchen-cum-washhouse as an extension at the front. Built in terraces row upon row they precluded expansion of single households into complex residential units. Yet in other areas architecture and space allowed expansion into compounds, extensions to a basic unit being built on to form a U-shape, so that residential arrangements could reflect an enlarging family group. Again, there is a complication with Chinese terminology: the word *jia*, which is normally translated as 'family', often seems to refer to the kind of group which is discussed below in Chapter 3 as a 'lineage'. Further, there were ways in which individuals or conjugal families within the extended family could control certain property and funds quite separate from the joint estate. Given the conflicting pulls of idealised family type and practical considerations of everyday living, and given subcultural diversity throughout China, deviations from the common pattern must be expected.

MALE VERSUS FEMALE

There is one aspect of family organization which the reader will no doubt have begun the understand for himself: the Chinese kinship system heavily stressed the importance of the male and of relationships traced through the male.

Women were theoretically of little import. They were necessary for the reproduction of the species, and in most cases for their labour in the home, but in both ways they were considered to be there to serve the male and the male principle. In classical thought they were considered to be minors throughout their lives, subject first of all to the men of the family into which they were born, then on marriage to the men of their husband's family, and finally on widowhood to their sons. These were known as the 'three obeyings' of women, and seem to have been expressed first in the *Yi-li*, a Confucian classic some two thousand years old. Even in death the fate of the woman's soul was dependent upon its worship by her descendants through males.

In fact, of course, women could be much more significant than the above would seem to indicate. China has had an Empress, indeed, and the formidable Empress Dowager towered over the decline of the last Imperial dynasty. Again:

> At one point in the family cycle a widow might find herself the most senior member alive and in reality (as well as for the purposes of government registration) assume control of the family's estate and affairs in general. Indeed, widowhood was paradoxically a great opportunity afforded to some women in Chinese society. Unless they chose to live in sisterhoods . . . widowhood was their only chance of exercising supreme authority over adults. In the nature of things, the period of this uncharacteristic mastery was not likely to last long, but while it endured the perpetual jural minor of her society could in fact enjoy the fruits of domestic power.[22]

Accidents of fate and personalities could upset theories; but we must accept that it was normally only the strong personality of a woman which could raise her above her allotted status.

Surname was passed on down the male line. Just as in Western society, children took the surname of their father not of their mother. There was a possibility of a son taking his mother's surname, but this deviant form, resorted to usually only in extreme circumstances, worked in fact to bolster the mother's family group not the mother herself.

The basic family was a group of males which in order to reproduce itself imported brides from elsewhere and, since it was primarily a male group, it did not hesitate of course to export its own females (its daughters) elsewhere as brides. The family needed women in order to beget children, but its own women, with whom it was prevented from marrying, had to be got rid of in marriage as they were in the last analysis not part of the group. The normal pattern was for a married couple to live in the village of (if not the home of) the husband's parents.

Inheritance followed the male line. While sons inherited equal shares of their father's estate, daughters could normally inherit no land or property or immovable goods at all. They might be said to have inherited some movable property in that they took with them some goods when they were married, but they did not share significantly in their parents' estate.

There was a huge imbalance in the number of people actively recognised as kin on the maternal and paternal sides of the family. There existed a large spread of kinship terms for the father's side, and the individual recognised as close kin all the members of the group descended through males from his great-great-grandfather out to his third cousin—and for each of these many relationships there was a distinctive kinship term. On the mother's side, however, the individual was concerned with only a very few people as kin, the number of specific kinship terms was smaller, and there was little importance attached to kin more distant than the mother's brothers. The following examples of the imbalance will perhaps help to explain this better.

First: a man could not marry anyone of the same surname as himself, since it was assumed that all holders of a given surname must somehow be related to each other. This assumption was manifestly absurd—it is known for instance that the common surname *Li* was conferred upon families as an honour by a Tang dynasty emperor, so that the present-day Li surnames spring from many different stocks. Again, there are two surnames both pronounced Wang in the Cantonese dialect, and the Cantonese Wangs of the two surnames would not intermarry: however, the same two surnames in the Peking dialect are pronounced differently—one is Wang and the other Hwang—so that in the north of China the two surnames did intermarry. Even where marriage to someone of the same surname was not so seriously disapproved of, it was still the case that marriage to a girl related within that large group descended from the great-great-grandfather was considered highly improper. On the other hand, and this is where the imbalance shows, it was perfectly possible for a man to marry his first cousin on the mother's side. Marriage to the daughter of one's father's sister (also of course a first cousin) was possible because the bride would have a different surname, but it seems to have been rare.

Second: there were quite distinct kin terms for one's father's elder brother and his younger brother, and their wives were similarly distinguished. But on the mother's side, where Age was not important, there was no distinction between elder and younger brother—both were merely called 'maternal uncle'.

Third: so heavily was relationship through males emphasized that heredity was supposedly affected by it too. Thus in the famous 18th-century novel, the *Hong Lou Meng* (The Dream of the Red Chamber), there is a delightful passage where the old grandmother has her daughter's beautiful daughter described to her in the following terms:

> Her whole bearing, madam, is such that she seems to be not a granddaughter on your daughter's side, but rather your granddaughter by your son.

*   *   *

The family was a residential and economic unit composed of males. In order to reproduce itself it was forced to import women as brides, and it disposed of females born to it by marrying them off to other families. It laid heavy stress on relationships through males, and tended to play down those through females, while there was a concomitant stress on the importance of men as opposed to women. Relationships were differentiated according to Generation and Age, and the attempt was made to reduce the importance and disruptive effect of the necessary imported women by subordinating the Sex relationship.

The basic family of man, wife and unmarried children could be built on until it was several generations deep, with five generations probably being the maximum. Expansion depended mainly on the wealth of the family, poverty tending to preclude expansion beyond the simple or stem family level. It broke up at the point where the estate was divided between the male descendants of the founder, and where it ceased to be a single economic unit. The point at which it broke up was determined largely by personality factors.

The role of the imported women in precipitating conflict and fission was important, but again wealth was a significant factor. Among the poor, where a wife was expected to work hard for the family, it was likely that she would be in a stronger position as an individual than among the rich, where she contributed no labour to the family and where she was easily replaceable by concubines or (more rarely) through divorce. Among the poor there was, then, more likelihood that women would contribute heavily to the pressures for fission, and hence poor families were much more likely to be organized on a simple or stem family basis.

The economic factor was important in allowing expansion of the family and in holding it together, but it could also be an important cause of fission. There must always have been the problem for the individual of whether he would gain more by staying in the family or by seceding from it. The wealthier the family the greater the chances of its remaining intact, not only because it could control its women better and because its members were better educated and more deeply imbued with Confucian morals, but also because:

> Among the rich and the influential, it is reasonable to assume, possible alienation from a source of power would weigh with a man in his decision to press for a division of the household.[23]

All Chinese families could theoretically achieve the ideal, but for the vast majority it could be less than a dream. For some it was partially realisable. For a very few it was achieved. We might say that while not all wealthy families were ideal families, almost all ideal families were wealthy. Eventually even the ideal family must break up through sheer unwieldiness, through the collapse of its financial resources, through outgrowing its accommodation, or through the distance of the kinship ties which succeeding generations made greater.

2

The Individual and the Family

THE CONTINUUM OF DESCENT

In Chapter 1 we said that the Chinese saw the family as the basic unit of society, and we touched on the important role which Confucian philosophers gave to it. We must now explore this idea further and see just how far the life of the individual was dominated by his family.

It is perhaps not unreasonable to say that in the West we see the family as an institution which exists in large part to provide an environment in which the individual can be conveniently raised and trained to go out into the world as a full member of society. An indication of the validity of this notion is the break-up of the family when the children reach adulthood. But the emphasis in the traditional Chinese situation was reversed—it was not the family which existed in order to support the individual, but rather the individual who existed in order to continue the family.

At this point we may consider an idea which will help to throw light on Chinese attitudes, even if in itself it is rather far-fetched; and that is the idea that there is an underlying assumption in Chinese thinking on the family that there is such a thing as a 'Continuum of Descent'. By this I mean simply that Descent is a unity, a rope which began somewhere back in the remote past, and which stretches on to the infinite future. The rope at any one time may be thicker or thinner according to the number of strands (families) or fibres (male individuals) which exist, but so long as one fibre remains the rope is there. The fibres at any one point are not just fibres, they are the representatives of the rope as a whole. That is, the individual alive is the personification of all his forebears and of all his descendants yet unborn. He exists by

26

virtue of his ancestors, and his descendants exist only through him: and we shall see later that we can treat these statements vice versa with almost equal validity. To continue our crude analogy, the rope stretches from Infinity to Infinity passing over a razor which is the Present. If the rope is cut, both ends fall away from the middle and the rope is no more. If the man alive now dies

Figure 4. The Continuum of Descent

without heir, the whole continuum of ancestors and unborn descendants dies with him. In short, the individual alive now is the manifestation of his whole Continuum of Descent. His existence as an individual is necessary but insignificant beside his existence as the representative of the whole:

> Life must go on. The generations stretch back thousands of years to the great ancestor parents. They stretch for thousands of years into the future, generation upon generation. Seen in proportion to this great array, the individual is but a small thing. But on the other hand no individual can drop out. Each is a link in the great chain. No one can drop out without breaking the chain.[1]

To say that the individual was dominated by the family, then, is another way of saying that the individual was dominated by his Continuum of Descent—but it happens that 'family' is a concept representative of the Continuum which we can more easily grasp. We can now see that it makes great sense that the actions of the individual in Chinese society were geared to the requirements of the family. In a way the individual *was* the family, just as he *was* his own ancestors and his own descendants. He received his descent and his body from his parents and he held them in trust for his sons—they were not his to dispose of lightly:

> The most rigorous of the practices of filial piety was connected with the same ideas: a pious son had to preserve his body intact. 'He does not bind himself to death by a bond of

friendship'; 'he avoids climbing to great heights, he avoids going near precipices, he avoids cursing or laughing incautiously; he avoids moving in the darkness; he avoids climbing up steep slopes: he fears to dishonour his parents!' A sage who hurt his foot remained sad even when he was cured; this is the reason why: 'what makes up a man is given to him by his parents in a state of perfect wholeness: if he gives it back to them in the same state, one can say that he is a pious son. . . . A good son does not move a foot, does not say a word without heeding the duties of filial piety; he takes the main roads and never the byways: he goes by boat and never swims; he has not the boldness to expose to danger the body he has received from his parents'.[2]

The *Xiao Jing* (*Classic of Filial Piety*), written some two thousand years ago, stated quite simply:

It is the first principle of filial piety that you dare not injure your body, limbs, hair or skin, which you receive from your father and mother.

ENTERING THE FAMILY

Having justified the ascendancy of the family over the individual in this rather high-flown way, we can now come down to earth and look at the life cycle of the individual in the family. We shall deal first with the men, and (appropriately in the Chinese context) relegate discussion of the women to second place.

The birth of a son was clearly of great importance to the family. Here was the means for perpetuation of the group, the best guarantee of a future existence for the parents. But the hold on life of young babies is precarious, and parents did not dare to consider the son truly alive until he was thirty days old. Only then did he receive a name. The naming was done at the feast which the parents gave to announce their good fortune to society, the feast being called the Full Month Feast.

Sometimes he would not be given a normal name:

A guest of the celebrated eleventh-century writer Ou-yang Hsiu, having just learnt that one of the children in the family was called *Brother Monk*, expressed his astonishment. 'How', he said jokingly to the great scholar, 'how could you have given such a name to your son, you whose feelings about Buddhism are so well known?'—'But', replied the other, laughing, 'is it not customary in order to protect children as they grow up . . . to give them childhood names that are despicable, such as *dog, sheep, horse?*'[3]

Another way of fooling malign influences was to give the boy a girl's name:

The following is the reason of such appellations. People imagine that by using a little cunning and trickery, they may succeed in deceiving the wily elves, who seek to injure male children, but care little to molest girls or animals. To put them on a false track, the name of an animal or of a girl is given to the new-born male child, whom one wishes to protect from their vexatious pursuits. Hearing him called by these names, they are led to believe that he is indeed a little animal, or at most a girl, and will thus abandon the idea of cutting short his life.[4]

Some men even grew to adulthood without losing this name.

A Chinese in the course of his life could have many names, so many that scholars have devoted much time to compiling lists of the various names behind which historical characters have sheltered to the confusion of posterity. For example, a man could have his *milk name*, given to him at the Full Month Feast; his *book name*, given by his teacher when he started his schooling; his *style*, a name which he took when he was married; his *other style*, by which he was known to his more formal acquaintances; one or more *pen names* if he wrote; an *official name* if he had official rank; and probably a *nick-name*, since the Chinese are very fond of these. Throughout all this only the *surname* remained constant.

Two significant points should be made here. The first is that the surname, being very much in the family sphere, was considered highly important. The Chinese contrived to make a great deal of social organization hang on the surname, as we shall see later on. And it is entirely in keeping with this that surnames were placed before personal names, so that a Chinese name was (and is) always given in the order SMITH John Henry, and never John Henry SMITH. The second point is that the major personal name which a man carried was that by which he would come to be known to posterity—his so-called *posthumous name*. Customs differed from place to place in China, but more often than not this name seems to have been in fact the milk name. In any case, the name will have been given to the man not by himself, as happened with the style, for instance, nor by friends, as with the nick-name, but by the family: and this important name which the individual received was often not 'just a name', but rather a name which fitted into a family and wider system of names, and which put the man firmly in his place as a member of a particular generation. As an example, in one family of five sons which I know, a *generation name* meaning 'to govern' has been adopted. Each of the five sons carries the word 'to govern' as part of his personal name, and the other part consists of a compass point. Thus, the five sons are known as:

Wang Govern the East
Wang Govern the West
Wang Govern the South
Wang Govern the North
Wang Govern the Centre.

(Luckily for this family, the Chinese cardinal points include the Centre, otherwise there might have been difficulty with naming the fifth son.) Clearly then, under this system the individual did not even receive his name in his own right, as it were, but only as part of the group. Even better illustrative of the subordination of the individual in this way is the fact that often the generation names were determined many generations in advance—not even the parents had a choice in the naming of the son:

The rule to use the same code word for all sons of one generation of one family branch is widely spread, and such families usually have a poem consisting of ten, twelve, twenty, or twenty-four words which every older member of the family knows by heart. Each word of the poem is the code word for the children of one generation. This means that if our man Wang Ching-li is visited by a Mr Wang he will first try to find out whether that guest belongs to the same family . . . Mr Wang Ching-li then will ask Mr Wang for his personal name. . . . If

the name contained the code word, the host would immediately know whether the guest belonged to a generation
higher than he himself (in this case he would address him as an
uncle or granduncle, even if by age he was still young) or to his
own generation (in this case he would treat him as an older or
younger cousin). If there should still be a doubt, the host could
ask the name of the father of the guest; the father should have
the code word for the next earlier generation in his name.[5]

From the beginning, then, the individual's role as the filler of a
predetermined slot in the family was stressed. But what if no son
were born to fill the slot? The answer was given in the previous
chapter—adoption. If at all possible an heirless family would
adopt a son, and the next best thing to a son of one's own was
'another fibre of the same rope', preferably a son of the husband's
brother. Once adopted, this son slotted in in just the same way as
a son born to the family. Chinese genealogical charts abound
with juggling of sons from strand to strand of the rope.

BIRTHDAYS

When a child was born, the exact hour, day, month and year of
birth were carefully recorded in a standard form of eight
characters known as the *ba-zi*. They were used for fortune-telling,
and were thought to be especially important in ascertaining the
likely success of a marriage, the two sets of *ba-zi* being required to
harmonize according to set rules.

By contrast birthday anniversaries generally had little significance in Chinese society. The individual might be pleased, sad, or
indifferent about the fact that he has now lived for a full twelve
years where yesterday he had not, but the family feels nothing—
the rest of them are a day older too, and no change in
relationships within the group has occurred.

In fact, the Chinese added a year onto his age not on his
birthday but at Chinese New Year, and since everyone else did so
at the same time there was no cause to celebrate as an individual:

New Year is everybody's birthday, as it is from that date that
age is reckoned, regardless of the actual day the individual first
saw the light. Once that morning dawns every man, woman,
and child is a year older. Part of the celebrations of the festival

consist in firing crackers in honour of the domestic animals and grains, on which man depends for subsistence. The first of the year is the birthday of the chickens, the second of the dogs, third pigs, fourth ducks, fifth oxen, sixth horses, whilst on the seventh there is a universal birthday of mankind. . . . It is lucky to visit relations on the Horses' birthday, but on the universal day of mankind one should stay at home and eat red beans, to the number of seven for a man and fourteen for a woman.[6]

This practice could lead to some rather odd results. A Chinese was considered to be one *sui* old when born. If he were born on the last day of the year, he added a year to his age the next day, so that he was two *sui* old, his Western counterpart being only one day old. To complicate the reckoning the Chinese lunar year could have as few as 354 days, so that it was possible for a Chinese age calculated in *sui* to differ by as much as three from age calculated as completed years of life as in the Western system.

There was once a celebration of something akin to our own moribund 'coming-of-age'. Boys were 'capped' at the age of twenty, and girls went through a ceremonial putting in of hairpins at fifteen, but in recent centuries the ceremonies survived only as a minor ritual incorporated into the immediate preparations for marriage.

For the young at least birthdays were of no great moment, and this points again to the playing down of the individual vis-à-vis the family.

BETROTHAL AND MARRIAGE

After the Full Month Feast the next important ceremonies for the individual were in fact betrothal and marriage. Here again it was the family which controlled the individual, for marriage was arranged for the individual, not left to his own free choice dependent on the vagaries of 'love'. It was the parents, grandparents or perhaps maternal uncles of the man who decided when he should get married and to whom. Frequently he was not consulted at all, and might only be informed of his impending marriage shortly before it took place, and after the arrangements had been made. The hero of *The Dream of the Red*

Chamber was put through a marriage ceremony by his family, and only discovered that it was not to the girl of his choice that he was wed when it came to the unveiling after the ceremony. Many men had not even seen their bride until the wedding was over:

> Critics of China condemn the custom of keeping the couple apart until after the wedding. They charge that this ignorance of one another is the cause of many marital failures and tragedies . . . and without love no marriage can be successful. According to the writer's careful observation, this is only partially true. The young couple's lack of knowledge of one another may make an early adjustment difficult, but it does not prevent successful marriage. When a husband and wife have worked together, raised children together, tried to build up the prosperity of the family, shared happiness and sorrow, they feel that they have had a successful marriage, be it romantic or not. . . . A marriage based on mutual attraction between young people of different standards and ways of thought often calls for greater mutual adaptation than in the case of the traditional Chinese marriage, which is arranged by the parents but in which the parties concerned know exactly what is expected of them, and have similar traditions and ambitions.[7]

Once more, given the emphasis on family importance, it is fitting that the individual should not be allowed to choose his mate. Free choice would imply a strong partiality of the husband for his wife, and this would mean that Sex considerations might impinge on Generation and Age considerations, resulting in the individual giving weight to the wrong relationship as far as the family was concerned. How much better for the family to select the bride—the husband then was less likely to get his priorities wrong. No matter that the husband found that he did not like his wife much—he and she were there to continue the family, not to like each other. In a very real sense the husband/wife tie was not one of affection (though affection could and often did arise between them) but of duty. The family required a daughter-in-law in order to continue the line and in order to help out with the household chores. If in the process the family could forge a link with another family of influence or wealth or other attraction so much the better. A young man would not necessarily have the judgement to choose the appropriate spouse for the family—let the experienced family head do it for him.

Three examples of the role of the family in marriage should suffice to drive home the point we are making. The first is that, since individual choice was not allowed, there was no need for the family to wait until a son was of marriageable age before selecting a spouse for him. In some cases betrothals were made even before the birth of the couple, two families agreeing that should one have a son and the other a daughter they would be betrothed and eventually married. The following case is not so extreme, but clearly takes no account of the desires of the individuals:

> As soon as a son was born, the family began to think about his betrothal, which could be contracted as soon as the child had passed its first New Year's Day. Marriage contracts were seldom confirmed before a boy was five, however, and most betrothals occurred at the age of ten or eleven, by which time it was expected that such matters would be settled. The mother and father discussed the problem, reviewing all the families in neighbouring villages with unmarried daughters fitting the prescribed rules of preference. . . . In any event, the qualifications of family were primary and those of the individuals secondary.[8]

The second example deals not with betrothal but with the wedding ceremony itself. In the West the ceremony is witnessed by the Church and/or State, but in traditional China the wedding took place in the home of the groom, and a major part of the ceremony consisted of the worship by the couple of the groom's ancestors, and the offering of food and drink to the elders of his family:

> The bridal pair are conducted to the ancestral hall, where they prostrate themselves before the altar on which the ancestral tablets are arranged. Heaven and Earth, and the gods of the principal doors of the house, and the parents [of the bride-groom] are the next objects of their worship. A further act of

homage, which consists in pouring out drink-offerings to the ancestors of the family, having been duly performed by the bridegroom only, the happy couple are escorted to the bridal chamber.[9]

The third example points most clearly the relative un-importance of the individual. It happened from time to time, of course, that a son died while betrothed but yet unmarried. In such cases it was possible for his family to perform a 'ghost marriage', wedding the fiancée to the spirit of the dead son, thereby securing for the family the services of the bride to help in the house, and at the same time making it possible for the bride to adopt a son and bring him up to continue the family line, just as would have happened perhaps if her prospective husband had lived. The desire to have practical support for the parents in their old age was probably as much a factor in this arrangement as was the need for provision of spiritual and ancestral comforts for the son. The son's place at the wedding ceremony was taken by his ancestor tablet or by a white cockerel. This latter substitute could also be used when a living but absent son took a bride, a fairly common procedure in emigrant areas of China.

Concubinage was one answer to the problem of barrenness in a wife. For the wealthy it was often a status symbol; for the poor it was usually an economic impossibility: for those trapped in an inimical arranged marriage it could be an escape. A man could have as many concubines as he could afford, desire or tolerate, and he could choose them himself:

Mr Lin did not hesitate to admit true love for his first concubine whom, it is said, he took with the approval of both his own and his wife's family in a ceremony which did not differ from that of his first marriage except that the concubine had to serve tea to his wife. He had paid a great deal of rice for the girl, who was sixteen. The two women, at least in the beginning, had different rooms in the same house and were friendly. Asked if they ever fought, he answered, 'How could they, they had too much to do in order to eat and clothe themselves.' Mr Lin pointed out that in the place where he lived, many men had concubines without suffering from domestic troubles, while in other cases the wives were always slapping newcomers. Asked what would happen if a concubine slapped a wife, he said that he did not think that would happen, but if she did people would not like it.[10]

Both custom and law required that the first wife be treated as superior to a concubine:

He who degrades his wife to the position of a concubine shall be liable to 100 strokes. He who raises his concubine to the position of wife while the wife is alive shall be liable to 90 strokes.[11]

Most concubines were taken with less ceremony than Mr Lin's in the above example, though it was normal for there to be some form of symbolic deference to the wife, such as the offering of tea or, in one area, crawling through the wife's straddled legs. Concubines were protected by incest law from abuse by other males of the family, and their position was legally regularised in other ways too. By custom the sons of a concubine usually had the same equal rights of inheritance with the sons of a wife. They were expected to treat the wife as a mother, and she could expect their ritual services after her death. For this reason, and because hostility on her part might anger her husband to the point of repudiating her, a barren wife might actively welcome her husband's taking of a concubine.

We might note in passing that resort to prostitutes was another means of escape from inimical marriage. It was neither uncommon nor considered particularly reprehensible, especially in and near large towns or cities:

If reproduction is confined to the family, the same is not so generally true of sexual satisfaction. A large number of the young men of my acquaintance, including gentlemen, young clerks and merchants, had experienced sexual intercourse before marriage. Some of them, though married, occasionally visited prostitutes when travelling to Nanking or Shanghai. . . . There was one man who had been a merry gentleman with a local reputation as a poet and smoker of opium. His nephew relates that upon the death of his wife, this man had been plunged into utter melancholy, which threatened to see him waste away. The father of my informant acted as go-between and went to Ch'uen-chiao, a nearby county seat, where he arranged for the service of a professional prostitute. The melancholy man was taken to Ch'uen-chiao, where he lived with the girl for a short time. The affair was paid for by a coalition of friends and relatives, and a swift recovery was said to have been achieved.[12]

THE AGED AND THE FAMILY HEAD

As he got older and his seniors died off, so the man gradually became more and more powerful in the family. It was in the later years of his life that the individual might begin to celebrate his birthday, particularly at certain ages which local custom decreed were more important. In general these ages seem to have been 51, 61, 71 and 81, but for the man who had attained a position such as family head, that is the senior male by Generation and Age in the family, each birthday might well be the occasion of family ceremonial. Again, the point should be made that such a man was important by virtue of his position, and not really in his own right as an individual.

The family head had a great deal of power over the other members of the group:

> The Father or senior male ascendant has control over his sons, his grandsons and their wives as well as over hired servants and slaves. Municipal law does not greatly concern itself with what takes place within the domestic forum or family group; the head has certain discretionary powers, and unless these powers are grossly abused it will not interfere. In the Father is vested all the family property, and he alone can dispose of it.[13]

Of course the family head did not *own* the family property, it was not his to own; it belonged to the family and he was merely chief trustee. Despite this, the author of the book from which the above is quoted goes on to point out that:

> There appears to be practically no limit to the extent to which a man may dispose of or squander his property during his lifetime. In this there is a logical inconsistency. In the Roman

Law, where, as here, the head of a family was considered as forming in some sort, with those under him, an undivided unity owning the property in common, the next of kin could, by imposing a *curator*, restrain a prodigal or spendthrift from wasting his patrimony.[14]

The inconsistency surely lies in the fact that the basis of family order, the Generation–Age–Sex hierarchy, worked to give the family head virtually absolute power, a power reinforced by the law; but the sanctions which restrained that power were almost entirely confined to the religious sphere without secular backing. We shall be looking at the religious aspect of the family in due course, but we should meanwhile not be misled into thinking that, because there was no secular power to restrain them, large numbers of family heads were prodigals.

In any case there was one natural factor which exerted an opposing force to the power of the family head, and that was his surrendering to the advance of age. The older he became, the less physically capable he was, and physical superiority gradually passed to his son or sons. Lip service to the authority of old age was always paid, but in practice much moral authority tended to follow in the footprints of physical strength, particularly in that majority of families which were engaged in agriculture:

> The father's authority in the fields, now that he does not work there, is considerably lessened. He has lost his role in business transactions because he is too old to take the farm products to the market town and deal directly with the dealers. To a certain extent, his importance in relations with the neighbours is diminished, because people find that he is no longer the real authority and that his position as family head is more nominal than real, although he is still respected by all the household. His wife must see to it that he is well fed, well clothed, and well cared for. He preserves also the privilege of venting his anger upon any member of the family, except his daughters-in-law. Nevertheless, he sometimes recognizes his real position . . .[15]

Care of the aged was the responsibility of their sons:

When the family property was divided equally among the

sons, a portion was set aside for supporting the aged parents. This was the custom of *yang-lao-ti* ['land to support the aged']. If the household head had died and only his widow survived, land amounting to 2 or 5 mow, and sometimes as much as 10 mow, was so provided. This land could be leased to other peasants, but the rent was used to support the aged parent. This land was not to be mortgaged or sold until both parents died, and only then was it to be sold to pay for funeral expenses. Any remaining land was divided between the sons. If the land was not leased while the parents lived, one of the sons farmed it and divided the produce between the sons caring for the aged couple.[16]

DEATH

The Chinese recognized three 'great events' in the life of the individual—his birth, his marriage and his death. We have seen how closely interested in birth and marriage the family was: it was no less so with death.

The deceased was briefly remembered as an individual, but in the funeral and mourning the accent was on the family and its continuance. His funeral was made the occasion for a display of family wealth and strength:

Poverty and death are haunting spectres of the poor. They roam through the village and inspire fear that is not physical but social.

It is not that the villager fears death; his belief in Fate relieves him of that worry. But to think of his parent drawing near to the time of departure without adequate funds for proper rites and burial,—this is a real fear. To fail in the provision of rites, feasts, coffin, and funeral would be conduct the most unfilial and condemned by social opinion. The family would be disgraced and the prestige of the village lowered in the estimation of the regional community, so far as gossip would extend on the matter.[17]

The dead were buried near their homes, either in waste land or, where there was none, in the fields:

The quick destruction of human corpses having, since very ancient times, been odious to the Chinese as imperiling the happiness and safety of the living, while their preservation in the ground was always esteemed by them as the highest duty prescribed by filial piety, it must appear a strange thing, that that very same people has for many centuries much practised cremation. . . . Cremation was in the first place largely practised with the Buddhist monkhood, from which it passed over to the laity, assuming for a long time considerable proportions. But in a subsequent period of general abatement of the influence of the Church cremation fell a prey to the general odium, so that at the present day it hardly occurs anywhere, except within the pales of Buddhist monastic life.[18]

As far as length of mourning time and degree of mourning dress worn were concerned, these depended on the degree of relationship which the survivors had with the dead, not on the degree of affection which they bore him. He made no will, for he had no property of his own to bequeath. Of course, there was a personal, sentimental side to the remembrance of the dead, just as there was in the treatment of the living, but the dead man was also something of a cipher, an 'ancestor', to be used by the family as a ritual prop, a religious symbol reinforcing family unity. His place in the family was filled by another—the razor had moved along the rope to another fibre.

THE WOMAN AND THE FAMILY

The general remarks we have made about the life of the male vis-à-vis his family do not hold good for the female. She started life at a disadvantage and received quite different treatment throughout it. For comparison we shall match topic for topic her life with that already given for the male.

Her birth was attended by little of the rejoicing which surrounded that of a son. There was a greater chance of her being killed at birth than the son (though we should avoid exaggerating the incidence of infanticide), and a much greater risk of being sold out of the family. She was unlikely to be wanted in adoption, and she was unlikely to be honoured with a Full Month Feast.

A girl had no proliferation of names: her milk name sufficed. When she married, she tended to lose even that, for she was generally known by her husband's surname, or more formally by her own surname prefixed by her husband's, or by a kinship term which placed her firmly in a family-determined slot, or even in due course by such a name as 'mother of —— (whatever her son's name was)'. Her one claim to individuality might be a nickname.

Her parents might well bring her up with some reluctance—in the southeast of China, for instance, the Cantonese and Hokkiens referred to their daughters as 'goods on which one loses one's capital', the point being that it cost money and effort to raise and train a girl only for all the investment to be handed over to her husband's family when she married. The girl began to share in the housework and baby-minding responsibilities at a very young age, while her brothers were allowed a much longer, much freer childhood. The boy went to school if he were fortunate, but girls rarely had such an opportunity and were for the most part condemned to illiteracy. The whole training of a daughter by her family was aimed at fitting her to be a wife, mother and worker for another family.

Many girls were subjected to foot-binding:

The foot became so compressed that the woman usually hobbled about with difficulty or had to lean on a wall, cane, or another person for support. One result of this virtual crippling, especially severe among upper-class ladies, was to confine women to the boudoir. They were thus physically prevented from moving about freely and unchaperoned and were rendered immune from the social disease of conjugal infidelity . . .

Another reason why this custom survived the vicissitudes of a millennium of history was its profound appeal to the Chinese male. . . . The sexual appeal of footbinding to the Chinese male was never questioned. Those in favour of abolition condemned the tiny foot as lewd and lascivious, because it led man astray and prevented him from fulfilling his social responsibilities.[19]

Not all women had bound feet, and there were degrees of severity of binding, but the practice emphasised the dependent status of the female.

With regard to marriage the girl was just as much a pawn in the hands of her family as was the man. The following extract is translated from a Chinese account of marriage customs in a district of southeastern China:

> However, one month before she leaves her natal home, the bride's family go through the ceremony called 'knowing the day'. This is because her wedding is something completely outside the bride's control—it is her parents who decide on it—and she has been kept in utter ignorance of it. Now, when the time to be married out of her home is near at hand, she may be deceived no longer, and it is only when she is formally acquainted with the fact that she becomes aware that she is about to be married out as someone's wife. From the moment of her telling on, her freedom of movement is limited, and her rising and living, drinking and eating, sitting, sleeping and working all are confined to one place (usually upstairs in the house).

But in marriage the girl had much more at stake than the man. Where a man's life had three 'great events', there was one 'greatest event' for a woman—her wedding. The man after all usually remained with his own family; it was the woman who was cut loose from her natal surroundings and plunged into a completely strange family in which she knew no-one. Seated in an enclosed sedan-chair, she was carried weeping to her new home. The weeping was customary, as often were the obscene songs which she sang about the unknown family into which she was being married, but grief, fear and anxiety doubtless had as much to do with the quality of her performance as did custom.

Since the man had little or no say in the choice of his bride, it has often been commented that it was his family and not he who married her. Thus:

> A man in China does not marry so much for his own benefit as for that of the family: to continue the family name; to provide descendants to keep up the ancestral worship; and to give a

daughter-in-law to his mother to wait on her and be, in general, a daughter to her.[20]

What we have said so far goes a long way towards backing this interpretation. A preoccupation with the mother-in-law/daughter-in-law relationship is observable in many of the Western books which have touched on Chinese family life: it should now be apparent why. The husband/wife relationship was placed low on the scale of priorities, while the parent/child relationship was considered very important. Given a cultural situation where there was expected to be little communication between the sexes, it follows that the parent/child relationship affecting the daughter-in-law most in everyday life was going to be that with her mother-in-law. Often this seems to have resulted in a tyranny of the older woman over the younger.

In some parts of China it was preferred for:

the son to become betrothed to his mother's brother's daughter. . . . In fact, a betrothal was almost compulsory in Kao Yao if a boy had a maternal cousin no more than three years younger, and it could be arranged if the girl was older.[21]

It has been suggested that this form of first-cousin marriage (shown diagrammatically in Figure 5) worked to make less unpleasant the relationship between bride and mother-in-law,

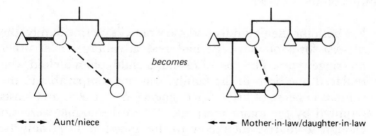

becomes

◄ – – ► Aunt/niece   ◄ – – ► Mother-in-law/daughter-in-law

Figure 5. Cousin Marriage

because the two women would have come from the same background, would be already related to each other, and would almost certainly have known each other before the marriage. Be that as it may, it was not a universal preference, and the majority of brides would not have been chosen in this way. The tyrannous aspect of this relationship could be explained in a number of ways—in terms of necessity to break the newcomer to the ways of her new home, in terms of a revenge for her own lifelong subjection taken on the part of the older woman against the one adult person over whom she was given much power, or in terms of the results of rivalry for the affections of the son:

> The relationship between mother and son . . . is comparatively close. . . . The affection between mother and son is threatened when the son marries. If the mother is selfish or narrow-minded, as many mothers are, she will become jealous of the young wife. Not a few of the difficulties between mother-in-law and daughter-in-law are unconsciously based on such jealousy.[22]

The necessity to break the bride to her new life was avoided in one form of marriage which again illustrates the degree of family control over the fate of the individual. In this form a young girl or girl baby would be purchased by a family who would raise her themselves and eventually marry her to one of their own sons. This procedure seems generally to have been despised, perhaps not least because it was associated with a considerable divorce rate. It was commonplace in some periods of Chinese history, however, and recent research on Taiwan has shown that it was quite common there:

> For both the men's family and the women's uterine family, the sim-pua form of marriage had real advantages over other marriage types. The cost of raising a child, often a child who replaced one born to the family, was not comparable to the ruinous expense of bride price, engagement cakes, and feasts required by the major marriage. When the couple were old enough to marry, their bow to the ancestors need only be acknowledged by a simple family feast. . . . Both wealthy and poor families saw advantages in the sim-pua form of marriage beyond those of economy; they valued the safety of having a daughter for a daughter-in-law. No outsider had to brought into the heart of the family. The family did not need to depend on the word of a go-between and the dubious

judgements of relatives about the character, honesty, industry, health, and good nature of the woman who was to spend the rest of her life in their house and take care of them in their old age.[23]

While on the subject of despised practices, we should note that there was an exception to the rule whereby the wife was married into her husband's family. The reverse could take place (usually where a family had only daughters and not sons) when a son-in-law might be married in in order to continue the family line. In such a case the son-in-law (*chui-fu*) agreed to allow the first son of the marriage to take his wife's surname, the wife thus functioning for descent purposes in her own family very much as though she had been a male. Often in these cases the *chui-fu* reserved the right to bring up a second son to his own surname, and so two families would emerge, each with the same parents but with different surnames. Again, this gives an indication of the importance of family continuance.

The position of a wife in her husband's family was theoretically a very insecure one. Legally, under the so-called 'Seven Outs', she could be divorced (that is, 'outed' from the family) for the following reasons:

1. Barrenness
2. Wanton conduct
3. Neglect of parents-in-law
4. Garrulousness
5. Theft
6. Jealousy and ill-will
7. Incurable disease.

In return she was protected only by the 'Three Not Outs', which ruled that she could not be divorced if:

1. She had kept the three years mourning for either of her parents-in-law
2. Her husband's family had become wealthy after she was married into it
3. She had no home to return to.

Barrenness was one of the worst fears of the young wife, and her marriage was in a certain amount of danger until she had borne a son—after all, like 'neglect of parents-in-law', barrenness offended against the family:

> Mencius said, 'There are three ways of being a bad son. The most serious is to have no heir.'[24]

Despite legal prohibitions, the sale and pawning of wives sometimes occurred:

> More especially pawning occurred on a grand scale in the provinces of Hunan, Chekiang, Kiangsu and Anhui. It was to be found in the lower and the middle classes of society and even married women having children were pawned. Poverty is given as the reason for this custom contrary to the law and Chinese moral teaching, but at least one man sold his wife because he was very angry with her for her going so often to her own family.[25]

With the harsh treatment which wives could receive, we might expect many of them to have wished for divorce, but even if they did so desire there was nothing that they could do:

> It was considered improper and unwomanly for a wife to repudiate her husband. If she left his home of her own free will, she was guilty of having run away and punished accordingly— in T'ang and Sung, by two years' imprisonment; in Ming and Ch'ing by one hundred strokes and the provision that her husband could sell her in marriage. If she married before she returned to her deserted husband's home, she was sentenced to three years' imprisonment under T'ang and Sung law, and 'detention in prison for strangling' under Ming and Ch'ing law.[26]

In any case, the divorced woman would be hard put to it to survive—her own family would be unlikely to welcome her back, and there was much disapproval of re-marriage for women, though it was quite in order for men to re-marry. Her options were all unpleasant, and extended little further than a choice between suicide, begging, prostitution, and becoming a nun. On the part of the husband's family, however, there were moral if not legal sanctions to be reckoned with, and the combined weight of public disapproval of divorce and of possible pressure from the wife's family probably were sufficient to make divorcing her unthinkable. In practice, divorce was very rare. Even concubines, who mostly did not go through a full wedding ceremony, seem seldom to have been cast aside.

With the birth of a son a wife was in a much stronger position in her husband's family. She was now fully connected to it through her son. As she got older and came to a senior position in the family so her influence grew. In the home at least she was in control. Even when her husband died and she supposedly came under the authority of her sons, her age and her relationship with her sons often enabled her to hold sway. If she were senior in Generation and Age in the family she would almost certainly be treated as the family head. Her sons would defer to her on most matters, and especially so in the domestic sphere.

Old age, then, gave a woman at last a measure of equality with a man. However, her strength even then derived through the family system and her having sons. Without sons she was doomed to powerlessness and eventually to extinction, for if she had no sons she could not be an ancestress, and if she could not be an ancestress it meant that her soul would have no means of support when she died. With sons her importance to the family was established, her existence after death was assured, and she became as immortal as did her husband.

*   *   *

This look at the individual in the family has been in some ways a biased one. We have tried to bring out clearly the basic differences in the emphasis on family importance between the traditional Chinese family and the family we know in the West. To do so we have picked out those aspects of family life which seem to show the difference most pointedly, and the result is a picture of automaton figures dancing in patterns set by the family. Obviously Chinese people were not and are not automatons, so that in accepting what has been said above as a guideline to the Chinese family system we must make allowance for a great deal of difference in practice between families and of variation under the influence of individual personalities.

The heavy-handedness of the family in its control over the individual would surely not have continued if there were not benefit accruing to the individual from submission to it. The family in fact repaid the individual for his subjection in many ways, a convenient umbrella word for which might be Security.

With the accent on continuance of membership, property and religion, the family achieved a stability on which the individual could rely right through his life. His own loyalty to the family and to his elders within it was returned by the support of the family both while he was young and when he was aged and dependent. Relationships within the group may have been difficult as personality struggled with duty, but the family offered a sure source of help and comfort and a lasting refuge from a most uncertain outside world.

3

The Lineage and the Clan

THE LINEAGE

We have seen that despite the great weight which was placed on family relationships, the family was full of tensions. All the urging of the Confucian ethic could not prevent the group from breaking down constantly into small units which resembled the simple family much more than the undivided five-generation extended family. Almost always the personality clashes within the family proved stronger than the forces for unity which were founded in a dispassionate sense of duty. The ideal continued to be believed in, but few could realise it: and the Chinese seem to have been no less blind to the actual scarcity of extended families than were those Westerners who reported them as though they were the norm in Chinese society.

But the principles upon which the family was built could be applied to groupings of kin much larger than even the extended family. In fact, in large areas of China, and especially in the southeastern provinces, these principles formed the basis of successful kin groups which we shall call *lineages*.

The lineage basically consisted of a group of males all descended from one common ancestor, all living together in one settlement, owning some property in common, and all nominally under the leadership of the man most senior in Generation and Age. Together with these males were, of course, their wives and unmarried daughters.

This definition bears so much resemblance to what we have called the Chinese family that it is only at second glance that we see where the differences lie—the word 'settlement' takes the place of 'household', and 'some property' is substituted for 'all property'.

49

THE LINEAGE AND THE ANCESTRAL TRUST

Let us invent an example of the formation and growth of a lineage. Farmer A has two sons. During his lifetime he has worked extremely hard, he has had a certain amount of good fortune with his crops, and he has managed to build up a sizeable farm. His sons, B and C, are also hard-working and they get on well together; but they have no great desire to continue together as one family after A's death. When A dies, therefore, they compromise on the problem of dividing the estate. They wish to observe the proprieties and not break up their father's holdings, but they also wish to live and farm separately. They do it this way: they set aside a portion of the estate as a trust, calling it the 'Farmer A Trust', and they divide the remainder between them according to the normal rules of inheritance. Each son now has his own private holding and also a one-half share in the trust. The trust consists of land, and they take turns to farm this land. The income from the trust is used to finance the rituals for the worship of Farmer A as an ancestor—it is the Farmer A trust after all— but if there is money left over after the rituals have been paid for, then B and C share it between them.

In due course B and C die, and their sons succeed them. Their private estates are divided between the sons, but the trust may not be divided—it belongs to the Farmer A line in perpetuity—so each son of the new generation also has a share in the trust. To return to our rope analogy, we can say that, while some property is being inherited down the strands of the rope, a proportion of it continues to be held in the name of the rope as a whole. By the rules of the continuum, Farmer A *is* his own descendants as well as himself, and it is therefore only fitting that these descendants should come to call themselves 'the Farmer A Trust', which in fact they are likely to do.

And so the process goes on. Figure 6 shows the situation by the time the fourth generation inherits. The sizes of the individual inheritances vary according to the number of brothers among whom they have to be shared. The size of the trust remains constant, but the number of shares in it depends on the number of male descendants of Farmer A alive at the time. In this example, if we can imagine the unlikely situation where A to G are all dead and no sons have been born yet to any of H to O, then Farmer A's

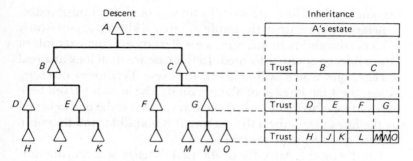

Figure 6. Trust and Private Inheritance

original estate now is divided into one unit of 8/32 (the trust), two units of 6/32 (H and L), two units of 3/32 (J and K) and three units of 2/32 (M, N and O).

While the division of the private estates has gone on, and each son has been setting up his own household and becoming head of his own simple family, the trust's existence and his share in it have meant that he has had to stay physically close to his brothers and cousins in order to take advantage of it. The whole group probably still lives in one village.

At this stage of development the group's position is critical. The critical factor is that the growth of group membership over the generations has constantly reduced the size of the shares in the trust. The trust is supposedly indivisible but, if it were divided now, each member would still receive a worthwhile share—one seventh of the trust. If the trust is allowed to continue then, given a continuing growth in membership, the share of each member would become smaller and smaller and perhaps not worth the trouble of division. Once again there is a conflict between duty ('the trust must continue') and personal preference ('I can personally benefit from splitting the trust now'). If the trust is divided, there is no longer anything to hold all the descendants of Farmer A together, the group loses cohesion and another kinship group has disappeared.

But in many cases the trust was not divided. Generations of descendants of Farmer A would continue to have a share in his trust, would continue to live in the same area in order to participate in the benefits of the trust and, if procreation were favourable, would continue to grow in numbers. Farmer A could become the founding ancestor of a lineage of almost limitless size.

Before we enter upon the implications of a kinship group which achieves durability in this way, we will study another example of how a lineage could be formed. In this case we shall look at a real lineage, one which still exists in the New Territories of Hong Kong, the Liao lineage of Sheung Shui. The account given here may not be of strict historical accuracy, but it is the one believed by the lineage members themselves, it is plausible, and therefore a quite good enough example.[1]

The Founding Ancestor of the Liao lineage was an itinerant tinker who came to the area and decided to settle there during the latter part of the 14th century. He had one son, three grandsons and six great-grandsons. By the time the eighth generation was in manhood he had many descendants, but they had not all stayed together and apparently had not set up an ancestral trust in his name. They lived scattered around the plain in many different settlements. One far-sighted man, however, laid plans to unite all these strands, and the various families finally came together to found the village of Sheung Shui and an ancestral trust somewhere around 1600 A.D. Thus, the Liao lineage as a unit really dates from this time, but the Liaos themselves date it from the Founding Ancestor, whose trust it is which forms the basis of the group's unity. Over the centuries the lineage grew in numbers, prosperity and influence, until the present-day when it is some 3,400 strong.

In this case the rope of descent had frayed, but was spliced back together in the eighth generation. Needless to say, all members of the lineage bear the same surname (*Liao*) since, as in the family, only the males and their wives stay with the lineage, the females being married out to other surnames.

Let us return to our imaginary lineage. The Farmer A Trust has been seen to play an important role in holding the kin group together, each member of the group wishing to stay in the close vicinity of the trust land and his fellow members in order to participate in the benefits from that land. But we have looked at the trust and at the rest of the property being inherited as though they were fixed finite amounts. If that were so then a lineage would probably never develop, for in the private sphere it would not be possible for more and more people to live off the original holding of land, and in the case of the communally owned trust the share of each member must eventually get so small as to be no incentive to remain with the group.

Clearly then the economic situation could not remain static. For a lineage to develop it was probably necessary for there to be available land lying idle so that new land could be opened up to support the growing population. Otherwise, of course, either some of the population-limiting factors which we discussed in Chapter 1 might come into play, or people would be forced to move away to seek a living. The ready availability of land may partly (but only partly) explain why lineages developed most easily in the southeast of China, that is, in the frontier regions most recently settled by the Chinese.

Often more land would also be added to the ancestral trust, so that there was not expansion in the private ownership sector alone. But it could have happened that the Farmer A Trust remained static, while private land holdings increased, and we have said that as lineage membership swelled so the share of each member in the trust was decreased and the incentive to hold the group together was diminished. We should have said 'the *economic* incentive', because there was a clear political incentive to balance this—the great advantage which a large-sized group had in terms of power and self-protection in Chinese society. The reasons why this should be so have partly been given in Chapter 1 and will be further dealt with in a later chapter: for the moment we will note that once a lineage group had become established the political advantages became as important as the economic ones.

But even on the economic side there was always benefit to be gained from the small original Farmer A Trust. Throughout the development of the lineage the trust has provided a surplus of income over the cost of the ancestral worship of Farmer A. In the early years this excess was shared out between the lineage members, but as the lineage grew in size so it became ludicrous to share it out—the portions were not large enough to be valuable. Instead the surplus was kept back as a lineage fund. This fund became a more and more important factor in lineage well-being. It could be used to purchase more land for the trust, of course, or it could be used for essential public works such as well-digging, road-making, irrigation works etc. In fact the trust provided the lineage community (note again that the members are all living in one settlement) with a public fund and the means to joint action which were almost unknown to non-lineage communities in China.

The Farmer A Trust was unlikely to remain the only trust maintained by the lineage. Other descendants of Farmer A might also become the foci of trusts, the membership of which would consist of all their descendants. Let us suppose, for instance, that B and C were both made the focus of a trust and some of their land therefore taken out of the private inheritance sphere. In B's case, the members of his trust would be D, E, H, J and K and their descendants; in C's case, F, G, L, M, N and O and their descendants. D could not be a member of the C Trust, because he is not descended from C, and by the same token M could not be a member of the B Trust. But all of the descendants of A remain members of the Farmer A Trust, whether or not they are members of other trusts.

If both B and C form the focus of a trust, then there is a nice symmetrical pattern of trusts set up, but in later generations it is unlikely that such symmetry would prevail. Figure 7 looks at the Farmer A lineage and shows the haphazard way in which trusts might have been formed over the first five generations. The ancestors with trusts are shaded in.

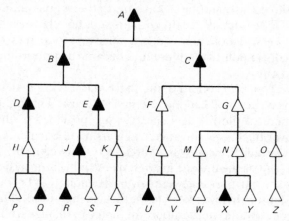

Figure 7. Trust Distribution

Thus the descendants of Z belong to only two trusts (A and C), while the descendants of X belong to three (A, C and X), the descendants of Q to four (A, B, D and Q) and of R to five (A, B, E, J and R). As a general rule the number of trusts which exist in any one line of descent is an indication of the wealth of that line— the more trusts the wealthier the line—so that we might expect descendants of R to have access to considerably more power and wealth than the descendants of Z.

The group which focused on an ancestral trust was organized in much the same way regardless of whether it was a lineage or, as in the previous paragraphs, a lineage segment (sub-lineage). Some groups had more importance in the ritual sphere, others in the political sphere. All seem to have had some importance in the economic sphere, though some segment trusts lost this importance if their membership grew without expanding the trust itself. What happened when a sub-lineage trust was formed was that a group of lineage members was marking itself off from the rest of the lineage and salting away some of its wealth in such a way that no-one outside the group could have a claim on it. The bonds of close kinship, ideally at least, laid any wealthy segment open to claims for help from less well-off lineage members, but the formation of an ancestral trust provided an ethically sound defence against such claims—the benefits must go to the descendants of the focal ancestor.

Economically then the lineage might be quite highly internally differentiated. Not only segments focused on trusts but individual families could be richer or poorer, some families being landless while others would have an excess of land over what they could farm themselves.

ORGANIZATION AND LEADERSHIP OF THE LINEAGE

In the family the leadership situation was clear, the Generation–Age–Sex priorities ensuring that everyone knew who should be Family Head. In practice we have seen that the theoretical did not always apply, and that real authority might pass to the more able younger generation in the family even if lip service were still paid to the authority of the nominal Family Head.

In the lineage the split between nominal and real authority tended to be very much more marked. As in the family, the lineage head came to his position by virtue of being the oldest male in the most senior living generation. If we look at the

Farmer A lineage when A, B and C have all died, then the lineage head will be whichever of the generation D, E, F and G is oldest. E and G are the younger brothers of the two pairs, so the lineage headship will go to whichever of D and F is the older. We may not assume that D will be older than F merely because B was older than C—after all B may have had six daughters before D was born, while F might have been the first child born to C. The odds are in favour of D being older than F, however, because in Chinese families elder sons always married before younger, as we have seen. If D is the oldest he is the lineage head. When he dies the next eldest left alive of the third generation becomes lineage head, and so on until the last male representative of that generation is dead. When D, E, F and G have all died, then the eldest man from among H, J, K, L, M, N and O becomes lineage head.

In some lineages the lineage head was not the oldest male in the most senior living generation, he was the oldest male in the most senior living generation *of the senior branch*. In the Farmer A lineage that would mean that the lineage head always came from among the descendants of B.

Now if we consider what has been already said about poverty postponing marriage, we shall see that, as the generations went by, those lines of descent within a lineage which were less well-off were likely to be continually marrying later than wealthier lines. We can show this graphically as in Figure 8. Let us suppose for the sake of simplicity that the line descended from X is richer than the line descended from Y, so that the descendants of X are marrying and reproducing earlier, at age 20, than those of Y, who marry and have sons at age 30. If we now ask 'Who will be lineage head two hundred years after the births of X and Y?' the answer must be 'a descendant of Y', for the heavy line drawn through *200 years* shows that at that time Y's descendants are only in the seventh generation, while X's have got up to the eleventh generation. The fifth generation member of Y's line might still be alive at eighty years old, but the fifth generation member of X's line would have had to have lived to the age of one hundred and twenty in order to qualify for lineage headship!

The example of X and Y is a very much simplified situation, but we can say that as a general rule the lineage head tended to come from the poorer sections of a lineage. But common sense

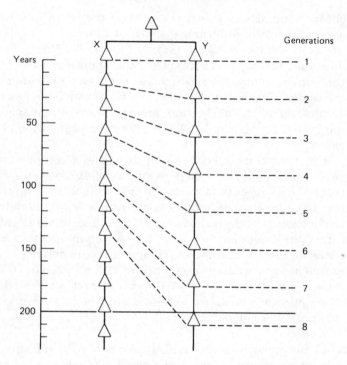

Figure 8. Differentiated Generation Depth

tells us that such a man was unlikely to be well fitted to the
running of a large organization. In the first place, he must in the
majority of cases have been old in order to qualify for his position,
and old age is rarely associated with energy and clarity of mind.
In the second place, it could be argued that a man from a poor
line had proved his unfitness for leadership because of his very
poverty and lack of success. *Per se* this argument is specious, but in
terms of the lack of education, connections and wide experience
which was implicit in the concept of poverty, it has much
validity. A man without wealth was likely to be a man without
influence, and he could hardly hope to have the ordering of other
wealthier and more influential men in the lineage.

In small lineages it may well have been sufficient for the
running of the group to have been left to the lineage head assisted
by other men who had attained an age, such as 51 or 61,

arbitrarily laid down by lineage custom as the age of elderhood.
These old men would form a Council of Elders:

> The clan [lineage] was directed by a council of elders and
> the business manager. In principle, the council of elders was
> the center of authority that made all important decisions con-
> cerning the affairs of the clan, and the business manager ad-
> ministered its financial activities under the supervision of the
> elders.
>
> The council of elders, who served without compensation,
> consisted of males over sixty-five years of age. When a man
> reached his sixty-fifth birthday, he gave a big feast to the entire
> clan in order to qualify for council membership. Should this
> celebration be beyond his means, his close relatives might
> contribute money for the feast. . . . The requirement of giving
> a feast for the clan had the actual significance of making wealth
> as well as age a qualification for council membership. In fact,
> there were several poverty-stricken old men in the village
> whose age was well above sixty-five, but who had never sat on
> the council of elders.[2]

But in large lineages there was likely to emerge a split leadership
system which, again, reflected the conflict between moral duty
(the ideal) and common sense practicality. Here the lineage head
and the other elders would be allowed nominal authority, and
would remain particularly important in the ritual sphere, where
the source of their authority in any case lay; but the real power
and leadership of the lineage would rest with the men of wealth,
position, education or political ability, the kind of men who
would be likely to form the leadership in any society or
community. When it is remembered that the lineage-village was
a community as well as a kinship group, so that the leaders of the
lineage were also really leaders of the village, and that 'the
village' in this context could be a very large settlement of several
thousand people, then the necessity for an able leadership
becomes more obvious.

What did the lineage leadership have to do? Its first responsibility was to organize the ceremonies of worship of the
founding ancestor, and to ensure that the funds to pay for these
were forthcoming. Accordingly, economic matters claimed

much of its attention. Fields had to be rented out or placed in the care of lineage segments, rent or income had to be collected, lineage property maintained, and the surplus income put by or spent to the best advantage. Where an entire area was under lineage ownership, it was often worth-while for the lineage to invest in irrigation systems (dams, channels, bridges, wells) which would benefit all the land in the area, regardless of whether it was trust land or private land. Money could be invested in other ways too. Lineages often set up schools for their sons, paying for the education, and sometimes even providing rewards in cash or kind for members who were successful enough at their studies to pass the stringent Civil Service examinations. Widows were sometimes cared for at lineage expense; temples and shrines were built and maintained; non-ancestral religious ceremonies on special occasions such as drought and flood were paid for; caretakers for lineage property were employed; feasts were given; halls for ancestor worship were built; and so on.

Lineage investment, therefore, was complex and valuable, and the lineage leadership had to protect that investment. So it organised its own Watch system, which patrolled the lineage-controlled area and gave warning of and some protection against thieves, bandits, flood, fire and civil commotion. On a wider scale, the lineage also had to guard against other lineages (a matter which we shall take up again in a later chapter), and to this end it built defensive walls and moats, and collected together weapons and armour.

As a community leadership the lineage leadership had to deal with disputes and internal anti-social problems. In small lineages maintenance of order might be entirely in the hands of the elders, who would mediate disputes, give judgement and pass sentence on offenders, all on the basis of an uncodified body of locally accepted standards of behaviour. Without official legal sanction these men were able to use the weight of public opinion in their own communities to enforce judgements which in some cases might go as far as corporal or even capital punishment. In larger lineages there was likely to exist a written code of conduct which was held to be binding on all lineage members. Offence against this code was punished by the leadership, powerful men in their own right, who passed sentence either according to their own sense of justice (which again must have taken great account of the accepted community standards) or according to the punishments which some of the codes laid down.

The code of conduct was usually to be found in the lineage *genealogy*, a book periodically revised, which kept records of the descent lines of the lineage, preserving for posterity the names, titles, deeds and writings of the lineage ancestors. One of the sections of the Liao lineage genealogy code runs:

> If any male becomes an entertainer, or a lictor, or is adopted into another surname group, or becomes a priest, or commits a serious offence against lineage rules, his name should be expunged from the genealogy.

A major study of lineage rules has this to say:

> One clan [lineage] rule states: 'Cases involving death and flagrant violation of ethical relationships should be sent to the government for due punishment under the law.' Another clan rule makes a clear demarcation: 'The clan head shall administer corporal punishment at the ancestral hall to a member who commits an illegal offense which is punishable under the law by flogging. However, if it is a criminal offense subject to penal servitude, the guilty member shall be sent to the government.' On the other hand, a few exceptionally stern clan rules exceed the legal limitations. One clan, so states its rule, would order the death of a member who harboured criminals or who was himself guilty of serious crimes 'so as to avoid legal trial which brings shame upon the ancestors'. However, such cases must be regarded as rare exceptions. While a clan might compel one of its members to commit suicide, the law did not permit the clan to put him to death.[3]

Whether or not a lineage was prepared to go to such an extreme as capital punishment, it is clear that the individual member of the lineage was under considerable constraint to behave according to a code which reinforced the solidarity and power of the group as a whole. But, as with the family, there were high returns to the individual for his loyalty and obedience. The lineage group gave protection and support to its members against the outside world. As we have seen with the descent continuum, each living male of the lineage was one with his ancestors, who in turn were one with each other living male: the mathematical formula *if A equals B and B equals C, then A equals C* is an expression of the ideal relationship within the Chinese lineage. Even if within the lineage some members were wealthier or more powerful than others, the fact remains that vis-à-vis the outside world an attack or insult or deceit directed at one member (however lowly) of a lineage was likely to be treated by the lineage as directed at the whole group. The humble farmer could 'swagger through the market-place' (as the Chinese phrase has it) secure in the support of his powerful lineage kin, even if they themselves treated him within the lineage as far less than an equal. For this support and for the economic advantage and security which lineage membership gave, the individual was doubtless more than happy to toe the lineage line. It follows that a punishment which took the form of expulsion from the lineage (that is, name 'expunged from the genealogy') was a very serious matter indeed for the individual, almost equivalent to the criminal deportation practised in nineteenth-century Britain. A Liao who was converted to Christianity early in this century and became a colporteur for the Hong Kong and New Territory Evangelization Society was hounded from the village with his family, and his house was closed up and apparently sold by the lineage leaders.

Each individual was a member of the lineage trust but, as we have seen, there were often many more trusts than one in a lineage. The larger a lineage became, the more importance came to be given to certain sub-lineage trusts. To put it another way, some sub-lineages or lineage segments came to play a more important role as the lineage which they composed became larger and more unwieldy. The further the living generations receded from the founding ancestor the more distant apart from each other the various lines of descent from that ancestor became, and the less strongly must a man have felt himself to be related to many other of the lineage members. In these circumstances the sub-lineage trusts became crucially important. We have looked at them so far as devices for splitting one segment of the lineage off from another, but if we look at them from the bottom, as it were, we can see that they were the points at which the split-off segments joined back into the body of the lineage. The segment trusts were important, then, as links into the lineage which were close enough to the individual to have meaning for him, but which themselves were only meaningful in a total lineage context. The following quotation gives an example both of how segmentation of a lineage could be divisive and of how none the less the overarching lineage organization worked for unity:

> The head of the clan [lineage] or of the large family . . . is heeded when he settles disputes between members or between branches of the family. If he is the head of a large clan his authority extends to the settlement between subsidiary branches and between villages. . . . A feud threatened between two branches of the same clan in emigrant community X. The conflict had been caused by a dispute between their children. Both branches threw up barricades of sand bags around their homes and to close off their streets; and on both sides men were sharpening their weapons. The heads of the families were called together, and after negotiations extending over four days the controversy was peaceably settled.[4]

But some segments were especially important. We said when talking of the Farmer A trust that B and C would take turns to farm the land in the trust. As the lineage grew it would become more difficult for the sharing of trust work to be done in this way, and a convenient way out of this would be to lay down that the descendants of B and the descendants of C should as groups take turns at the farming; that is to say, the B and C segments rather than individuals have become the working units. As the prime purpose of the trust is to worship Farmer A, the B and C segments also take turns in organizing the rituals. B and C thus become important segments in the ritual and economic spheres. Now, if the lineage grows really big, greater decisions have to be made, and there is more trust money to be administered. Things may become too important to be managed in this turn-and-turn-about fashion. Big decisions need to be made not on a year-to-year basis by a succession of alternating segment leaderships, but on a continuing basis by a continuing whole lineage leadership. This lineage leadership, however, in order to be felt to be representative of all members by all members must include men from each of the segments, which we have already said are groupings to which the individual can relate more easily. So the segments become important in the political sphere too.

In Sheung Shui the Liao lineage gives importance to two sets of lineage segments. Their early genealogy is given in slightly simplified form in Figure 9. The founding ancestor had only one son, but three grandsons. The segments focussing on the trusts of

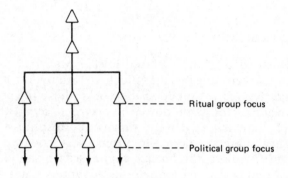

Figure 9. Liao Lineage Segmentation

these three grandsons have become important ritual groups, and all lineage ritual includes a representative from each of the three segments. But in political matters it is the fourth generation, the generation of the great-grandsons of the founder, that counts. The reason for this seems quite clear—the descent line from the middle grandson of the founding ancestor has flourished and grown much stronger than the lines of either the eldest or the youngest grandson. If political significance were given to the segments focused on these three ancestors, then on the one hand the majority of lineage members would have a minority representation in lineage matters, and on the other hand the middle grandson's segment would tend to be too powerful for the other two and tend to overwhelm them in importance. However, by focussing on the fourth generation, where the middle grandson's line is itself split into two, then four political segments of more roughly equivalent weight are created. In all political matters in Sheung Shui it is the segments focussing on the fourth generation which each have to be represented.

Segment trusts were organized in the same way as lineage trusts, and they had a leadership selected in much the same way. In large lineages the segments were more important than in small, and in fact could be said to be lineages within lineages. Just as large lineages had two kinds of leader, so did large segments; and just as lineage leaders mediated disputes between their members, so segment leaders dealt with tensions among their own members.

THE LINEAGE AND THE VILLAGE

We have tried to show that the lineage was very similar in structure and certainly in basic ethos to the family. It contrived to make the most of the Confucian ideal of kinship as an organizing factor, while at the same time it managed to avoid the major pitfall of the extended family, that is, the disruptive effect of personality clashes where the group was confined to one household. In short, the lineage capitalised on the idea of the extended family, having many of its advantages and few of its disadvantages.

Internally a lineage could go on dividing into segments, and the family pattern could be extended or simple, but the group itself remained a viable whole. Given this, there was little reason for fission, and the lineage could go on getting bigger for just so long as it was able to do so on its available land and space. Here of course external factors were important, and these will be dealt with in a later chapter, but we should note that the lineage was an expansionist organization; it looked inward for cohesion and co-operation, and outward for antagonism. It reached its peak efficiency when it operated in its own totally controlled environment—its own village surrounded by its own land—and therefore it tended to expand towards this objective.

The possible constant expansion of the lineage gave rise to some huge groups. We have already seen that the Liao lineage of Sheung Shui grew in the space of some six hundred years to a membership of over three thousand. The reader may have guessed by this time that the reference in Chapter 1 to 'families' of 500 to 750 members was in fact a reference to 'lineages', though the authors of that quotation did not use the word lineage. These are large groups, but there were others even larger, and references to lineages of 10,000 and even 30,000 members are to be found.

Much of the discussion of the lineage given here assumes one-village/one-lineage conditions, but it should not be forgotten that multi-lineage settlements were common even in southeastern China where lineage organization was strongest.

A village in which more than one lineage lived was ultimately almost bound to be a village in which conflict was present. Each lineage would, almost by definition, be trying to expel the other lineages from the village. I once visited a small single-lineage village in the New Territories of Hong Kong and listened to a long and gleeful account by an old man of how his lineage had ousted the other two lineages which used to share the village. He pointed with pride to two delapidated ancestral halls, and claimed that interference with their geomantic siting had been largely responsible for the failure of the unfortunate lineages which used to worship in them. (For geomantic warfare, see Chapter 6 and Appendix II.) In another part of the New Territories:

> Tung Sam Tsuen is a mixed-surname hamlet, with as many as three different surnames represented in a single row of nine houses. People still say they dislike living cheek by jowl with people of different surnames, and the movement out of Tung Sam Tsuen seems to be continuing: it has more empty and tumbledown houses than any of the outlying hamlets, all of which are inhabited by people of a single surname.[5]

Fights, disputes, bullying and all-round uneasiness would mark village life in many such cases. The following quotation describes conditions in a village in Kwangtung Province not one hundred miles from Sheung Shui:

> Familism and clannism were visibly built into the physical plan of the village. The houses were grouped by clans [lineages] so that each section was separated from another by gates. Even families of each subdivision of a clan were generally concentrated on the same street or alley. Interclan rivalry was intense, sometimes flaring into open conflict. At such times, children of one clan did not dare to play in another clan's territory.[6]

Members of such lineages would be unlikely to marry each other, for conflicting loyalties would produce even more tension. The village was disunited in leadership, and unified action in the political and economic spheres was not easy. By contrast the single lineage village was a unity, and its internal divisions were purposeful, functional divisions, segments of a whole. The possibilities for strong and united action were much greater. Of course, not *all* multi-lineage settlements were strife-torn: much might depend on environment. Even in an area of strong lineage dominance, for instance, small lineages of different surnames might band together for protection and co-exist peacefully and with good cooperation. But such settlements were likely to be as defensive, negative and static as single-lineage villages were aggressive, active and expansionist.

We have been looking at the lineage as an institution and treating the village in which it resided as a secondary feature. If we turn this idea upside down and look at the village as the main focus, then the lineage may be seen as a way of organizing a community which was probably the most efficient and viable form which the Chinese village achieved. Reference to Chapter I and our discussion of the ideas of Chinese political philosophers on the role of the family in society will show how closely the lineage corresponded to those ideas, even if the family itself did not.

Why was the lineage not found in equal strength throughout China? is the first question which springs to mind when it is seen to have had such obvious advantages over the non-lineage settlement. The answer to this has not yet been fully worked out. Some have suggested that the lineage was a response to a 'frontier situation', and that therefore it occurred mainly in the southern, newest-settled, wildest regions of China. Persuasive argument to the contrary springs from field research in Taiwan:

Far from fostering the development of strong localized lineages, frontier conditions tended to inhibit such a development by requiring extensive cooperation for defense and environmental exploitation among unrelated family and lineage fragments. Conversely, one might argue that only where frontier conditions do not exist—where hostile forces are not present and working the land does not demand extensive cooperation with nonagnates—is a 'patrilineal ideology' likely to become dominant.[7]

It has also been suggested that lineage development was connected in some way with rice-farming and the need for co-operative labour, and that this explains why the north of China where rice does not grow has few lineages. Others have concluded that the older-settled north lost its pattern of lineage settlement over the centuries as war and strife played havoc with the population. Some part of each of these arguments may be true, but none of them alone seems to give a satisfactory explanation. One factor which carries much weight is economic surplus. It does seem that strong lineage organization did not exist where there was a mere subsistence economy, and since the south was the most fertile region of China, especially where there was double- and even treble-cropping of rice, the incidence of strong lineage settlement there is at least a very significant correlation. Chapter 6 gives a further explanation.

THE HIGHER-ORDER LINEAGE AND THE CLAN

The connection between family and lineage is close and obvious—one could grow out of the other. The lineage itself could grow and split in such a way that several new lineages emerged. For example, in the New Territories of Hong Kong there is a large number of villages inhabited by lineages bearing the surname *Deng*. The founding ancestor of the Dengs settled in the area about one thousand years ago, and over the centuries his descendants either grew too numerous to survive in the territory which the original village possessed or fell out among themselves, so that gradually other lineage villages were founded on widely scattered sites. Each of these villages may be said to be a complete lineage, and yet each of the lineages still retains a share in the original ancestral trust. For such phenomena the term *higher-order lineage* has been coined.[8] The growth of the higher-order lineage out of the lineage is a fairly obvious process but, as with the lineage, there was no reason why it could not be formed retrospectively when a group of lineages which had scattered would get together to reactivate their relationship through formation of a trust.

But there were other large-scale groupings which stretched the idea of kinship organization much further. The family, the lineage and the higher-order lineage all were 'natural' kinship groups, groups which found their basis in and traced clear descent from the ancestor from whom they all sprang. The *clan* on the other hand was not really concerned with close recent kinship ties. The clan was an artificial kin group, and consisted of a deliberate amalgamation into one loose federation of a number of lineages all of which bore the same surname. Typically the clan's membership was drawn from a given wide area of the country-side, often taking administrative boundaries as the limits of its spread. Thus some clans had a membership drawn from an entire province, others from one or more prefectures, and perhaps others from areas as small as the county.

The clan would be founded by gentry members of lineages, and it seems to have existed as an organization for the benefit of the gentry. Membership of 'natural' kin groups was given by birth, but there was no such automatic entry into the clan: first, the membership was composed of lineages and not of individuals, and second, the lineages had to *buy* their way into the clan. The clan would build an ancestral hall, nearly always in the major city which was the focal settlement of the area from which clan membership came, and the lineages would each have shares in the hall. The main purpose of the hall was often to provide a city residence for members of the clan who were studying or taking examinations, and libraries were part of the hall's equipment.

Of course, ancestor worship was carried on in the hall, but it was very different from that in a lineage hall. The clan did not necessarily have one ancestor from whom all members could trace their descent, or, if it did, it was often a mythical or ancient historical figure who was credited with initiating the clan surname; instead it had a conglomeration of ancestral tablets which were put there as concrete evidence of their financial shares by the component lineages, and which were mostly without especial significance for the majority of members of the clan. The collective genealogies produced by many of these clans in attempts to trace common ancestry remain in the world's oriental libraries to baffle scholars with their size, complexity and frequent defiance of meaningful analysis.

The clan, then, was a federation of lineages of one surname

from one given geographical area. It built an ancestral hall, a library and study rooms. It worshipped its conglomerated ancestors, and concocted massive genealogies. Its membership included all male individuals from the member lineages, but in practice only the gentry from these lineages seem to have been actively involved with it.

What was the function of the clan? It seems to have been an organization which existed to raise the bargaining power of its lineages vis-à-vis the rest of society, and particularly the government, through unity and strength of numbers. In other words, it tried to enlarge still further the benefits which wider kin groups have been seen to have given in Chinese society. At such high levels of organization it was bound to be the gentry—that is, the wealthy and influential—who administered the clan, for how could the common man have experience enough to operate successfully? But, was it feasible for such large groups joined together by such remote threads to work? Again, there is not a clear answer. The clan seems to have been set up for potential action rather than for any specific purpose; or perhaps it would be better to say that the occasions when activation of the clan organization was necessary were rare, and that the rest of the time the organization was kept ticking over through the humdrum routine of annual ancestral rites, and the to-ing and fro-ing of gentry members on their ceaseless struggle with the examiners.

*   *   *

The tentacles of kinship stretched far indeed. From the simple family to the extended family and then to the lineage were logical and simple steps. From the higher-order lineage to the clan was a rather bigger step, but the heavy emphasis on the importance of surname, which we have seen in so many aspects of kinship, made the leap from true to artificial kinship easier.

The true kinship groups had all-inclusive membership, and so stood to be of advantage to all individuals born into them. They were ongoing, active groups which were concerned with the day to day organization of their members' lives. The clan did not concern itself with the humdrum, and benefited only indirectly the vast mass of its membership. The higher-order lineage tended to occupy a middle position between lineage and clan. On the one hand, like the clan, it had little connection with everyday life or the affairs of the ordinary lineage member: on the other, like the lineage, it was basically oriented to local society and local affairs, and it did not much turn its attention outwards to the state or to society beyond its own area.

Kinship could reach even further than the clan. Since surname in common could be considered kinship in common, there were always opportunities for alliances both at the personal and the group levels. Accordingly, lineages might well look for help in times of need to other groups with the same surname, and they might refer to their combined strength as a 'clan' despite the lack of any formal tie between them. In 1929 a group of families with the Liao surname moved into the Sheung Shui area from a distant part of Kwangtung province. On the strength of common surname and a common ancestor of some 900 years ago, they asked for and received considerable help from the Sheung Shui Liao lineage. No formal organization of the two groups has resulted.

We shall see in Chapter 7 how surname could operate between individuals too as a basis for joint interest. In brief, kinship principles operated at many levels of social organization, large or small, formal or informal, permanent or transitory.

4

Ancestor Worship

In Chapter 2 we talked of the Continuum of Descent and of the crucial razor-like function of the living individual in whose person descent is concentrated. In making the statement that 'he exists by virtue of his ancestors, and his descendants exist only through him', we added that this unexceptionable idea could be stood on its head and still remain valid. The first part of this chapter, then, is to some extent concerned with the proposition that the invidual exists by virtue of his descendants, and that his ancestors exist only through him.

The importance of reciprocity could be seen very clearly in Chinese family relationships, and the sense of mutual responsibility between parents and son was central to the operation of the family as a continuing and strong unit. When the son was young and incapable he was fed, clothed, housed and educated by his parents. As he grew older so he began to take on more and more tasks and achieve a state of comparative self-reliance where he was putting into the family quite as much as he was taking out. Eventually his parents would become old and weak, and he would come to have more authority, as we saw in Chapter 2. It would then be his turn to feed, clothe, shelter and care for his parents, thus directly reciprocating their previous care of him. In the case of a daughter the reciprocity was indirect in that it was to her husband's parents that she repaid the care expended on her by her own father and mother.

Such mutual responsibility between parents and children does not strike us as particularly alien or peculiar. Where the Chinese situation differed markedly from the Western was in the continuation of the parent/child dependence after the death of the parent. Death did not release the son from his duty to his parents, it merely altered the form which his duty took. While alive parents were served and respected; dead, they were served and worshipped. And in return for the sacrifices and service of the living the ancestors gave to their descendants such blessings and assistance as were in their supernatural power. A continuing reciprocal relationship, then.

We know that ancestor worship has been practised by the Chinese since the earliest recorded times. Inscribed bones used for taking oracles have been discovered which show that over one thousand years before Christ the kings of the Shang dynasty were sacrificing to their ancestors and worshipping them as powerful gods:

> the ancestor's real power began when he died. For then he was transformed into a spirit, of powers undefined but vast. He was more or less vaguely dependent on his descendants for food, in the form of sacrifices, but he could very well see that these were forthcoming, or make his descendants wish that they had been.
>
> The activities of these spirit ancestors are not altogether unlike those of the Greek gods. They were not, it seems, either omnipotent or omniscient, yet in practice they were very nearly so. Success in hunting, agriculture, war and other activities was theirs to give or to withhold. Famine, defeat, sickness and death were the penalties which they could and did hurl at any who had the temerity to displease them.[1]

Clearly the ancestors of kings were powerful, and they were perhaps important enough to be only 'vaguely dependent' on their descendants. We do not know whether or not the common people of Shang practised ancestor worship; but it is likely that the ancestors of the majority of the common people of China since those times have needed a considerable amount of attention from their descendants.

For the Chinese, the after-life was seen as in many ways a duplicate of this world:

> the prevailing notions attributing to the inhabitants of the Land of Shades the possession of an amount of power quite

equal to that which their position caused them to enjoy in the present world.[2]

Spirits were subject to the same needs as men; they had to eat, have clothing, shelter and money. They were not all equal, and the powerful oppressed the weak. Where the living looked to religion and the supernatural for assistance in the hard realities of life, the dead in turn looked to the living for aid. As one writer has summed it up:

The dead are commonly regarded as actually present at the sacrifices; they enjoy the offerings, and are dependent upon posterity for their continued well-being. Though this belief is seldom definitely expressed, and though it may not often take the form even of conscious feeling, it is an instinctive pre-supposition of the rites of tendance. We may therefore assume that one motive of ancestor worship is the desire to supply the needs of ancestors.[3]

Dead parents, then, needed the worship of their children in order to be comfortable and happy. But children also needed the supernatural support of their parents. It was believed that blessings were in the gift of the parents, and that the care and protection which they had given while alive they would continue to bestow after death.

But, if the parents needed the worship of their children, it would seem to follow that they must usually be benevolent in their attitude towards their children. They might show displeasure by visiting sickness or misfortune on neglectful or offensive descendants, but in most cases the descendants could hope for assistance from the ancestor whom they worshipped, provided of course that they kept up the sacrifices due to him. If dead parents could be so malevolent as to cause the death of their descendants, they would be cutting off their own means of support; yet occasional such cases have been reported:

The most severe punishment I heard of was supposed to have been meted out by the Ui ancestors. 'Several years ago a Ui man accidentally bumped and moved the incense pot for the ancestors in the hall. As a result, another man in the lineage died shortly afterward. When they opened the tablet box to insert that man's tablet, two more people died.' Usually ancestors do not bring about serious infirmity without being seriously provoked (by having their oath broken, for example). Still, people do find it plausible that ancestors will inflict death as punishment even for simple carelessness.[4]

But a father is also of necessity a son, and the parents when alive had the responsibility of worshipping their parents in the same way. In order to continue the duty of the parents to worship so that the grandparents should not suffer deprivation, it became necessary for the children to undertake this service. And on the grandparents in turn had lain the same responsibility. Thus, on the living could fall the heavy burden of worshipping the entire ancestral line:

This system of ancestral worship, when rightly understood in its true significance, is one of the heaviest yokes which ever a people was compelled to bear. . . . The hundreds of millions of living Chinese are under the most galling subjection to the countless thousands of millions of the dead. 'The generation of to-day is chained to the generations of the past.'[5]

In fact the living seldom considered it necessary to be so all-embracing, as we shall see; but we might just note in passing that if worshipping so many ancestors were a burden, given the reciprocal nature of ancestor/descendant relationships, at least the benefits obtained should have been felt to be correspondingly weighty.

NON-ANCESTORS

Ancestors whose line became extinct, ancestors whose descendants failed to sacrifice, or those who died heirless, were condemned to wander through the supernatural as 'hungry ghosts', spirits without sources of food, clothing, shelter or money, the beggars of the after-life. Public-spirited men might donate sums of money to hold ceremonies for the peace of these ghosts, but such ceremonies probably did nothing to preserve their existence, and their souls would gradually melt away. The Sung dynasty philosopher Chu Hsi said:

At death material-force necessarily disintegrates. However, it does not disintegrate completely at once. Therefore in religious sacrifices we have the principle of spiritual influence and response. Whether the material-force of ancestors of many generations ago is still there or not cannot be known. Nevertheless, since those who perform the sacrificial rites are their descendants, the material-force between them is after all the same. Hence there is the principle by which they can penetrate and respond.[6]

Under Buddhist influence public ceremonies of propitiation have been held in the seventh lunar month annually since the eighth century, but the ceremonies have concentrated as much on clearing the world of these hungry ghosts and having them consigned to the guardianship of the Rulers of Hell as they have on their long-term salvation:

The gates of Hell are opened and all the demons are allowed to return to earth for the space of thirty days. . . . In the temples and on the streets, the priests pray for their release from punishment. These festivals continue until Ti Tsang's [the King of Hell] birthday, at which time the ghosts are compelled to return to the Underworld. As there is a great deal of danger from their presence, the people treat them most courteously during this period.[7]

Such depersonalized placating of the unwanted dead was obviously felt to be much inferior to the loving and dutiful attention which those with posterity could receive. Indeed, the term 'ancestor worship' should be clearly distinguished from 'worship of the dead'. Other people's dead were of little concern: the only dead to be worshipped were one's own dead, one's ancestors.

In the *Analects*, Confucius is quoted as saying 'to sacrifice to ancestors not one's own is presumptuous'. The most exhaustive work on Chinese religious practices was written by De Groot in the years around the turn of this century. He also was quite clear about this question, and speaks of:

> A prevailing social rule which forbids their contributing in any way to other people's ancestral sacrifices . . . everything a child possesses belongs to his parents, even though they are dead; hence, offerings presented to a strange soul are regarded as a theft from the holy ones . . .[8]

In the village of Sheung Shui which was mentioned in the previous chapter, it was believed that without the presence of a son of the deceased a coffin could not be lifted, and one informant claimed that he had seen forty men unable to pick up the coffin at a funeral where the son had absented himself.

Ancestors, then, were jealous of the personal attentions of their own descendants, and were not very receptive to the attentions of outsiders:

> If the offerings to, and worship of, the dead ancestors are discontinued because the living descendants are unfilial or because there are no more descendants, then the deceased ancestors become hungry and angry, and vengeful, and inflict much pain and harm upon the descendants and on other people. In short, they become demons.[9]

Both the living and the dead suffered when ancestor worship was not practised. It was to avoid such suffering that the state, which was interested in giving support to the family, went so far as to legislate that even after ordination Taoist and Buddhist priests must continue to worship their ancestors on pain of corporal punishment and defrocking.

But even if we set aside those unfortunates whose lines died out or whose descendants failed to worship them, there must have been others who could not come into the category of ancestors:

> Those who died unmarried or under the age of twelve received simple rites or none at all. The latter were not even marked with a spirit tablet in the family altar.[10]

Difficulties arose also with men who could not or did not marry, or those who had no sons and were unable to adopt a son. Some of these men must have had to resign themselves to eventual ritual extinction; but others who were less unlucky might be included *ex gratia* in the worship of their brother by his descendants, this form of worship being known as 'supplementary sacrifices'. Eunuchs were cut off [sic] from their families and, except when castration was performed late in life, had no means of becoming ancestors:

> As eunuchs, after death, cannot be sacrificed to by their children—they have none—the government allows a yearly sum to enable a certain number of eunuchs to go to the cemeteries in the spring and autumn to burn paper money, and offer sacrifices at the tombs of those who have been buried there.[11]

The worship of eunuchs by eunuchs was thus a substitute for ancestor worship, and this kind of mock kin relationship between living and dead was practised by other similar groups of childless people, such as monks and nuns.

There could be explanations for non-worship of those who died young:

> In Ch'inan, a boy who dies young is held to be the incarnated soul of someone to whom the parents owed a debt. 'He is born and lives with us for a few years, eating our food until the debt we owe him is paid off. Then he dies, having no more to claim from us.' Because the child is but a guise adopted for this specific purpose, when a boy dies lineage members need have nothing more to do with him. No one is further obligated to him; it is assumed that he lived only until the debt owed him was repaid in full.[12]

In pointing out the difference between the usual Chinese term for spinster and our own understanding of this idea, we mentioned in Chapter 1 that the Chinese system of ancestor worship failed to cater for unmarried women. Women, in fact, must be seen as only temporary members of the families into which they were born, and as such no provision was made for their permanent accommodation there, still less for anything so permanent as to last after death. Neither logically nor in fact

could unmarried childless women become ancestors. The impli-
cation of this was of course that women were bound much closer
to the families into which they married, for it was only through
their husbands and children that they could ultimately achieve
ancestral status. We saw in Chapter 2 that men could be
married posthumously to live girls. They could also be married to
dead girls, and it was even possible for dead girls to marry live
husbands:

> Spirit marriage occurs when a girl who has died in childhood
> appears to her family in a dream some years later and asks to be
> married. A groom is found by the family by laying 'bait' in
> the middle of a road. This usually takes the form of a red
> envelope (used in China for gifts of money). A passer-by sooner
> or later picks up the envelope, and immediately the family of
> the spirit come out of hiding beside the road and announce
> to the young man that he is the chosen bridegroom. If he
> refuses, he is of course in danger of vengeance by the ghost, but
> his enthusiasm for the venture can be increased by an offer of a
> large dowry if necessary. The ghost is married to him in a rite
> designed to resemble an ordinary wedding as closely as
> possible, although the bride is represented only by an ancestral
> tablet. No affinity is established between the groom and his
> spirit-wife's family in this way, and the only obligation he and
> his family have is to accommodate the ancestral tablet of the
> bride on their family altar and to provide it with sacrifices as
> though the spirit bride had married in life.[13]

The life-long spinster, where she existed, was able to look forward
to an after-life which would be as uncomfortable as doubtless her
aberrant position in this life had been.

There have been, nonetheless, some women in Chinese society
who have been precluded from marrying. The most obvious
example is the nun. Chinese nuns did not marry and, on the other
hand, they did not necessarily all have a strong faith in a religious
system which would offer them a guarantee of after-life comfort
equivalent to that which they would have had as ancestors. Such
nuns often created their own quasi-ancestral line by treating
former nuns from the same temple as ancestors, raising tablets to
them on an altar, and worshipping them in much the same way

as the family did its real ancestors. In turn, of course, the nuns could hope to be similarly worshipped by those who were to come after them.

It is worthwhile here quoting at some length from a fascinating article on Vegetarian Halls in present-day Hong Kong:

> The halls of all faiths are particularly popular in Hong Kong with unattached women especially working and retired domestic servants (amahs). They provide a home in old age and a *pied-à-terre* for the working woman. . . . Halls also provide funeral benefits and house the soul-tablets of deceased members . . .
>
> Another attraction of the halls, both Buddhist and sectarian, is that they recruit members through what one might term a pseudo-kinship system. One joins through a master who is regarded as something like a father; the fellow disciples of this man are termed (paternal) 'uncles' and one's own fellow disciples 'brothers'. Halls normally house 'family' households, and one hall may be connected with others through extended 'family' relationships, and, in the case of the Buddhist halls, with monasteries and nunneries occupied by monk and nun 'brothers' in the 'family'. Genealogies may be constructed and kept.
>
> Such 'families' practise 'ancestor' worship (unmarried persons may receive such ritual attentions and have tablets placed for them in the hall: not customary in the traditional Chinese actual kinship system).[14]

All this makes it apparent that the ancestors were of great importance in Chinese society. It goes without saying that no man can exist without having had ancestors, but we may now perhaps see more clearly how for the Chinese no ancestor could exist without having living descendants. As we said in Chapter 2, the existence of both the future and the past depended on the present.

ANCESTOR WORSHIP FOR THE LIVING

If it were true that the ancestors depended on the living, it must also have been true that the living ultimately depended on the yet unborn. That is to say, the living individual knew that he had a continued existence after death only if he could ensure his own posterity. Hence, the desire for a 'hundred sons and a thousand grandsons' may be seen to be a very understandable one.

Virility and fertility were accordingly of great concern to the Chinese male—almost to the point of obsession in many cases. Indeed, Chinese culture had the dubious distinction of hosting a hysterical condition known as *Koro*:

> Koro, well known among the Chinese as Shook Yong, is a belief that those afflicted with the disease experienced a sudden feeling of retraction of the penis into the abdomen with great fear that, should the retraction be permitted to proceed, and if help was not forthcoming, the penis would disappear into the abdomen with a fatal outcome. In their fear and anxiety to prevent such a mishap, they held on to the penis either with their hands or with instrumental aids, such as rubber-bands, strings, clamps, chopsticks, clothes-pegs, etc., sometimes with severe injury to the penis. . . .
>
> In Singapore for many weeks in October and November 1967 there were widespread rumours that Koro was caused by eating the flesh of pigs recently vaccinated in a mass campaign to combat swine fever. This led to almost a standstill in the sale of pork in markets, eating stalls, and restaurants, and affection by Koro became epidemic.[15]

It is perhaps not surprising that there was a vast number of medicines and foods which were taken primarily for their supposed aphrodisiac or strength-giving properties:

> The basis of both external and oral aphrodisiacs was usually herbal, the commonest ingredients being ginseng, sulphur, cinnamon, cedar seeds, seaweed, pine-needles and powdered charcoal. To these were added one or more of the following: liver extract of various animals, distilled urine—human or animal—secretions from the human sex organs, from tame bears, goats and bulls, hymenal blood, and the excreta of certain animals and birds notorious for their powerful or predatory characters. A third popular constituent was related to shape, its likeness to fertility symbols, and in this category

were the horns of various animals, plants, fungi and cacti of penis-like mould, and certain marine objects. These were powdered and sieved before being swallowed.[16]

The list of special foods was endless, and ranged from highly expensive items such as dried stag's penis for making soup with, down to common items of everyday diet thought to have aphrodisiac properties. Still there were those who could not produce children, and ways round the problem had to be found.

Concubinage was one remedy for childlessness or heirlessness. By no means everyone could afford to take on another mouth to feed, but for those who could afford it it was an obvious course. A wife who had had no children or no sons (for both of which 'failings' she rather than her husband was considered to be responsible) might actively encourage her husband to take a concubine. On the one hand this enabled her to keep in her husband's favour and reduced the slight risk of her being divorced for barrenness. On the other hand the production of a son by a concubine was to the benefit of the wife also, for as the true wife she was the social mother of all her husband's children regardless of who the biological mothers were. A concubine's son made potential ancestresses of both the concubine and the wife. Such an arrangement did not mean that the fact of motherhood was denied or that the biological mother was denied her role, but it does once again demonstrate the importance of the family above that of the individual—it was important for the family group to have a son, and not so important which member of the group produced it. Given the normal power structure of the family the wife must have her superior position reinforced, so she was still considered the 'head mother' as it were.

Adoption was a more certain method of ensuring posterity. However, it was not a simple matter of finding any boy to adopt, for there were clear rules which limited the field of choice. The Qing dynasty (1644–1911 A.D.) code, for instance, says:

When any person is without male children of his own, one of the same kindred of the next generation may be appointed to continue the succession, beginning with his nephews as being descended from the nearest common ancestor, and then taking collaterals, one, two and three degrees further removed in order, according to the table of the five degrees of mourning. If all these fail, one of the kindred still further removed may be chosen, and finally any one of the same family name.

and:

> Anyone adopting and bringing up a child of a different surname, thereby confounding Families and kindred, and any one giving his son to be Successor to a Family of a different surname, shall be liable to be punished with 60 blows, and the child shall revert to his proper kindred.[17]

The custom in particular families might be even more restrictive. The rules to be found in the genealogy of the Liao lineage, for example, did not allow even those of the same surname to be adopted if they were not members of the lineage:

> Male children may not be given in adoption to families of another surname, nor may males of a different surname be taken in adoption. Anyone lacking an heir should adopt a son of one of his own brothers. If there should not be one to adopt, then he must choose a suitable male of the next generation and nearest collateral branch of the lineage. . . . If even in the whole lineage no heir can be found, the line should be marked 'ended'.

The living were Janus-faced with regard to ancestor worship. On the one side they anxiously attempted to placate and please their ancestors; on the other they looked to their descendants for similar treatment in due course. Their worship was both a payment to the ancestors and a premium towards an eventual endowment.

ANCESTOR WORSHIP AND THE FAMILY

Confucius himself was not to be drawn on the subject of the afterlife. 'The Master did not talk of prodigies, feats of strength, revolts or spirits', say the *Analects*. He said men should sacrifice to ancestors 'as if present', but that does not mean that he believed in their existence. What he clearly did believe in were continuity and the importance of the family. When asked to define filial piety he replied, 'When parents are alive serve them according to ritual, when dead bury them according to ritual and sacrifice to them according to ritual'. Continuity is a theme which has recurred in this book, and in the practice of ancestor worship it is particularly important.

If the parents when alive needed food, clothing, shelter and money, and if the after-life closely resembled this life, then the parents when dead would continue to need food, clothing, shelter and money. To supply them with these essentials was one of the fundamental purposes of ancestor worship.

Transfer of the goods from this world to the next was achieved for the most part by burning. Paper clothes, paper houses, paper servants, paper money (not earthly bank notes, but specially printed notes for after-world use), paper sedan-chairs and paper horses could all be sent on to the ancestors in this way. With food, however, it was possible to be more realistic, and real foods often in great variety and abundance were offered to the ancestors. The foods were not burned, merely offered, and the dregs were finished by the descendants once the ancestors had extracted the 'essence' from them. The after-life is, it seems, subject to modernisation in the same way as this world, and it has become not uncommon for paper cars and even paper aircraft to be burned for the ancestors' use, while I have also seen cigarettes offered with the food—and, like the food, consumed by the living once the dead had taken their fill.

To make sure that the offerings went to the right person was clearly important. In some cases, as with the paper horses, cars and so on, it was a simple matter to write the name of the relevant ancestor on the paper. But mostly this procedure was made unnecessary since the offerings were only set out at such places as were known to be frequented by the spirit of the ancestor. Here we need to look at what happened to a person when he died.

Various accounts of the fate of the soul are to be found. It was said by some to consist of two elements, the earthly and the heavenly. Other versions pointed out that there were actually seven earthly and three heavenly elements. Yet others had it that each man had three souls. And doubtless there have been many Chinese who have been unaware of the existence of more than just one soul. There even appears to have been a belief that the ancestor might be present wherever his name was written down, and this would chime in with the almost sacred quality which the written word came to acquire in China. When I asked permission to copy down the genealogy of the Sheung Shui Liao lineage, one old man said to me: 'I don't know if the ancestors will like it in London'. He clearly felt uneasy that the ancestors would be taken back with me in the copy.

The fact is that an ancestor could be worshipped in a number of places, and a coherent theory to account for this must indulge in notions of divided soul, or of separate souls, or perhaps of an undignified flitting of the soul from one place to another following its worshippers. For the purpose of description here we shall talk in terms of separate souls, but it is probably safe to assume that the majority of the Chinese themselves never gave a moment's thought to this matter.

On death one soul went directly to Hell, where it was judged according to its conduct during life, the King of the First Court of Hell assigning the soul to the appropriate court for tortures and punishment which would ultimately expiate its sin. This soul demanded immediate worship upon death, and had to be heavily supplied with food, clothing, transport, servants, a house, and above all money. The money was particularly useful for smoothing the passage of the soul through the after-life, bribery being as effective there as in this life. The living could help in another way here too: a nineteenth-century missionary writer scathingly reported:

A ceremony designed to propitiate the good-will of the ten kings who rule over the affairs in the lower world is often performed for the benefit of either parent. It is believed that the punishment of the dead may be alleviated by obtaining favor with the governors of the ten departments of hell, through which they will be obliged to pass, and in which they will be obliged to suffer punishment for the sins of this life. If these kings are willing, they are supposed to have the prerogative, or, at least, to be in the practice of punishing the dead but slightly, imposing on him such penalties as are easily borne, or even of passing him along through the different departments without penalty. Thus do this people fancy they can bribe the rulers of hell![18]

The funeral service and a long period of mourning were concerned with this soul in Hell, and it would be worshipped at intervals for many years afterwards.

At the same time another soul remained with the corpse, following it into the grave through whatever process of burial was indulged in. Burial could be a very complicated affair, by no means always taking the form of a rapid and final disposal of the body in a grave:

> The very poor are often obliged, in order to save expense, or for other reasons, to bury their dead in the course of a few days after death. This is likened to a mandarin who proceeds to his official trust by the swiftest post, without the usual delays, receptions of honor, etc., *en route*. It is considered disreputable, and a mark of the very lowest poverty, or that the dead is destitute of friends and relatives who take an interest in the honor of the family.[19]

But in some cases the corpse would be laid up in a sealed coffin for many months, or even years, until a suitable burial site and an auspicious time for burial were found. Sometimes a grave-site might be proven inauspicious when ill-fortune struck the family of the deceased, and the body would then have to be exhumed and another site found. In parts of China it was almost standard practice to bury and rebury the body, a hastily dug grave serving as its resting place in the first instance, and then:

> Some five or ten years later the body is exhumed, and what can be found of the bones are cleaned and put into a large earthenware urn which is left out on the hillsides. Sometimes these urns stay there until they break and scatter their contents over the ground; but ideally they are looked after and worshipped every year by the descendants, while an auspicious time is awaited for the bones to enter the third and final stage, which is re-burial.
>
> Re-burial is the most difficult part of the process, for not only must an auspicious time be awaited, but an auspicious site for the grave must be chosen; and an auspicious site is not easy to find.[20]

The ancestor could be worshipped wherever his remains were, regardless of the stage of burial, whether in unburied coffin, temporary grave, urn or permanent grave. Usually a head-stone or plaque of some kind identified the ancestor and formed the focus for his worship. Often, the names of those male descendants of the deceased who had contributed towards the cost of building the permanent grave were inscribed on the head-stone, the stone thus serving both as a reminder to the living of whom they were worshipping and as a reminder to the dead of whom to benefit.

This grave-based soul was normally worshipped only once or at most twice a year. The principal occasion for grave-visiting was during the spring *Qing Ming* (Clear and Bright) festival, sometimes known as the 'Grave-sweeping festival', when it was the duty of the living to clean up the grave-sites, weeding and sweeping, re-painting and repairing, and putting down lime to discourage the growth of plant life. The ancestors were sacrificed to and worshipped by the whole family, and the ceremonial foods were eaten afterwards at a picnic held beside the graves. Some families repeated the ceremony during the autumn—usually somewhere around the ninth day of the ninth lunar month—and some confined their worship to the autumn only; but beyond these two occasions attention was seldom paid to the graves.

Yet another soul resided in an 'ancestor tablet' in the home, often placed in such a position that it overlooked much of the life that went on there, a permanent presence watching over the doings of its descendants. The ancestor tablet could take several forms. The most common was a narrow wooden block about one foot in height sunk into a wooden base support. Phallic symbolism has been attributed to this, perhaps not unreasonably given the importance of fertility and virility in Chinese culture. The name, generation number and attainments of the ancestor were written or carved on the front, the inscription saying that this was 'The place of the spirit of ——'. Usually the surname of the man's wife or wives and those of his concubines were also written on the tablet, but sometimes separate tablets were made for each of the spouses.

There is no doubt that this home-based soul was of the utmost importance in ancestor worship, and while it would be wrong to deny the importance of the other souls, it does seem to have been the ancestor tablet which was most heavily set about with ceremonial and which received the largest share of ritual attention:

> The tablet . . . is first 'dotted', and then placed in the niche among the ancestral tablets of the family. An acting mandarin, if possible to engage the services of such a man for the occasion, is called in; the higher his rank, the greater or the more auspicious the omen for good to the descendants of the person whose tablet is to be *dotted*. It must be premised that, to this period, one of the characters which have been written upon its front is deficient in one dot or stroke. The deficient character, meaning 'king', by receiving a small dot above the uppermost parallel stroke, becomes 'lord', which is what is desired. The mandarin dotter, or the dotter whatever his rank, uses a vermilion pencil. The eldest son kneels down reverently before the dotter, who dots the 'king' character with the required stroke, making it into the 'lord' character. He then returns it to the kneeling son, who reverently places it in the niche provided. . . . After this time the tablet is regarded as a *bona fide* residence of one of the three spirits of the departed.[21]

Every day tea and incense would be offered to the ancestors in the home, and an eternal light of some kind was often kept burning before the altar. This was usually a small saucer of oil with a wick floating in it, though of recent years a red-painted low-wattage electric light has been much in fashion. By these means the ancestors were constantly borne in mind.

On the first and fifteenth days of the lunar month—days which were considered particularly auspicious for ritual activity—the ancestors would share in the enhanced religious atmosphere, receiving offerings of foods, fruits and money in addition to the tea and incense. Much religious life was determined by the pronouncements of the *Almanac*, and when this book announced any day as ritually auspicious (which it did several times a month) the ancestors would again benefit. At lunar New Year, which was the most active time of all for worshipping, the ancestors would receive yet more elaborate offerings; and on the anniversaries of their birth-dates and/or death-dates they were again remembered. Any event of importance to the household was reported to the ancestors, and they partook of all special foods which were prepared by the family for weddings or Full Month feasts or other ceremonies and festivals. They were, then, very much a part of the everyday life of the family.

The daily worship was usually undertaken by the women, falling as it did within the home, the woman's sphere. But on the most important occasions, such as New Year or an ancestor's birth-date, it would be more likely the men, and particularly the male head of the family, who officiated. There were no priests, the ancestors could be worshipped only by their own descendants, and the simple rites required no great ritual expertise.

Of course there would be more than just one or two tablets on the ancestral altar in the home, and ultimately this could become a problem, for as the generations went by so the numbers of tablets sharing the limited space grew greater, until there came a time when it was physically difficult to fit more of them in. Here we come face to face with a major aspect of ancestor worship which picks up a point we made earlier in this chapter: the idea that the soul if not worshipped might eventually just melt away and cease to exist as an independent entity. The fact is that there came a time when an ancestor had so little significance for his descendants that they did not desire to go on worshipping him.

What determined that time? Well, all things being equal, the determining factor in family ancestor worship was personal acquaintance with or close personal knowledge of the ancestor. This meant that of course you continued to worship your dead father and grandfather, they were both known to you personally. And your great-grandfather figured as a real person in your memory because what he did and said had been talked about by your elders in your hearing when you were younger, so you worshipped him too; but your great-great-grandfather? You were very uncertain of him, he was of little interest to you. (And would you be of interest to him?) So perhaps you would not be over-concerned to worship him. The feeling of non-concern would doubtless increase with every generation. Consequently there was usually a limit to the number of past generations represented by tablets on a family altar. Some accounts speak of as few as three generations only, while five generations seems to have been as many as most families cared for.

Five is a very significant number in the Chinese scheme of kinship. We have already explored the Five Human Relationships (*wu-lun*) and the Five-generation Family, and now we meet another five, the Five Mourning Grades (*wu-fu*). These were categories of mourning garments and mourning periods which kin of differing relationships with the dead were expected to observe. The deepest mourning was worn for the longest time for those kin most close, one's father and mother; slightly less severe mourning was observed for paternal grandparents, and so on, until the least severe mourning still observed in the lineal direction was that for paternal great-great-grandparents (whom few people can ever have lived to mourn). The mourning prescriptions worked similarly in a lateral direction, so that deeper mourning was observed for one's brother than for one's first cousin, and the least severe for one's third cousin. (This is shown in Figure 11, p. 109.)

Now what these mourning grades effectively did was to mark off for the individual a special group of kin with himself at the centre, a cell of close relationship within the larger cell of relationship which kinship in general formed. This cell was the ultimate in kinship, a group from within which it was utterly impossible to select a spouse. But the other side of the coin of close ties with a limited group of people is the weakness of ties with people outside the group, a point we shall be making again. Therefore it made sense that when an ancestor fell within the range of this close-knit *wu-fu* group he should be worshipped, but that when in the course of time he receded from the living so far as to be outside the *wu-fu* group of the eldest surviving members of the family, interest in him should quickly be lost. And of course, given the reciprocal nature of things, he for his part may be expected to have lost interest in the living too.

It might also be pointed out that from a practical point of view a man could expect to get better returns from worshipping his father, who had only to divide his supernatural aid between him and his brothers, than from worshipping his grandfather, whose help was being tapped not only by the man and his brothers but also by the father's brothers and their sons. A great-great-grandfather might be dissipating his blessings over a large number of descendants, and if these powers were not infinite the individual worshipper could hope for only a small portion in return for his devotions.

After a few generations, then, the problem of overcrowded

altars was solved by weeding out the oldest of the ancestor tablets and disposing of them in a ritually acceptable manner—usually by burning or burying—thus making room for more recent tablets. The older graves too went untended until they were overgrown and forgotten. Such a fate marked the ritual end of the ancestor, and his soul would presumably melt away at this stage.

But it would be wrong to suggest that *all* ancestors fell within the five-generation limitation, for it is clear that in some cases men of many generations earlier were worshipped. The descendants of Confucius in the direct line were in receipt of a state pension even in the twentieth century:

> There has been no family in China which can boast that its ancestors have never worked for the last five hundred years, like some aristocrats in France or the Habsburgs in Austria, except Confucius's family, which has not worked for the last two thousand years.[22]

It would be strange if they did not keep his tablet before them. Similarly, some families had particular reasons for remembering earlier ancestors; for example, the ancestor who had founded the fortune on the basis of which the family still had an easy life, or the ancestor who had been a powerful court official and who might therefore be expected to be powerful still in the after-life. Also, the more extended the family the greater the number of ancestors in whom they would share an interest and the further back they would have to look for an ancestor from whom all were descended. In a nutshell, the ancestors who were worshipped were those who were important to the living family for any reason—but it happened that in most cases this meant only those ancestors of the most recent generations.

This emphasis on important ancestors points up the function of ancestor worship—its role in reinforcing the unity of the family. If we think of descent as a tree with the founding ancestor as the trunk, his sons as the primary branches and so on, then we can also visualise the disastrous effect on that tree when the trunk died—the branches would all fall apart as there was nothing left to hold them together. If the tree were to be kept whole, a way of preserving the trunk had to be found: and this in effect is what ancestor worship did, it preserved the founding ancestor without whom there was no connection between the various lines of his descendants. But since ancestor worship was, as it were, merely an artificial device, it was possible for it to be manipulated to fit the group for which it was intended. Thus, the family if it wanted to needed only to preserve that portion of the tree in which it was interested. If the family consisted of two sub-branches of one branch, it might concern itself with preserving just that branch which held the two sub-branches together, and might not worry any more about the other main branches or even the trunk. Ancestor worship could accordingly be operated on a sliding scale without fixed reference point at any one generation, its main function being to symbolise and reinforce a particular family group.

More than that, ancestor worship provided a ritual sanction to back up the Generation–Age–Sex scheme of authority in the family. The very principles of ancestor worship, the fact that it necessarily gave respect to earlier generations (Generation), that it gave priority to eldest sons by keeping the tablets in the care of the senior line (Age),* and that it considered women at all only in that they were the wives and mothers of men (Sex), these principles stressed the same priorities which we have already seen to be the basis on which the Confucian family was ordered.

ANCESTOR WORSHIP AND LARGER KIN GROUPS

We have seen that ancestor worship was the religious sanction behind family organisation of any size, and we saw in the previous chapter how the principles of family organization could be extended to much larger groupings, of which lineages were particularly important. It was only to be expected that ancestor worship in lineages should play a similar unifying role.

In a small family of uncomplicated structure it was unlikely that ancestors of very many generations would be worshipped, but in the larger, extended families it would probably be necessary to look rather further back in order to find the ancestors most important to the entire group. In the case of the lineage it

---

* Younger sons could have tablets under their care, but they were usually of a different type, often being a kind of composite tablet which did not refer to individual ancestors but had some such wording as 'The place of the spirits of all the ancestors of the ——surname'.

was always necessary to hunt back to the founding ancestor, for it was only in him that all the ramifications of descent in the group were united. As a ritual figure the founding ancestor was highly important.

Although viewed objectively the most vital function of the lineage ancestral trust might be said to have been an economic one, members of lineages would be quick to say that this was not so, that it was for ritual purposes that trusts were founded, and that the economic benefits which frequently accrued were a secondary consideration. And it is true that the first call on trust funds was the financing of lineage ritual—the worship of the founding ancestor. He was to be worshipped at his grave and at his ancestor tablet, much like any other ancestor.

Very often lineages built ancestral halls in which to place the tablet of the founding ancestor. Again, the primary purpose of the halls could be said to be the ceremonies of worship, but they were also used for lineage meetings, for feasts, for schools, and even for sleeping guests in. The tablet took the same form as that in the home, and was worshipped in the same way, with incense and tea daily (a service provided by a paid lineage official), and with sumptuous offerings on the one or two occasions during the year when ancestral rites were carried out.

But the founding ancestor's tablet was unlikely to be the only one in the hall. His sons and grandsons were probably of almost equal significance for the lineage, especially if they formed the foci for the major branches or segments round which political or ritual organizations were built. Accordingly their tablets would also appear in the hall, in a position on the altar only slightly inferior to that of the founding ancestor. Nor was it likely in a lineage of long standing that these would be the only ancestors to be worshipped. Over the generations successful, powerful and wealthy men would have arisen, and these men, because they themselves had success, would throw their glory by reflection on the lineage as a whole. By installing the tablets of such men in the hall the lineage not only paid tribute to their glory, but also kept that glory before the attention of its members permanently, enhancing its own prestige and its pride in its own achievements.

In the home, tablets were given a place on the altar by right— even the meanest and most unsuccessful man was guaranteed a few generations of worship and attention. But it is fairly obvious that this was by no means always the case with the ancestral hall. A few men (and of course their wives) were given places there by right of being the founders of the lineage from whom all others sprang, but for the rest it was a matter of honour, of special privilege, to have one's tablet selected for a place on the altar. The hall was stocked primarily with the tablets of the most *distant* in the line, the home by the most *recent*.

At least one writer has suggested that there could be an almost automatic progression of ancestors from the altars of the homes to the altars of the ancestral halls:

> When a new generation is added to the family shrine, the tablets of the ancestors five generations removed are sent to the ancestral hall . . . there to receive offerings with all the other bygone members of the group.[23]

My own observations in Sheung Shui and elsewhere did not coincide with this view, but there was a way in which the honour of having a tablet in the ancestral hall could be attained even there. Whenever the ancestral hall needed restoration (and buildings do not last very long in south China) the lineage would gain the extra income needed by selling off spaces for tablets on a special altar in the hall. Those who could afford the asking price would do so, having their tablets made and installed in preparation for their death. In order that no inauspicious effects should come of this premature memorial, the donor would have a red wooden cover bearing the words 'long life' placed over the tablet, not to be removed until he died. In somewhat macabre vein, I have seen an altar of this type where just one of the covers remained patiently awaiting the last donor's death.

Now, the ancestors in halls were there by right of seniority, by dint of success, or by purchase. Thus, there were three altars in the main ancestral hall of the Liao lineage. The central altar contained the tablets of the founding ancestor and of other genealogically important men of several generations; and this was flanked on the one side by an altar with the tablets of the two men of the lineage who had obtained particularly high degrees under the old civil service examination system, and on the other by an altar bearing many tablets of men who had donated money in successive restorations of the hall. But once a tablet was admitted to a hall it tended to lose its individuality, to become just one tablet in a huge bank of tablets; and the ancestor himself seemed to become part of a body of ancestral spirit which stood for the lineage as a whole and which the lineage would worship as a whole. It is true that the founding ancestor and one or two other men might be singled out for individual attention, but for most ancestors this was not so. This contrasts again with the personalized worship of the ancestors in the home.

There were other differences from home worship. Women were seldom, if ever, allowed in ancestral halls lest they defile them in some way (menstruation, for instance, was a ritually unclean condition), and they certainly were not allowed in when the ceremonies of worship were going on. But this meant that not all the lineage could worship its forebears, though in the home everyone joined in making obeisance to the ancestors there, and the women seem to have been responsible for the greater part of the day-to-day tendance of the household altar. And not only were the women excluded, but only a proportion of the men were involved in hall worship. In practice hall worship was conducted on behalf of the entire lineage by those seen as most fitted to represent the group to the ancestors. Notable amongst these were the elders, with the Lineage Head paramount. Being themselves closest to the ancestors and embodying the superiorities of Generation, Age and Sex, the elders' worshipping underscored symbolically the whole organization of the lineage. But also in evidence at the hall ceremonies would be the political leaders of the lineage community, the examination passers and the wealthy. If the tablets were in the hall by right of seniority, by dint of success, and by purchase, so were those who worshipped them!

Hall worship was formal, with women and children excluded, with the men on their best behaviour and dressed in ceremonial silk robes whenever possible. There was music to accentuate the effect of the ceremony and to summon the spirits to it; firecrackers to punctuate the long proceedings. There were tables laden with foods; whole roast pigs, preserved and fresh. fruits, meats of several kinds, fish, eggs, tea, wine, cakes and rice. There were ornate and expensive altar trappings, silk cloths, incense burners, huge decorative candles, large sticks of incense, sandalwood. There were lineage officials to guide the elders through the complex patterns of kow-towing and offering. There were addresses to the ancestors. There were feasts afterwards for the elders and the leaders, and there was sharing out of the pork in strict amounts according to age and position in the lineage. Certainly quite different from the casual, intimate worshipping which went on at home. And lineage worship at its important grave—that of the founding ancestor—was equally weighty and formal.

A lineage could be a very large unit and demanded a formal organization. Lineage ancestor worship had to act as the religious sanction behind this organization, and so needed to be undertaken with great seriousness. A lineage genealogy was usually kept, and in it would be recorded all the most important names and lines of the group. Recognition of membership in the lineage was granted officially by the lineage head and the elders at ceremonies held annually in the ancestral hall, new-born sons being formally registered there. Recognition was taken away by them too in extreme cases, by striking through the name of a man in the genealogy, thus cutting off him and his descendants for ever from the lineage.

Lineages, as we have seen, were often internally differentiated into segments, segments which we pointed out were very similar in organization and function to the lineage of which they formed a part. In ancestor worship too the segments resembled the lineage; they worshipped their founder as the unifier and sanction behind the group. Some segments—the particularly wealthy ones—owned halls and held large ceremonies there once or twice a year, the segment head worshipping its founder's tablet on behalf of all its members, just as the lineage head worshipped in the main ancestral hall. Those segments without halls—and they would be the majority—would usually confine themselves willy-nilly to the annual grave-worshipping ceremony. For those members of the lineage who came from wealthy descent lines with many ancestral trusts the autumn grave rites were a time of continuous worship and feasting. In Sheung Shui the lineage worshipped its founding ancestor on the 9th of the 9th lunar month, and his son on the following day. On the 11th, each of the three branches worshipped at its focal grave. One line of descendants then went on over the course of the next two weeks to worship at the graves of every ancestor from the fourth to the fourteenth generation.

Feasting after such ceremonies was subject to constraints of income of the segment. Some segments were so wealthy that they would actually feast all their members, men, women and children, while others could barely manage a small meal for their few elders.

Segmentation, of course, did not occur in every generation, and in some cases many generations in one line of descent might go by without a trust being formed. It is in such cases that a systematic interpretation of the theory of Chinese ancestor worship runs into difficulties. If trusts were focussed on men of the fourth and seventh generations with the result that those ancestors were still being worshipped several centuries later, it is pertinent to ask what has been happening to the ancestors of the fifth, sixth, eighth and subsequent generations. If the answer is, as it probably should be, that they are not worshipped at all, then we must assume that their souls have melted away. But if they are no longer there, there can be no connection between the two men who are still being worshipped, nor between them and the present-day descendants. Perhaps, if coherent answer there must be, the fact that the names of the unworshipped men are still extant and shown in correct order in the genealogy is sufficient to keep the link vital.

With units greater than the lineage, or perhaps we should say greater than the higher-order lineage, ancestor worship became as debatably authentic as did the stretching of the idea of kinship to such groups. The clan I called an 'unnatural' kin group, and it has to be said that unnatural lengths were often gone to in attempts to rationalise clan genealogies and arrive at common ancestry. Some clan genealogies, for instance, traced their descent from the Yellow Emperor, a mythical ruler said to have reigned in the third millenium B.C.; others from the Monkey God, who of course was also mythical; and so on. The ancestor tablets brought to clan halls by constituent lineages were little more than pawns in a financial game, mere tokens of the shares in the clan property purchased by the lineages. At best, it seems to me, they were an attempt by clans to cash in on the established values of ancestor worship, to try to bring to the clan the same sense of unity and loyalty which the lineage so strongly evinced. But the feeling of involvement, which lineage members operating in their own community must have had when worshipping, was surely lacking amongst the blasé gentry who worshipped an assembly of largely unknown tablets in a remote clan hall.

ANCESTOR WORSHIP AND 'CHINESE RELIGION'

The Chinese tolerated a range of religious belief and practice which is staggering in its breadth. Ancestor worship may well have been the most systematically viewed, was probably one of the most ancient, and was certainly the most widely practised religious element, but it existed side by side with many other beliefs. Buddhism, which came to China from India in the first century A.D., made a deep impact upon the Chinese, and from time to time gained an ascendancy at court and looked likely to become the universal religion, but it never did achieve it. Taoism, a native Chinese religion strongly associated with a philosophy of inaction and with alchemy, inter-acted with Buddhism and each became indebted to the other for ideas and for deities. There was a very full pantheon of gods of all sorts, from heavenly emperors to deified mortals. There was a very old set of beliefs in spirits associated with natural phenomena—tree gods, river gods, earth gods, etc. There were ubiquitous evil spirits and ghosts which had to be appeased. And there were evil and good influences in nature which could influence men's lives. The picture can be made even more colourful by mentioning Judaism, Islam and Christianity, which all were present in China too, though only Islam made sizeable inroads into popular acceptance.

With the exception perhaps of the devout Buddhists, Taoists, Muslims and Christians (altogether only a small proportion of the population, though in some areas they might be in the majority), most people seem to have been able to believe in nearly all these elements simultaneously. Or perhaps 'believe' is too strong a word for what really amounted to a willingness to practise rather than an understanding and acceptance. There were few families in Sheung Shui which did not worship their ancestors; the Door Gods; the Kitchen God; the Goddess of Mercy, a boddhisattva taken from Buddhism and embraced by many Chinese; the Empress of Heaven, a deified girl who when alive had, like Grace Darling, gone out in a storm to save lives at sea; the Great Sage, a local god; the Gods of Earth and Grain; an

Earth God; a Well God; a Tree God; and Heaven: making offerings to or taking precautions against ghosts and evil spirits; employing spirit mediums in time of sickness in order to consult the gods about cures, Taoist priests and Buddhist nuns to officiate at funerals and other ceremonies, geomancers for grave-siting, astrologers for match-making, and so on. This hotch-potch of practice was called by some 'Chinese religion'.

Ancestor worship stands out from the rest as being more systematic and more obviously in tune with the structure of Chinese society. It was probably the one belief system which was fundamentally important to most Chinese. Yet it must be viewed against this background of lack of systematic belief. It was not itself entirely unaffected by other beliefs, nor did it fail to influence them.

In many ways Buddhism and ancestor worship were contradictory. In the early period of mourning, ancestor worship was largely directed at the soul finding its way to hell and then finding its level there, and this could be characterised as ancestor worship lending itself to Buddhist purposes. It chimes ill with the idea of ancestors as gods able to help their descendants: indeed one has to wonder whether anything was expected from the ancestor as a return at this time, and if not, is this to be called 'worship' at all? Perhaps it is little more than elaborate 'memorialism'?

But Buddhism presented a far greater challenge to ancestor worship than this. The idea of re-birth is clearly contrary to the concept of a continuing ancestral spirit. Could one logically go on worshipping an ancestor who had been reborn as an animal or as another person? The following case is taken from a Chinese tale. A young girl was so frequently unwell that her doting father consulted a learned man about it. He said:

> 'She is not ill, but no life-producing hwun [soul] has settled as yet in her body.' Ching asked him to explain himself better. 'So-and-So', thus was the answer, 'prefect of the district So-and-So, is the body preceding that of your girl. This man had to die several years ago; but he was doing so much good in this life that the Nether-world intervened on his behalf, so that the day of his death was postponed. He is now over ninety years old; when he dies, the girl shall regain her health on the same day.' Ching quickly despatched a man to the place mentioned,

to obtain information there, and he found indeed that the prefect was more than ninety. Next month the daughter suddenly had a sensation as if awaking from a state of inebriety; and her illness was all over. Ching Kiun then sent the man again for information; and indeed, without any previous illness, the prefect had died on the very day on which the girl was restored to health.[24]

Here, even if the man had three souls, the one which would normally go down to hell could not have done so, but it would be odd if he were not worshipped as an ancestor just the same. It is difficult to know how much weight to give to stories of this type, but they do at least stress the lack of a systematic approach to religious problems.

Christianity wrestled with ancestor worship from the outset. Faced with the one religious practice from which the Chinese converts were most loath to desist, many missionaries found solace in the idea that the practice was memorialism and not worship. In this they were encouraged by the use of the Chinese word *bai* 'to worship', for there was no doubt that it could also be used in the sense of 'to pay respects to'. By assuming this latter meaning to be the correct one, the practice could be equated with such actions as putting flowers on a relation's grave and so be perfectly acceptable to the Christian. Whether the ancestors were *worshipped* in China or not has been a matter for debate among Western observers for many years. The weight of the evidence falls heavily on the positive side, but it would be unkind to suppose that all those who have claimed that the ancestors were not worshipped were guilty either of unforgivable ignorance or of transmitting a fiction. In his most perceptive and sympathetic booklet on Chinese ancestor worship, J. T. Addison reaches the conclusion that:

The test, then, is whether or not some return is expected for sacrifices offered. Is there a *quid pro quo*?
    The answer to this question depends on the value assigned to the mass of evidence in support of the conclusion that the Chinese perform the ceremonies of ancestor worship with the aim to avoid calamities and to secure worldly prosperity. *That evidence is ample enough to establish the fact that in popular ancestor*

worship the element of religion is so strong as to justify the term 'worship'.[25]

With this conclusion it is hard to disagree. For the pre-Buddhist Shang kings at any rate there was certainly no doubt.

Christianity and Buddhism, both imported religions, were affected by ancestor worship, just as ancestor worship was in turn considerably affected by Buddhism. It is hardly to be wondered at that many of the native religious practices were closely linked with ancestor worship. Thus, the Lineage Head, whose functions normally were squarely in the fields of kinship hierarchy and ancestor worship, could go around the village once a year worshipping the whole gamut of gods on behalf of the lineage; the grave where the ancestor was buried and worshipped was usually protected by an Earth God, who also had to be worshipped in order to maintain his watch; the ancestor could be spoken to through a spirit-medium, who operated in other religious fields than ancestor worship alone; and the ancient dualistic *yang-yin* theories were involved too:

> The ancestors as bones are *yin*: they are of the Earth, passive, and retiring. The ancestors in their tablets are *yang*: they have affinities with Heaven and are active and outgoing.[26]

Perhaps closest linked of all was *feng-shui*, which is often called 'geomancy'. Geomancy was a body of belief which centred on the idea that the natural surroundings in which a man lived were capable of influencing his fate. If the environment was suited to him he would be happy and contented, a view with which few people would disagree. But geomancy went further and claimed that the suitable environment could also result in increased wealth, in a strong and successful posterity, in good health, a long life, and so on. In order to exploit this natural resource, it was necessary to develop a science which could assist in discovering the ways in which the veins of good fortune could be tapped. Professional geomancers, with the aid of a specialised compass and of a vast body of lore, could locate the most propitious areas and pinpoint the exact spots and directions which would give the desired results. The building of a house, a temple, or even a village in accordance with a geomancer's instructions should ensure for the inhabitants such blessings as the site was naturally endowed with. As a reflection of this, the geomancy of graves was important, the descendants of the grave's inhabitants benefiting from its good *feng-shui*:

> In West Town there are not only many cases of 'stealthy entombment' (i.e., a poor man deliberately entombs a deceased family member in a highly situated family's grave-yard, so as to share the good geomantic effects of the prosperous family) but also struggles between members of the same clan for a 'better' location for their own immediate ancestors in the same graveyard. The idea seems to be that the 'better' the parents are situated the better their immediate descendants will succeed in their worldly affairs.[27]

It is a moot question whether or not geomancy of graves was thought to operate independently of ancestor worship; whether, that is, burial automatically released the good effects or whether they were released only because the man buried was pleased with the site. It was possible for charitable persons to bury in good sites the bones of any who were found to be without proper burial, and these persons presumably expected to receive some supernatural return for their charity. Yet there is no doubt that from the recipient's point of view such burial would be thought inferior. However, in most cases it was his own descendants who buried a man, and it was they who would normally expect to benefit from the geomancy, so to that extent at least the geomancy of graves was closely tied in with ancestor worship.

Ancestral halls, too, were much affected by geomancy. The main hall of Sheung Shui was built on a spot which was said to be on the head of a dragon, a most propitious site. Since dragons always chase pearls, part of the village was built in front of the hall in the stylised shape of a Chinese pearl, thus ensuring that the dragon's head would not turn away and spoil the geomantic effects.

It is not easy to isolate ancestor worship from the many other religious beliefs and practices which went to make up 'Chinese religion'. For the most part the same kind of offerings went to ancestors as to other gods—incense, candles, food and drink were common to both kinds of worship, though in some areas very nice distinctions in offerings were observed. But we can, I think, be sure that if all the non-ancestral religious features were trimmed away, there would remain a basic core of belief and ritual which could stand as a meaningful religion in its own right.

XIAO

In Chinese society much was made to depend on the relationship between father and son. It was universally accepted as the most important human relationship, and was central to a concept which the Chinese called *xiao*, generally translated (inadequately) as 'filial piety'. *Xiao* took the kind of superior-inferior relationship which was inherent in the father-son relationship and extended it by analogy to other social relationships. We have already met it in disguise as the *wu-lun* in Chapter 1, and it forms the subject of the *Classic of Filial Piety* (*Xiao Jing*), a very early work which came to form part of the Confucian canon.

The duty of a man was first to his parents and only second to the state. Except in the case of treason, a son was absolved from responsibility for reporting the misdemeanours of his father. In Imperial China it was a serious offence for a state employee in office not to declare the death of a parent and retire to mourn for the statutory period of over two years. For his parents a son must stop at almost no sacrifice. Here are two instances of the lengths to which *xiao* could be carried:

One of the most striking acts of Chinese filial devotion is cutting a piece of flesh from the thigh or arm, in order that it may be prepared with other ingredients as a restorative for a parent in extreme cases of sickness. Such acts of piety are not very unusual. At Pit-kong in the county of Shun-tuk, I was acquainted with a youth who had cut a large piece of flesh from his arm out of devotion to his mother, who was supposed to be suffering from an incurable disease. He was evidently proud of the scar which remained.

It is quite usual for sons to go to prison, and into banishment, for offences committed by their parents. In 1862, I found in the district city of Tsung-fa, a youth suffering incarceration in the stead of his grandfather, who had been committed to prison for bankruptcy. Availing itself of this sentiment, the government seizes the parents of offenders when it is unable to effect the capture of the offenders themselves.[28]

Parents' names were taboo and, if they happened to be common ones, considerable ingenuity was required to avoid their use. Sometimes, where avoidance of the word was impossible, a filial child would deliberately mispronounce or miswrite the word. Similarly:

'Name taboo' was one of the things to be considered in any appointment. In ancient times, an official would not accept an appointment if the official title or the name of the place where his prospective office was located was similar to the name of his grandfather or father. For instance, if a father's name was Ch'ang, the son would not accept a post as *t'ai-ch'ang* or one located in Ch'ang-shan.[29]

In other *wu-lun* derived relationships, too, extraordinary devotion to duty was considered correct. In the following case, taken from the Sheung Shui Liao lineage genealogy, the husband-wife relationship can be seen to call for much the same quality of self-sacrifice as the father-son relationship:

In the Hung Chih reign of the Ming dynasty [1488–1505 A.D.] pirates were taking captives and holding them to ransom, and Ch'ung-shan was captured by them. His wife went to the pirates' boat and offered herself as hostage for him while he returned home to find the money for the ransom. The pirates agreed to this. She secretly told him that when he returned he should first make enquiries as to what news there was, and she gave him a silver ring tied with one of her hairs. When he returned and made enquiries he heard that she had jumped into the sea and been drowned two nights previously. His grief knew no bounds. Then he used the ring and the hair to call up her spirit, and made a grave . . .

The aim of emphasis on *xiao* was the orderly running of the family and, through it, of the state. Orderly running of the family depended to some extent upon knowledge of the history of the family and of the logic of composition of the various units which could be covered by the concept of family. Here written records of family development (genealogies) became important, and these were backed up by other records, such as grave-stones. That a family had a history gave support to the idea of it as a long-continuing corporate group, and encouraged the notion of its going on into the future. Hence, in some parts of China it was possible to sign away the use of a parcel of land in return for a loan of money, the land being redeemable at any time, however many years or generations later, on repayment of the money.

The continuity of the family being of great importance the religious system which sanctioned it was naturally also important. The cult of the ancestors laid stress on precisely those aspects of the moral equipment of the family that tended towards unity and good order. Where *xiao* demanded an order of precedence in the family which gave us the Generation–Age–Sex formulation in Chapter 1, so ancestor worship laid stress on generation— ancestor superior to descendant; on age—the eldest of brothers was the recipient of the mantle of ancestor worshipping responsibility; and sex—women could achieve ancestorhood only through their husbands and sons, and were not allowed to worship in ancestral halls.

Where a family expanded over the years and so tried to accommodate in the one unit people who were less and less closely related to each other as generations went by, the number of ancestors worshipped increased too, so keeping the unifying features present in the larger group. The number of ancestors and the number of past generations worshipped were generally in proportion to the size and lateral spread of the group worshipping them. Thus ancestor worship could function as effectively at the level of the lineage of several thousand members as it could at the simple family level.

But if the family was seen as the basic unit of society, and ancestor worship as the religious sanction behind it, then it follows that what was less than a basic unit would probably not be sanctioned by ancestor worship. Accordingly we find that aberrant features on the social scene were not catered for by the cult. Divorced women, unmarried men and women, young children, the childless, none of these contributed to the continuity of the family, and all of them fell outside the sphere of ancestor worship. Assuming that everyone believed in ancestor worship, the pressures to conform were doubtless much increased by the knowledge that non-conformity meant this kind of ritual death.

The sum total of *xiao* and ancestor worship, together with those other religious features which were entwined with them, powerful urges to conformity in family and state, are probably what was meant by those people who have spoken of 'Confucianism'. Yet Confucius himself (who never spoke of spirits) would perhaps have denied the validity of the means even while agreeing with the conformist ends those means were serving. The intellectuals of his time were not unaware of the value of religion in social control, while cynically placing themselves above it. The philosopher Hsün Tzu (fl. 298–238 B.C.) wrote:

If people pray for rain and it rains, how is that? I would say: Nothing in particular. Just as when people do not pray for rain, it also rains. When people try to save the sun or moon from being swallowed up [in eclipse], or when they pray for rain in a drought, or when they decide an important affair only after divination—this is not because they think in this way they will get what they seek, but only to add a touch of ritual to it. Hence the gentleman takes it as a matter of ritual, whereas the common man thinks it is supernatural. He who takes it as a matter of ritual will suffer no harm; he who thinks it is supernatural will suffer harm.[30]

There seems in fact to have been an awareness of the social effects of the ancestral cult on the part of the educated elite which made their advocacy of it very much more a rational than a religious factor:

At one extreme we have the rites performed as a conventional memorial with no belief implied in the powers or even the existence of the deceased. At the other extreme we have the same rites performed with motive and desires scarcely distinguishable from those which express themselves in the service of gods and spirits. Toward the latter extreme tend the beliefs of the unlettered masses, toward the former the beliefs of the

Chinese classics and of all those who think and feel in harmony with the classics. Between the two extremes and in obedience to one tendency or the other are innumerable gradations and variations of motive and meaning.[31]

5

The Family in State and Society

So far we have looked at the internal organization of the family and other kin groupings, but we have not considered the place of the family in society nor how it interacted with other institutions. A family is, of course, moulded by its relationships with other families and with society at large, just as the behaviour and life-style of the individual are affected by his relationships with others. Even the lineage, large and 'self-sufficient' as it was, must be placed in a social context if we are to understand its importance.

In this chapter we shall look at the legal position of the family, and at the way in which the family's dealings with the state were regulated, and then go on to discuss some of its non-legal relationships.

THE WU-FU

The state not only recognized that the family was the basic unit of Chinese society, it went to considerable lengths to encourage and ensure the strength, unity and viability of the family. Large sections of the laws and statutes were concerned with the regulation of kinship ties and with relationships within the family. Basic to these laws was the carefully worked out system of degrees of kinship—the *wu-fu*—which we touched on briefly in connection with ancestor worship.

Wu-fu actually means 'the five kinds of clothing', and refers to the five different types of mourning dress which were very early on in Chinese history prescribed by Confucian orthodoxy. Each type of dress was worn for a specific period of time, as in Figure 10.

The *wu-fu* were included in the written laws of the state, and

Grade	Dress	Mourning period
1	Dress of unhemmed coarse hemp, hemp head-dress, grass sandals, and mourning staff	27 months
2(a)	Dress of hemmed coarse hemp, hemp head-dress, straw or hemp shoes, and mourning staff	1 year
(b)	Dress as 2(a) but without staff	1 year
(c)	As 2(b)	5 months
(d)	As 2(b)	3 months
3	Dress of coarse cloth	9 months
4	Dress of less coarse cloth	5 months
5	Dress of plain silky hemp	3 months

Figure 10. The *Wu-fu* (Mourning Grades)

imposed a duty of mourning upon the people, sanctioned by punishment:

When one knows that his father or mother has died, or when a grandson who is the Continuator of his family is acquainted with the decease of one of his paternal grandparents, or a woman (wife or concubine) with that of her husband—if then such a person keeps the fact a secret and shows no signs of distress, a punishment of sixty blows with the long stick, followed by banishment for one year, shall be inflicted. And if, ere the rescripts of mourning have been observed to the end, such a person puts off the mourning dress and behaves as if not in mourning, forgetting grief, making music, clubbing together with others for amusement and enjoyment of festive meals—eighty blows with the long stick shall be administered.[1]

In Figure 11 the patrilineal kin recognized by the system are each marked with the appropriate grade of mourning due to them by Ego (the mourner). It can be seen that about Ego himself are clustered those for whom he has to observe the deepest mourning, and that as relationships recede from him in either an ascending, descending or lateral direction so the mourning

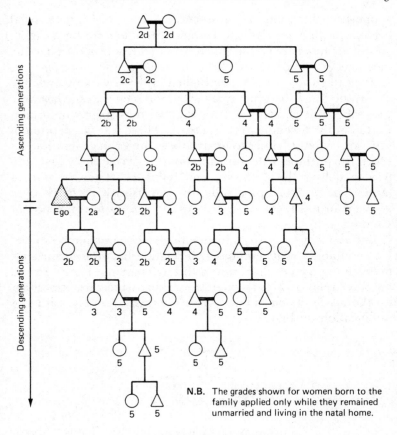

Figure 11. Patrilineal Mourning Grades

requirements are less severe. It can be seen also that horizontal mourning relationships (that is, those in the same generation as Ego) are for the most part reciprocal, Ego being due mourning of the same degree as he would give. But in vertical relationships there are some important distinctions. Thus, while Ego as a son observes Grade 1 mourning for his father, as a father he only observes Grade 2b for his son.

But it was not primarily for the enforcement of mourning that the *wu-fu* were of legal interest. They were mainly used to define degrees of relationship both within and outside the family unit, and therefore served as guidelines for the law in its concern with supporting the family as an essential feature of Chinese social organization. They defined degrees of relationship because the severity of mourning requirement was in direct proportion to the closeness and importance of the deceased to the mourner.

That the *wu-fu* were not embodied in the law solely to define mourning duties becomes clear when it is seen that the law only prescribed punishment for those who failed to observe mourning for kin in the ascending relationships. There was no mention of sanctions against failure to mourn those junior in generation. In short, the purpose of defining relationships so carefully by grade was to bolster the authority and influence of the patrilineal family, pointing emphatically the superiority of elder over younger in much the same way as did the *wu-lun* discussed in Chapter 1.

But in Chapter 1 we also mentioned the imbalance in the Chinese family in its emphasis on relationships traced through males as opposed to those traced through females. Figure 12 sets out those relationships through the mother which are prescribed by the *wu-fu*. Their small spread contrasts strongly with the ramifications of Figure 11.

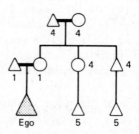

Figure 12. Matrilineal Mourning Grades

The mourning requirements towards females married out from the patrilineal family are shown in Figure 13. Comparison with Figure 11 will show the difference made by marriage. Thus an unmarried sister is mourned by Ego in Grade 2b, but in only Grade 3 when she has been married out. This is consistent with the reduced importance of the woman to her natal family once she has transferred her services and allegiance to another group. In the same way the *wu-fu* prescriptions register a considerable reduction in the scope of mourning obligations of a woman

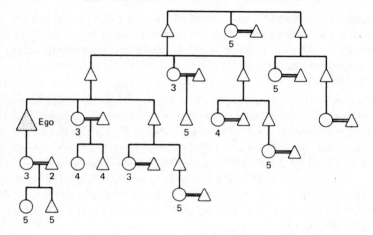

Figure 13. Mourning for Married Out Females and their Children

towards her natal kin once she has married out (see below, Figure 14).

The *wu-fu*, then, defined the limits of the kinship group which was considered officially to be of paramount importance to the individual. It is worthy of note that everyone in the 'five generations co-residing' of the Ideal Family which we discussed in Chapter 1 fell within the boundaries of the *wu-fu* network of any one of its members, and that therefore the state was providing reinforcement for relationships within that family. The *wu-fu* also circumscribed the group from which it was utterly impossible legally to select a bride of the same surname.

The law viewed crimes committed against *wu-fu* kin in a special light. First, it drew distinctions in gravity of crime according to the respective mourning grades of offender and victim:

A son who strikes or beats a parent (degree 1 relationship) suffers decapitation, irrespective of whether or not injury results. However, no penalty applies to a parent who beats his son (degree 2b), unless the son dies, in which case the punishment for the parent is 100 blows of the heavy bamboo if the beating was provoked by the son's disobedience, and one year of penal servitude plus sixty blows of the heavy bamboo if the beating was done wantonly.[2]

Second, it considered some offences more serious if committed against a *wu-fu* relative than if against someone outside the scope of the *wu-fu*. Thus, parricide was a worse crime than the murder of a non-relative, and

> any premeditated murder occurring among the mourning-relatives was punished more severely than ordinary cases. The degrees varied according to the generation and the degree of mourning. Anyone who designed the murder of any senior relative within the fourth degree, but whose plan miscarried, was punished by banishment to a distance of two thousand *li*. If the action occasioned a wound the offender was strangled; and when the murder was actually committed, the offender was beheaded.[3]

Third, it held some offences *less* serious if committed against a *wu-fu* relative:

> An interesting exception to the general principle that closer relationships involve heavier punishments is the treatment of theft within the family: the penalties for this offense are graduated *inversely* to the closeness of relationship, and at the same time made consistently lower than the punishments for ordinary theft outside the family. Thus the penalty for stealing from a fifth degree relative is two grades less than the ordinary punishment; for stealing from a fourth degree relative it is made three grades less; for stealing from a third degree relative it becomes four grades less, and so on.[4]

But it would not be right to assume that what was the law was always in line with what actually went on in Chinese society, and the *wu-fu* prescriptions sometimes were much at variance with local and popular custom. Thus, despite the official grades, few Chinese actually observed mourning for juniors, not even for their own sons or grandsons. Indeed, mourning even for seniors did not necessarily follow the system set out in the *wu-fu*. Local custom often modified the official prescriptions both as to dress and as to who should be mourned. An example from contemporary Taiwan will serve to illustrate one kind of diversity:

Seen from a distance, from the top of a building or one of the hills on which most graves are sited, the procession following a Chinese coffin is a colorful sight. The mourners wear long robelike gowns, some of rough dirty-brown sackcloth, others of gray flax or grass cloth, and still others of unbleached white linen or muslin; scattered among these are blue gowns, red gowns, and, on the rare occasion, a yellow gown. Female mourners cover their heads with a hood that almost hides the face and hangs down the back to the waist; men wear a hempen 'helmet' over a short hood or one of two kinds of baglike hats of unbleached or dyed muslin. A mourner's hood is sometimes of the same material as his gown, sometimes of a different material. The hood itself may be plain, or it may display a stripe or one or more patches of another material. A common combination is a tall spreading hat with a red stripe to which is sewn a smaller patch of grass cloth or blue muslin. I have never tried to count the number of mourning costumes in the Chinese repertoire, but there must be at least a hundred immediately recognizable variants. A funeral procession of fifty mourners usually includes twenty or more different combinations of textiles and colors.[5]

Clearly, more than just five grades of dress were involved here.

THE FAMILY IN THE LAW

The family was treated by the state as a mutual responsibility group:

The ancients usually considered that merely punishing the criminal himself in severe cases was not sufficient punishment to prevent a recurrence of crime. The arrest and punishment of the innocent family members of a criminal along with him was thought to increase the mental burden of the criminal so that he would hesitate to violate the law again. . . . At the same time, the practice was intended to make all family members watch each other's behaviour.

   Collective responsibility may have been exercised in two ways: either the family members received the same punishment as the criminal or they were punished less severely than the criminal. . . . Under the law, the parents, siblings, wife, and children of a criminal were to be executed with him. . . . In less severe cases the family members of the criminal were not subject to the death penalty, but were seized and made slaves.[6]

Much of this Han dynasty (205 B.C.-A.D. 220) thinking and some of the law and practice survived until the end of China's imperial history in 1911.

For the most part, however, the state relied upon the internal discipline of the family to keep individuals as law-abiding citizens. This meant that it had to maintain the authority structure of the family, and accordingly the law reinforced the Generation–Age–Sex hierarchy, and in particular gave support and responsibility to the family head as the topmost member of that hierarchy.

The punishment for any crime was laid down by the law, and ranged from the lightest flogging and fining, through transportation, to various forms of capital punishment. The most severe form of the death penalty consisted of slicing into many pieces, then came beheading, and, considered least severe, strangulation:

Although strangulation is thus a slower and more painful death than decapitation, it has always been regarded as a lesser punishment for socio-religious reasons: According to the tenets of Chinese filial piety, one's body is not one's own property, but a bequest from his parents. To mutilate one's body, therefore, or allow it to be mutilated, is to be unfilial. Strangulation, from this point of view, is superior to decapitation since it leaves the body intact. Furthermore, by the same token, strangulation is superior because it leaves the spirit of the executed man an intact body which it can continue to inhabit.[7]

For a son to strike a parent was an offence punishable by decapitation, even if no injury was caused to the parent. But a parent could beat his son with impunity, and would suffer only the mildest of punishment if the son were to die. A parent could have his son punished by beating or banishment for drunkenness, laziness, gambling, disobedience, or almost any behaviour inimical to him, such behaviour by definition being unfilial, and

> when parents asked to have an unfilial son prosecuted, the
> authorities demanded no evidence, nor did they raise any
> objections to the punishment asked. The law states clearly:
> 'When a father or mother prosecutes a son, the authorities will
> acquiesce without question or trial.' 'No parents in the world
> are wrong' is a very popular adage in China.[8]

But a son would be sentenced to strangulation merely for scolding
a parent or grandparent. And if a parent or grandparent should
commit suicide in a fit of anger at a son's behaviour, the latter
would be decapitated for causing the death.

Punishment for an offence against a senior within the same
generation was lighter than for one against a member of a senior
generation, but was designed to support the authority of senior
over junior. Thus, although an elder brother could strike, injure
or cause the death of his younger brother with legal consequences
only a little more severe than if his father had performed the
action, yet:

> The punishment for striking an elder brother or sister was
> imprisonment for two and a half years when no injury resulted,
> or three years' imprisonment if the victim was wounded. If a
> tooth, finger, toe, or rib was broken by the blow, the
> punishment was banishment to a distance of three thousand *li*;
> if a wound was caused by a sharp-bladed instrument, or if a
> limb was broken or an eye blinded, the offender was strangled;
> if death resulted, the punishment was beheading.[9]

The same principle applied to the husband-wife relationship.
A wife would be sentenced to a flogging of 100 strokes if she beat
her husband, to strangulation if she caused him permanent
injury, and to beheading if she killed him. A husband was
punished for beating his wife only if injury resulted, and the
maximum penalty he could receive for killing her was strangulation (not beheading). If a woman were beaten to death by her
parents-in-law, they were punished at all only if they could show
no reasonable grounds for the manner in which they beat her.

The sanctity and smooth running of the family was the aim of the laws. It was forbidden to marry anyone of the same surname, since confusion in the relationships between kin might result.* The penalties for such a marriage grew more severe the closer the relationship between the spouses, until capital punishment was merited in the case of marriage between close *wu-fu* relatives. The prohibition applied to concubinage as well as marriage. Similarly graduated punishments applied to marriage to the widow of a kinsman, such marriage within the *wu-fu* carrying the worst punishments. Again confusion in relationships and family authority patterns was being guarded against.

Even where marriage was allowed between kin or affines, the law prohibited marriage outside one's own generation. Adoption also had to observe the generation prescription, an adoptee having to come from a lower generation than the adopting parents. Sexual intercourse between members of the *wu-fu* not married to each other again attracted graduated punishment based on the mourning grades, higher grades carrying severer sanctions.

In recognition of the importance of the family, the law would on occasion allow junior relatives to suffer punishment in the stead of their seniors. For example, where a father with a large young family to bring up had been sentenced to death, one of the sons might be allowed to take his place. Often special clemency seems to have accompanied such substitutions, the son being punished less severely than the father would have been, or even obtaining a pardon as a reward for his filial action. Sometimes a son's punishment would be postponed or even remitted if it would have resulted in excessive hardship for dependent aged parents.

The right of choice in marriage was legally denied to a son (and, of course, to a daughter):

> Since the main aim of the marriage was to produce offspring to carry on ancestor worship, marriage itself became more a family than a personal matter. In no sense was a marriage concerned with the personal wishes of the man and woman involved; and since marriage was a union of two families, its

---

* We have seen already that there was an assumption that anyone of the same surname must have sprung from the same root.

conclusion depended on agreement between the heads of the two families concerned. Seniors in the direct line, and especially males, had absolute authority over an offspring's marriage. This was recognized by both law and society. Under the law of T'ang, Sung, Ming, and Ch'ing, a man, even though he was adult, held an official position, [and] ran a business far from home, did not have the right to marry without his parents' consent. If he became engaged while away from home, and his parents or some other authorized senior at a later date betrothed him to a girl in his local community, his self-initiated engagement, provided he was still unmarried, became void. Punishment for refusing to give up a self-initiated engagement was eighty to one hundred strokes, and only if the offender had married before his parents betrothed him to another girl was his union recognized.[10]

If parents were dead, then authority to arrange a marriage was vested in the next senior male highest in grade as defined by the *wu-fu*.

A wife who ran away from her husband's home was legally liable to punishment by beating, and her husband was entitled to sell her in marriage. Of course, her leaving home was considered detrimental to family order. We might note at this point that the 'Seven Outs' (the reasons for divorce) discussed in Chapter 2 were also mostly connected with family stability and good order. On the whole the laws seem to have been framed with a view to protecting the family against the wife, but she herself was protected by the law against any encroachment on her position by a concubine, and as a mother she came fully under the law's protection. Concubines were officially recognized, and had their place in the *wu-fu* also.

The family also needed protection from society at large, and over and above the normal laws on murder there was the provision that if anyone killed three or more members of one family, thus severely weakening the group, the punishment was death by slicing.

The law, then, was much concerned with the unity and cohesion of the family. Its strong support for the authority of those senior in the Generation–Age–Sex hierarchy meant that it claimed little jurisdiction over the internal ordering of the family.

Instead it recognized the responsibility of the familyhead, who was accountable for any crime committed by a family member. His burden included responsibility for the taxes and labour service (corvée) required of members of his household. He could be punished for failure to enter a member of his household on the population register. He was even liable for punishment for any infringements of the proprieties at a funeral by members of his family.

At various times in history the state attempted social control through the *bao-jia* system. The household, which for the most part was the same as the family, was the basic unit of the system. Ten households were known as a *pai*, and one household head from the ten would be made *pai*-head. Ten *pai* constituted a *jia**, with a *jia*-head, and ten *jia* made a *bao* under a *bao*-head:

> Its first function was the registration of the households and inhabitants in the neighborhoods and villages. Superficially, it resembled a census system, for it recorded the names of all inhabitants of a given place—all persons who dwelt in households, temples, and hostels—kept track of all the movements of individuals and households, made periodic recounts of the local population, and brought their registers up to date. But it was more than a census system, for it imposed upon the persons registered and those who made the registration the duties of a constable or sheriff: to watch, detect, and report any crime or criminal that might be found in the neighborhoods.[11]

The system rarely worked well. It was very unwieldy, and the heads of the various groups were chary of reporting crimes where prompt action by the state was less likely than prompt vengeance by the criminals. When strong group heads were in control, there was frequent abuse of power in the form of 'squeeze'.

POSITIVE SANCTIONS BEHIND THE FAMILY

In talking of the law we have seen how failure to maintain family sanctity was punished. Rewards and encouragement were to a lesser extent also given by the state.

* This word *jia* is not to be confused with the word meaning 'family'.

The imperial bureaucracy was staffed by meritocrats who had passed the civil service examinations. In that a major ingredient of the examinations was the Confucian classics, in that those classics laid great stress on family solidarity and on the family authority system, and in that there was universal respect for scholarship and scholarly success, it may be said that no family could be unaware of the state's encouragement of familism.

A more direct and positive approach was the institution in the 17th century of the *xiang-yue* system. This consisted of twice-monthly lectures to the populace given by local officials or by approved laymen, the lectures being based on the Six Edicts of the Shun Chih emperor. The edicts were:

1. Be filial and obedient to parents
2. Honour and respect elders and superiors
3. Be at peace and in harmony with neighbours
4. Instruct and admonish sons and grandsons
5. Let everyone peacefully go about his work
6. Do not do wrong.

Later, the Sacred Edict of the K'ang Hsi emperor, a similar though expanded set of prescriptions, was also used (see Appendix I). These edicts were grounded in Confucian family values and consequently formed a recurrent reinforcement of them in the minds of the people.

The veneration for old age associated with and perhaps arising from the elder-younger relationship in the family was also actively encouraged by the state, which could bestow the title *qi-lao* (*elder*) on the deserving aged:

The elders were a very small group. There was no definite age limit, but in general only people at least sixty years or more of age were counted as old enough for this age distinction. Furthermore, not all old people were given the honorific term of 'elder'. The elders had to be distinguished also by local prestige, ability, wealth, or general leadership in community affairs. They advised or helped to manage relief bureaus, helped in some localities to expound the sixteen maxims of the 'Sacred Edict', rendered assistance in arresting bandits, and so on.[12]

The honorific arch or tablet was a favoured form of state recognition of virtue, serving at once as a mark of distinction to the rewarded and as an example to the rest of the population. Frequently it was family virtues which were rewarded in this way, as in the following cases which illustrate the state's approval of conduct promoting family strength through filial piety, committed widowhood, selfless service and commensal harmony:

> In the seventh year of the period Yuen kia (A.D. 430), the authorities in southern Yü-cheu recommended the family of Tung Yang, living under their supervision in the district of Si-yang (province of Hupeh), to the Throne for having lived together during three generations without possessing separate doors leading out of the house or separate cooking places inside the house. By an Imperial order a board was placed over their gate, bearing the inscription: 'Village of the family Tung who live in harmony and concord'.

> He died, upon which his wife, fearing that her parents might bereave her of her chastity (by re-marrying her), wailed so bitterly at the burial that she died. By Imperial mandate an honorary board was exhibited over the door of her house and over the gate of her village.

> There lived . . . a girl, who occupied the same bed with her mother. The latter being attacked by a ferocious tiger, the daughter with a yell grasped the monster with her hands so firmly that its hair was scattered over the ground, and at a distance of over ten miles it dropped its victim. The maiden then clasped her mother in her arms and carried her home; the old woman was still breathing, but expired after an hour. The prefect Siao Ch'en assisted the girl in the burial expenses and reported the matter to the Throne. Thereupon a mark of distinction was affixed to her door and to the gate of her village by order of the Emperor.

> Receiving the news that his mother had died, he hurried barefooted to her mourning rites, vomiting blood at every fit of sorrow that overcame him. As his family was extremely poor, some old friends sent gifts to him; but he would accept nothing. He himself collected the earth he needed for the grave hill,

planted pines and bamboo on the spot with his own hands, and lived in a shed at the side of the grave. Mild dew [sic] trickled down upon the tomb, and crows and magpies swarmed there without any signs of fear. The prefect reported the matter to the Throne, upon which the gate of his village was decorated with a mark of distinction by Imperial order.[13]

It was not only the state which encouraged family solidarity. The language was full of proverbs which lauded family virtues; the ritual year included festivals which called for participation *en famille*, notably New Year, Qing-ming (the grave-sweeping festival), and the Winter Solstice; the almanac annually reprinted instructions for successful family living; and so on.

FAMILY VERSUS STATE

The Confucian state was firm in its conviction that the family should be strong, and it backed its belief with both positive and negative sanctions. Of course, law and official policy were not always reflected in common practice. The *xiang-yue* system was not consistently put into practice and, when it was, was sometimes very casually done. The *wu-fu* represented an ideal rather than a blue-print for performance. Similarly, the laws prohibiting marriage within the surname group were occasionally broken, but very seldom invoked. Divorce was infrequent despite the ease with which a man could legally slough off his wife. Concubines often did receive better treatment than wives regardless of the law.

The three family relationships contained in the *wu-lun* were dealt with at length in Chapter 1, and we have seen how greatly influenced by them was the law. Of the other two relationships, that between Ruler and Minister was analogous to that between Father and Son in the kind of duty which the inferior was meant to owe to the superior. Like the family relationships it was capable of extension, and so stood for Emperor-subject or State-subject, giving a lead to loyal and dutiful citizenship. But unlike the other relationships this one was almost infinite in its applicability, and demanded loyalty from the individual to the vastness and impersonality of the state, not to the circumscribed group of personally known kin. A group as inward-focussed and self-interested as the Chinese family was hardly likely to nurture individuals who could turn their loyalties elsewhere. Great inward cohesion was gained at the expense of equivalent outward antagonism. The state wanted to have the family strong in order to build with it. It achieved the strong family, but found it very difficult building material.

Indeed, there were some conflicts which had to be resolved in favour of the family against the state's interest. If the family were the basis of the state, then all fundamental loyalties were to the family, and the individual must put family before state. In that case concealment of the crime of a family member was not only justifiable, it was a duty. Hence it could not be an offence to conceal such a crime, nor could *wu-fu* relatives be testified against in court. Not only this, it became an offence for a person to accuse a relative in a court of law, punishment being scaled according to *wu-fu* grades. Only in case of rebellion was loyalty to state allowed to take precedence over loyalty to family, making reporting of relatives a requirement.

When a parent of a serving government official died, there was again a conflict of interest and again the state gave way to the family, the official being required to resign immediately under pain of flogging and dismissal in order to observe proper mourning. The ruling applied to high and low alike, and affected even those in key posts. Take the early career of Commissioner Lin Tse-hsu of Opium War fame:

> With his appointment as intendant of the Hang-Chia-Hu Circuit of Chekiang in 1820 Lin began his career as an administrative official. He had, however, to abandon his post abruptly in the following year on account of the illness of his father. After service as intendant of the Huai-Hai Circuit in Kiangsu and as salt controller in Chekiang (1822) he was promoted (1823) to judicial commissioner of Kiangsu. . . . Owing to the death of his mother he went home in the autumn of 1824, but the period of mourning was interrupted for several months by an imperial summons (1825) to superintend repairs of a broken dyke on the Yellow River in Kiangsu. Two years later (1827) he was appointed judicial commissioner of Shensi and was then transferred to the post of financial commissioner at Nanking. Late in this year his father

died and Lin once more retired to his home. Reporting in Peking in 1830 at the conclusion of the mourning period he was made financial commissioner of Hupeh and then of Honan.[14]

The inclusion of the Ruler-minister relationship in the *wu-lun* may thus be seen to be more a pious hope than a realisable aim. The subjection of the individual to the family was not in practice capable of extension to the whole state. The Friend-friend relationship *was* realistic—it, like the family relationships, was close, personal and limited in extent. But the four workable relationships stopped short at Friend-friend: how were a man's dealings with strangers to be regulated? Hostility, distrust and indifference were likely to characterize such dealings. If a man was not 'one of us' he was by definition 'one of the other side'.

Social consciousness, then, was not a dominant feature of traditional Chinese society. On the other hand nepotism, stemming straight from the culturally laudable emphasis on the importance of kinship and friendship, was rife. The family needed the state and was backed by the state, but it was not loyal to the state, because it throve on particularist relationships which were hampered by and inimical to a more universal approach. The following passage in its contrasting attitudes towards family and state can serve as a summing up:

But in private circles a man who can embezzle from public funds and get away with the crime is far from being ostracized. In fact, such a person, especially if he is generous with those who know his dealings or are related to him, is, to them at least, an object of admiration and respect. The illiterate public is too ignorant to know that the corruption exists and tend to look upon such a man either with indifference or with awe. The result is that by his own circle of acquaintances, relatives, clan members, and fellow natives of the same district he is shielded against all public denouncements.

Unlike the complicated and remote public affairs, which are always baffling to the ordinary small-town citizen, the affairs of firms owned and managed by members of the community become known easily and quickly, especially if they involve some grievance of one party or another. Anyone who corrupts the shop of a relative, a clan member, or a fellow member of the same community would never be able to raise his head in West Town, even if he ever dared to return home.[15]

FAMILY AND AFFINES

As well as its dealings with the state the family also had to face its social environment, that is, other families. In most respects its contacts with other families were regulated by the particular combination of state and customary political forces which governed all relationships in the community. But the family being turned in on itself was outwardly hostile, so that it was essentially in competition with other families—in competition for land, for wealth, for prestige, for power, and indeed for very survival. Isolation from the rest of society was, of course, neither possible nor desirable, and from amongst its hostile surroundings it sought and created special bonds, in particular through marriage.

Marrying outside the surname group was not only required by law, it was the custom of the people; and this meant that a link with another family was necessarily forged with every marriage. In some cases the two families might already be linked, as with marriage to a mother's brother's daughter, where the previous generation had already established a tie. This form of marriage was not particularly common, though we have seen in Chapter 2 that it was preferred in some parts of China. Perhaps more common would be marriage between families which were introduced to each other through some more distant connection, or marriage between the families of friends. But in the majority of marriages probably the two families would be strangers to each other. We have said that dealings between strangers were fraught with suspicion and hostility, and we have seen that this was reflected in the failure of the wu-lun to provide ethical backing beyond the Friend-friend relationship. As a result, the making of an alliance between families through marriage was approached with considerable caution.

Marriage customs differed widely from place to place in China, but were usually elaborations on the 'Six Rites' laid down in feudal times. The Six Rites were:

1. The offering of a gift through the go-between to the girl's family. Acceptance denoted serious intentions of going through with the betrothal.
2. The exchange of 'Eight Characters' (see below).
3. The ritual vetting of the Eight Characters.
4. The payment of 'bride-price', usually in kind, to the girl's family through the go-between (through whom negotiations as to its amount had been conducted). Acceptance of the goods sealed the betrothal.
5. Fixing the date of the wedding.
6. The welcoming of the bride to the groom's family home, together with the paying of ceremonial deference to his family and ancestors, and the consummation of the marriage.

The whole process of betrothal was hedged about with checks and precautions, so that the two parties could 'sniff each other over' and, if in any doubt, withdraw. Once the betrothal stage was passed it was almost impossible to withdraw from the match. A go-between or match-maker was always employed (even when both families were already acquainted):

From the outset all negotiations are carried on by one or more go-betweens. 'Without clouds in the sky', runs the Chinese proverb, 'there is no rain. Without go-betweens there is no marriage.' Now, it is obvious that in marriage, as in numerous other aspects of Chinese life, intermediaries are required to allow negotiations to proceed without loss of face to parties with conflicting interests. But the go-between is not a man (or woman) of one role. He may also be a broker in the marriage market: it is his business to know which boys and girls are available for matching and how the parity of 'gates and doors' of different families allows them to be linked. In addition, the go-between, in return for his fees and commission, is held accountable for the quality of the brides and grooms and for the success of the marriage, at least in its initial phase. . . . In reality, few families are foolish enough to rely solely on go-betweens for their information; any obvious physical or moral defect in a proposed bride or groom will not easily escape gossip or the test of inspection, however surreptitious. A family does not take a new member blind, nor does a family marrying off its daughter cast her into the completely unknown.[16]

But in addition to the vetting of the other family through the go-between and other secular means, the auspiciousness of the match was tested ritually. The method used was to write on a piece of red paper the Eight Characters representing the year, month, date and hour of birth of the other family's candidate and to lay this before various gods—the ancestors, the Stove God, a temple god, and so on. The god's judgement was obtained in various ways, such as by casting divining blocks or by shaking out a divining stick from a bundle.

> The next step is for the boy's mother to bring the red papers to a professional fortune-teller, who will answer questions (according to a special system of calculation based on the eight characters) as to the compatibility of the girls in question and the members of the boy's Chia [family]. He will suggest the relative merits of each girl, tactfully leaving his client to express her real attitude, and give a decision accordingly. Even if the fortune-teller gives a judgement against his client's wishes, which are usually uncertain, the latter is not bound to take this as final. She can seek a further consultation with the same fortune-teller or with another.[17]

It can be seen that the ritual investigations were sometimes treated as merely confirmatory, and could be manipulated to conform with judgements arrived at by other means.

The man's family would look for good health and good upbringing in the girl. If there were some difference in status, then it would tend to be the girl's family which was poorer, there being fears that a girl from a better circumstanced home might both make unfavourable comparisons in her new environment, and not be trained for the greater work-load she would have to shoulder. The girl's family, on the other hand, would be interested in the social position of the man's family, in the number of other sons with whom their future son-in-law would have to share the estate, and in the steadiness of character of the man. Thus, the man's family was basically interested in the girl's potential as a mother and as a worker, her usefulness to them in return for the price they had paid: the girl's family was more exercised with the quality of life for their daughter's own sake.

On the whole each family would be expecting to find a marriage partner from a family of roughly comparable social status— 'wooden gates match with wooden gates, and bamboo doors with bamboo doors', as the proverb had it. Too great a disparity might result in the poorer family making use of the tie to solicit financial and other assistance from the richer.

Marriage of children was a necessity, but it was likely to be dangerous to family equilibrium because it brought the family into contact and alliance with strangers, or, if not strangers, outsiders. Hence the need for elaborate checks in the betrothal procedure, and, of course, hence the necessity for the experienced members of the family rather than the individual to arrange the match.

Although 'bride-price' was paid, although residence was normally in the husband's village, and although the marriage system can be seen as one where women were transferred between static families, the girl was not sold completely away from the control and care of her natal family. The bride-price might be seen more as the purchase of the girl's reproductive, labour and ritual services than as outright purchase of her

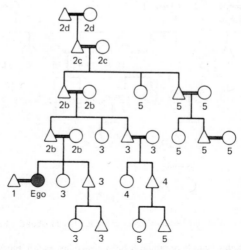

Figure 14. Married Woman's Mourning for her Natal Family

person—she could not after all readily be sold by her husband's family, and her own kin would retain an interest in her happiness. Indeed, her continued contact with her family of birth was desirable and valued, since at any time the two families might want to utilise the alliance which was latent in the marriage tie between them. In a society where the exploitation of personal relationships counted for more than objectively assessed merit, the extension of a web of contacts was important, and alliances at a premium.

Figure 14 shows the mourning due from a married woman to her natal family. (Before marriage she would have mourned in the same way as her brother.) Figure 15 shows the mourning

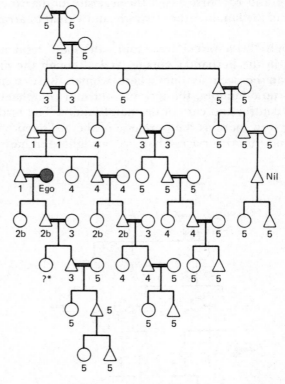

Figure 15. Married Woman's Mourning for her Husband's Family

* Ego's granddaughter should presumably be mourned in Grade 3, but this relationship is omitted in the Qing *Laws and Statutes*.

required of her for her husband's family: as well as its strong contrast with pre-marital mourning, it is otherwise noteworthy for the great emphasis placed on relationships junior to Ego.

Figure 16. Mourning for Wife's Natal Family

The mourning required of a man for his wife's natal family was minimal, as in Figure 16. Certainly mourning requirements across the marriage tie were much less severe than those within the family, but from the *wu-fu* prescriptions it can clearly be seen that the link between families joined through marriage was meant to last. Equally lasting doubtless would have been the enmity between families caused by the rare divorce. The ties between two families were more than just formal, and in some parts of China were very strong indeed:

> The child keeps close contact with his relatives on his mother's side. His maternal grandmother comes to assist his mother in childbirth. The child will visit his maternal relatives many times a year. His maternal uncle has special obligations towards him. He is the guest of honour at the ceremony held when the child reaches one month, and is the one who selects a name for the child; he escorts him when presenting him for the first time to his schoolmaster. He will present a valuable gift, ornament, or cash, when his sister's son gets married. On the child's side his maternal uncle is a protector against harsh treatment by his father. He can run to his maternal uncle in case of need. His maternal uncle will act as mediator in conflict between father and son. When property is divided between father and son or among brothers, the maternal uncle is the formal judge. When the maternal uncle dies, his sister's children will mourn for him.[18]

Relationships with maternal kin, and particularly the mother's brother, were especially useful in that being outside the family proper with its heavy discipline and hierarchical order they could be more relaxed, warm and intimate. The 'image' of the mother's brother was one of a kindly generous man. It was to him that a man would usually turn first for a loan. And, where farming was concerned, it was a great bonus that maternal kin lived in other villages, because the distance between villages often meant differing planting and harvesting times:

> If a villager should for some reason be unable to arrange for the necessary labor to harvest his crop, he knows that he may call upon some of his *ch'in ch'i* [maternal relatives] who are not at the time engaged in their own harvesting to come to his aid. Since a whole area must usually be harvested over a period of a single week, labor shortage is a frequent problem. The latter is especially serious if a typhoon threatens; then a crop may have to be harvested immediately. Under such conditions, one's *ch'in ch'i*, if available, come to help without expecting wages. The *ch'in ch'i* who gives his labor knows that at some future date he can expect to receive similar help. This is not only true in times of emergency; there is frequently an informal exchange of labor in house building or other economic functions. If at all possible, a *ch'in ch'i* always holds himself ready to extend such aid.[19]

With the various alliances formed over more than one generation through marriage out of daughters and through marriage in of daughters-in-law a family could spread its net of contacts: every tie was a further stay against the unkind winds of misfortune which could blow against it.

FAMILY AND NEIGHBOURS

We should not neglect the fact that there were other factors in addition to kinship which could unite families. Marriage ties were necessarily formed with spatially distant families, since marriage within one village was not popularly acceptable (and, of course, often was impossible owing to a preponderance of one surname in the village).

Within a village, however, getting the benefits of peaceful and happy co-existence entailed co-operation between neighbours. The *bao-jia* system was soundly based at least in that it did group together close neighbours. Shared experience at this micro-community level resulted in bonds between neighbouring families which at times could be warmer and deeper than those between kin. I observed that in Sheung Shui the women from next-door households would regularly co-operate in household tasks, in ritual observances, and in minor economic activity. Similarly, residential alliances had actually become the basis for political organization within the lineage there.

In one area for which we have records, weaving was conducted as a family business by the household, and:

In order to overcome the cold and low humidity of the winter days, in some villages several families joined together to dig, roof, and equip a cooperative weaving cellar. One about 28 feet long, 14 feet wide, and 10 feet high would be large enough for four looms.[20]

Thus the family strengthened its position in its immediate surroundings through neighbourliness, and stretched relationships out further into society through marriage.

FAMILIES IN COMPETITION

It is interesting to note that no family in our village has been able to hold the same amount of land for as long as three or four generations. Usually a family works hard and lives frugally until they can begin to buy land. Members of the second generation continue in the same pattern so that more land is added to the family holdings and it becomes well-to-do. Those of the third generation merely enjoy themselves, spending much but earning little. No new land is bought and gradually it becomes necessary to begin to sell. In the fourth generation more land is sold until ultimately the family sinks into poverty. This cycle takes even less than a hundred years to run its course.[21]

Here is a clear picture of a development cycle in the family, a constantly recurring pattern of rise and fall. While there were exceptions to this pattern—education and entry to the ranks of officialdom, for instance, made it possible for a few families to 'step off the bus' for a generation or two, or even to maintain high status over centuries in very rare cases—the overall picture seems valid. But there was more to it than a simple case of hard work in poverty and luxurious idleness in wealth.

We have seen that the high culture of China provided solid ethical backing for a strong family system through the *wu-lun*, the *wu-fu*, state law and education. Popular custom, low culture, and human nature, however, allied with the inheritance system to break up the strong family. First, personality conflict within the family group often precipitated division, and such conflict was very common. More property to argue about and more mouths to argue with exacerbated friction as a family got bigger and more successful.

Second, as the above quotation implies, being born to wealth was a temptation to luxurious, non-productive living. But it was not necessarily idleness and inertia alone which gave rise to such living—there were social and cultural pressures at work too. The high culture might suggest that people in affluent circumstances should live simply and capitalise on their wealth through education and perhaps civil office: the view of the masses was more likely to be that those with money should demonstrate their wealth by spending it lavishly, and should show their freedom from necessity to work by being conspicuously idle. Proof of such freedom might take such trivial forms as allowing the finger-nails to grow long (no manual worker could do it, of course), or might include foot-binding for women (rendering movement far too difficult to allow normal physical toil). For many the opium habit was tailor-made for a combination of flagrant leisure and conspicuous consumption. After investigation of a village where the opium pipe was the regular resort of the better-off, a considered Chinese opinion was:

> that the real incentive to work is a striving not for material gain but merely for subsistence. When subsistence is secured, the peasants relax and even retire from active work. They are satisfied at the level at which a comfortable living is maintained, 'comfort' being defined by the absence of strenuous effort rather than by the satisfaction of numerous material wants.[22]

Society, in other words, *expected* the better-off to behave in a

leisured way. The family which could resist such an attractive
virtue was strong indeed.

Third, once a family was split up, the inheritance system
ensured the rapid fragmentation of the estate:

> Equal property partition among the male members of the
> household is strictly observed among the farm families.
> Property division may take place either before or after the
> death of the father but generally occurs at the time of the
> marriages of the second and third sons, as harmonious family
> life is difficult to maintain when married brothers live together.
> All kinds of property, farm appliances, domestic animals,
> movable property, and liabilities as well as estates and
> buildings, are divided equally under the supervision of family
> relatives. Occasionally, the division is conducted by lottery. As
> far as possible, each successor receives an equal share; and
> sometimes differences in crop yields form an important aspect
> of property partition.[23]

The shares of such an estate were likely to be so small as hardly to
be viable units at all. Even with extremely wealthy, high status
families there remained:

> the economic problem posed by the Chinese inheritance
> system, which led to the continual fragmentation and dim-
> inution of family holdings. Division of properties among all the
> sons entailed an inevitable decline in the economic status of the
> individual member unless new property was continually
> acquired. A second factor was the difficulty of maintaining
> social status through official service. This became more and
> more a question of preparing one's sons to achieve success in
> the examinations, which depended to a certain extent upon
> the family's possessing sufficient resources to underwrite a
> lengthy education.[24]

What this process of rise and fall in family fortunes meant was a
society like a seething cauldron, with families bubbling to the top
only to burst and sink back to the bottom. When they burst they
shattered their land-holdings too, and the patch-work quilt effect
caused by the constant fragmentation and re-agglomeration of

land-holdings was a distinctive feature of the Chinese landscape. This very process of constant flux within families, while at the same time each family was fiercely competitive with others around it, ensured a kind of social control through a fluid balance of power.

Under normal conditions, the 'ups' and 'downs' took place gradually and in orderly fashion, being considerably controlled by a social mechanism of selection and distribution of individuals. The considerable ascending or descending displacement of a family or an individual demanded several years in the quickest case and more often one, two, or three generations. This slowness was due to the fact that the ascending or descending displacements did not take place without the testing and training of individuals. A climber had to show his ability. Many years of training or work were necessary to acquire it. The 'social promotion' of the climbers was therefore gradual and relatively slow. The same was true of the sinking men. Having been born to high positions, they automatically occupied places similar to those of their parents. With average ability and work, they might very easily keep them. Social inertia worked in their favor. Extraordinary moral or mental failures were necessary for such men to be ousted and displaced. Their first 'failures' usually were not enough to produce their degradation. Persistent and recurring failures were necessary to call forth such effects, and they naturally took years and years. Social inertia explains partly why 'ups' and 'downs' came gradually.[25]

In general no one family was able to grasp and retain sufficient power and wealth to dominate local society for long periods. There was accordingly no real inherited class system. True, at any one time there would be influential and powerful families, but a long term view would show the majority of those families back at the bottom of the cauldron, and new ones on top. The conception of continuity of the family over past, present and future no doubt helped to make the taking of that long term view possible:

Our guess is that the high social mobility among the elite made it possible for the able and ambitious among the common people to rise, thus reducing the pressure for rebellion against the political regime, which enabled the latter to continue much longer than its counterparts elsewhere. In this, the Chinese family and kinship system, which promoted an inward-looking or centripetal tendency on the part of the individual, was helpful. It discouraged the individual Chinese from spilling permanently out of his kinship group and local area, though it also augmented his incentives for fattening the latter at the expense of the larger society.[26]

6

The Lineage in Society and State

Although the lineage, which we have already described in some detail, was not to be found all over China, it was an extremely important form of social organization in much of south and south-eastern China:

> In Kwangtung, four out of every five peasants, or more, live with their clans [lineages]. Usually one village is inhabited by one clan. Even if there is more than one clan, each clan occupies a distinct section of the village; there is hardly a mixed neighborhood. In Chao-an, for instance, nearly one-half of the villages of the entire district are inhabited by people bearing the same clan name. More than one-half of the villages of Hwei-yang are so inhabited . . . we can safely say that one-third of the cultivated land of the entire province is clan land.[1]

Long-established lineages inevitably took more and more land into trust as the generations went by. The Liao lineage of Sheung Shui held over 50% of its lands in trust, while in another nearby lineage village over 90% of the land was in trust. The amount of land held by lineage trusts was enormous, and if we bear in mind that lineage members also held land privately, the influence of lineage organization on local society can be seen to have been high. Of greatest importance and interest were those villages inhabited exclusively by single lineages, and it is with such villages that this chapter is primarily concerned.

THE LINEAGE TERRITORY

Nearly all Chinese villages were close-huddled settlements, houses taking up a minimum of land. A perceptive if disapprov-

136

ing 19th-century description of villages in China says:

> Sometimes in a village a quarter of a mile long, there may not
> be a single crossroad enabling a vehicle to get from the front
> street to the back one, simply because the town grew up in that
> way, and no one either could or would remedy it, even if any
> one desired it otherwise. At right angles to the main street or
> streets, run narrow alleys, upon which open the yards or courts
> in which the houses are situated. Even the buildings which
> happen to stand contiguous to the main street offer nothing to
> the gaze but an expanse of dead wall. . . . A village is thus a
> city in miniature, having all the evils of over-crowding, though
> it may be situated in the midst of a wide and comparatively
> uninhabited plain. Whether land is dear or cheap, a village
> always has the same crowded appearance, and there is in
> either case the same indifference to the requirements of future
> growth.[2]

All around the village was the land which the villagers farmed.
In the case of a single lineage village, the settlement and its
surrounding land seem to have constituted a 'territory' within
which no outsiders were permitted to hold land. In the village
itself there may have been non-lineage members living. Many
villages had small stores selling minor household necessities, and
the storekeepers were often outsiders who rented (but were not
allowed to own) their premises. Similarly, priests and nuns from
outside might be living and practising in the village. Another
non-lineage group was composed of hereditary servants:

> In the distant past, members of the dominant lineage bought
> boys from poor families in far-away villages. They acted as
> servants in the master's household, where their special duty
> was to attend the young sons of the master's family. When
> these servant boys became of marriageable age, they were
> married to servant girls of approximately the same social status
> and were given small houses at the rear of the village in which
> to set up their households. They were also assigned lands to
> farm as tenants of the patron household and in return had to
> perform certain traditional tasks.[3]

But both outsiders and servants were low status groups under the domination of the lineage, and were tolerated as such. Neither group could *own* land or fixed property within the territory, and neither group was given a say in village government.

This exclusive territory was completely under the control of the lineage leadership. Offences committed within it would be dealt with by the leaders, the irrigation system would be maintained and improved at lineage expense, and any disputes over water rights could be settled through the lineage leadership hierarchy. Other public works within the territory, such as bridges, roads, wells and temples, would be paid for out of lineage funds. Protection of all property and crops would be in the hands of the lineage defence force, and the lineage could also build and maintain walls and a moat for its village. In all this the lineage funds drawn from trust land income were the basis for action, and could be expended freely since only lineage members would benefit. The land and property in the territory could, of course, be either privately owned by lineage members or belong to ancestral trusts.

Given a reasonable rate of reproduction the lineage was a group which could continue to expand in numbers without fear of fission. But increased numbers required more food and more income, so that the lineage was also territorially expansionist. To meet its requirements it would in fact keep expanding its holdings out from the village as far as it was able. On these lines a model diagram of a territory could be very simply drawn as a circle:

Figure 17. Lineage Territory

The extent of a lineage's territory was likely to be in proportion to its strength of membership, but there were bound to be constraints of geography and politics which would affect its size and shape. Geographically, a range of hills, a wide river, a marsh, an area of infertile soil, the sea coast—any of these might prevent expansion. Politically, around the lineage there were always other similar lineages with similar expansionist aims, and sooner or later neighbouring territory boundaries must meet. The size of a territory, then, in large reflected the strength of the lineage; and the shape of the territory boundary represented the interaction between the lineage and the product of the opposed geographic and political forces.

Map 1 is a rough sketch of the territory of the Sheung Shui Liao lineage. It is hardly a circle!

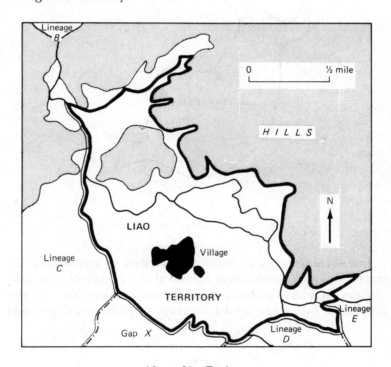

Map 1. Liao Territory

To the north the hills prevent expansion. Almost everywhere else the territory is in direct contact with the territories of other lineages. The boundary with lineage C is formed by a river and is very clear-cut, 100% of the land on one side being Liao owned and 100% on the other side belonging to lineage C. Elsewhere boundaries shared with other lineages are mostly equally clear-cut. Gap *X* represents an area which belongs exclusively to no one lineage, though several lineages, including the Liao, own land within it.

From Map I, I have simplified to Figure 18, and thence, by substituting the model circles of Figure 17, I arrive at Figure 19.

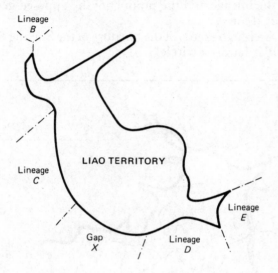

Figure 18. Liao Territory—First Abstraction

From Figure 19 it is only a short step to postulating the situation which would have existed if the ranges of hills near Sheung Shui had not been there. Figure 20 takes that step and gives us a first stage model diagram of a lineage-dominated

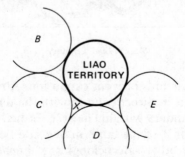

Figure 19. Liao Territory—Second Abstraction

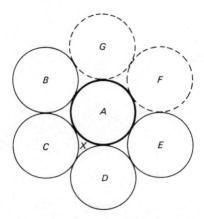

Figure 20. Liao Territory—Third Abstraction

landscape. That is to say, on a flat plain without natural barriers we might expect a developed lineage system to have arrived at a state of equilibrium in which the landscape is mostly covered by lineage territories which have expanded until they touched. The gaps (X) between lineage territories would be inhabited by small lineages of little power and wealth or by small villages of mixed surnames. The land in the gaps would belong predominantly to no one group, though many might be interested in owning it.

Of course, such a model situation could hardly exist: we have seen, for example, that the Sheung Shui territory is not circular, and that there is no gap X in the triangle ADE. No two lineages would have exactly the same size of membership and territory; nor was the situation ever likely to be static, comparative lineage strengths fluctuating with the vagaries of reproductive success and other fortuitous factors, and territorial boundaries retreating or advancing accordingly. However, this is a useful model on which to demonstrate the way in which the lineage-based society of South China worked.

Before going further, there is one more stage to the model. The seven lineages A–G cannot be considered in isolation, because of course they would not have been isolated from the rest of society. Figure 21 adds an outer ring of lineages to the diagram. This addition, besides being necessary to our analysis, also saves us from the trap of considering lineage A to be the pivot of the

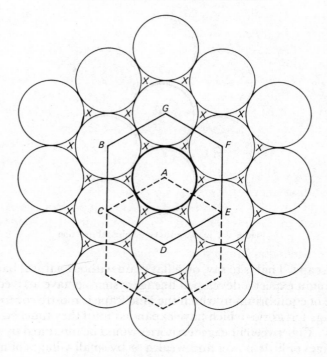

Figure 21. A Lineage Landscape model

system. Although for convenience we shall be looking at the system in terms of *A*'s relationships, we could equally well have focused on any other lineage in the diagram, for *A* is as much a member of a ring around *D* as *D* is a member of *A*'s surrounding ring.

Within its territory a lineage would allow only its own members and trusts to hold land: land could be sold, but to within the lineage only. Not all the land would necessarily be of good quality, but even the worst could not be removed from the lineage sphere of ownership. Non-lineage residents were tolerated only as political nonentities and social inferiors. Once expansion had been brought to a halt by meeting with other lineage territories, the lineage had to look elsewhere for extra land. The obvious places to look were the gaps between lineage territories. What might start out as merely a hunger for more land to support increased population could well end up as a colonization attempt if sufficient land could be acquired. But in each gap many lineages would be interested, and the competition for the land was such that no one lineage would easily be able to acquire an ascendancy.

In its territory all land, good and bad, was taken up by the lineage: in the gaps the tendency was to acquire only the best quality land. In the territory both private and trust ownership was found: in the gaps there was a tendency for trusts rather than individual families to buy. The insidious effects of these factors can easily be surmised. The inhabitants of the gaps, already much less powerful and less economically stable than the surrounding lineages, were subjected to the gradual loss of their best land through sale to lineage trusts which then rented the land back to them, so ensuring their continued depression and increasing dependence on the lineage landlords. Gap inhabitants thus became subordinated to the lineages and, where one lineage gained an ascendancy in this way, they became to all intents and purposes hereditary tenants who might perhaps be called on for assistance and service when the lineage masters required them.

A recent account depicts conditions in the county of T'i-ch'üan, Shensi: 'For three hundred years the adult males in our *tsu* [lineage] never exceeded thirty. Living between two big *tsu*, and being poor members of the intelligentsia who have been agriculturalists for four generations and teachers for three, they could not help being bullied and insulted by the big *tsu*' . . . 'Year after year, month after month, they come to borrow money. If you ask for a return of the capital only, you still are abused. If you don't lend money they come to steal, particularly at the end of the year. When they abuse you, bow your head; when they hit you, don't return the blow. Your wife and daughter you have to let them violate. Without money do not go to court.' Such are the indignities that the small *tsu* has to suffer in some parts at the hands of the powerful *tsu*, who certainly include among them a good proportion of the gentry.[4]

By purchasing land in the gaps a lineage acquired extra income and influence. Even without buying the land a lineage could, if it were sufficiently strong, place the inhabitants of a neighbouring gap under its protection, which again would add to both income and influence. As an example we can take the village of Poon Uk Tsuen which:

> has a population of about 160 people, all members of the small Poon lineage. The Poons were traditionally a client lineage living in the shadow of the more powerful Man lineage, but they owned much of the land they tilled and managed to co-exist with their patrons by paying regular protection fees. In return, the Mans did indeed 'protect' the Poons from the other lineages in the New Territories region. Although Poon Uk Tsuen is a single-lineage village, it was too small and too weak to become an important community in the power circles of the New Territories.[5]

INTER-LINEAGE RELATIONSHIPS

We have said that the family by being inward-turned was outwardly aggressive. The same applied to the lineage: but the lineage was also expansionist. The combination of these two factors meant that two neighbouring lineages with touching boundaries were of necessity in conflict, and hostility in many forms would characterize their relationship. From our model (Figure 21) we can see that lineage A was therefore surrounded on all sides by a ring of hostile lineages $(B-G)$, since each of these shared territorial boundaries with A. At first glance this would appear disastrous for A, but two compensating features of the system are clear from the model. First, lineages $B-G$ are themselves at loggerheads each with its neighbour, and are therefore not united in their opposition to A. Second, each of the outer ring of lineages is hostile to one or more of lineages $B-G$ for the same reasons as is A, and they may therefore be considered potential allies of A against $B-G$.

This basic concentric pattern of inter-lineage relationships would be reflected in the marriage system. We have already established that a marriage linking two families created or cemented bonds of friendship or alliance. A lineage village bore only one surname and therefore had to look elsewhere for its brides. But neighbouring lineages were mutually hostile, and marriage alliances forged with them would be fraught with conflict even where they could with difficulty be arranged. There is a fascinating tale told in Sheung Shui of how a Liao daughter married out to a man of lineage *D* was once seen to be on her knees praying to Heaven for a 'double-headed victory' while her husband and her father took the field on opposite sides in an inter-lineage fight. It follows that for the most part a lineage probably had to look to its outer ring of lineages for brides and for disposal of its daughters in marriage. Not only did such a system avoid the problems associated with dealings with actively hostile affines, it actually helped to cement alliances with outer ring lineages, alliances which were desirable and necessary in the power-balance game in which lineages were involved. An interesting sidelight on this kind of marriage pattern is that the Liaos began to inter-marry with lineage *D* quite frequently once warfare was ruled out by the presence of a British administration in the area from 1899 onwards.

'Inner ring hostile, outer ring friendly' is a simple clear-cut pattern. But we might consider some interesting complexities. Figure 22 shows a portion only of the full model:

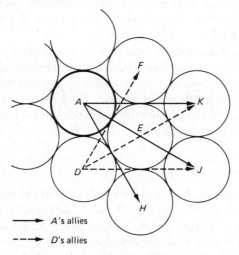

Figure 22. Conflicting Alliances

Now *A*'s relationships with *D*, *E* and *F* are clearly hostile, and with *H*, *J* and *K* equally clearly likely to be friendly. If we look at *D*'s relationships with the same group, we can see that *H* is hostile to D, not friendly, and F is friendly, not hostile: there has been a change of perspective. But J is an unequivocal ally of both A and D since it falls in the outer ring of both sets of relationships. For A and D, locked in enmity, J is a permanent friend, a mediator and arbitrator who can step in to cool down conflict. K is similarly placed.

To follow A's relationships round the whole model would be tedious and unnecessary. The important feature of this system is already evident—there existed an interlocking network of relationships which gave multiple possibilities of finding allies to counter a neighbour's hostility either through mediation or through co-operative military enterprise. Thus A might well be in tandem with K in warfare against F, while K in a different role might at the same time be interceding with A on D's behalf. A lineage would not necessarily always be in alliance with another lineage: the complexity of alliance patterns could result in changes of allegiance; and realignments of lineages to counteract an upswing in the fortunes or strength of a particular enemy could upset earlier alliances. We may suppose that enmity with inner ring lineages was more or less permanent, but that active alliances with outer ring lineages were more likely to be of a sporadic and ad hoc nature.

The lineage landscape was thus composed of cells held in tension by a complex web of alliances and enmities, the end result being a balance of power which tended to prevent the acquisition of over-weening influence by any one lineage or the prolongation of active hostilities to a point where bloodshed and damage could reach serious proportions.

INTER-LINEAGE HOSTILITY

It is hardly an exaggeration to say that in areas where lineages were common and strong the whole of society was in a constant state of war, though actual battles were infrequent. It was through this system that the lineages, which we have seen to be virtually self-governing internally, conducted their 'foreign affairs' to determine their position in society.

Let us look at relationships between neighbouring lineages (i.e. between A and B–G). They were entirely hostile, and the hostility manifested itself in many ways. At best it was merely symbolic. In Sheung Shui at New Year the lineage youths used to go to the river and there engage in an exchange of stone-throwing with lineage *C* youths on the other side. I heard of no serious injuries caused by the stones, the whole exercise seems to have been just a gesture, a symbolic playing out of latent hostility.

More serious was economic rivalry. Apart from competition for available land, there was much strife over control of rural market sites. Markets served quite large areas of countryside and, by charging a duty on produce sold, generated considerable incomes for the controllers. In the 17th century a local market was sited in lineage *C* territory, but by the early 19th century Sheung Shui had managed to have the site moved to its territory and was in full control of the profits. Stories of other such struggles and shifts of economic advantage are common in the New Territories, and always the contestants seem to have been neighbouring lineages:

> Around Tai Po, the influence of the Mans and Tangs seems to have been unequalled. They were, however, rivals and it may be that for a long time the Tangs had a slight lead . . . they established and controlled Tai Po Old Market, and it was upon the market that discontent with their power came to be focused.
>
> There were a variety of reasons for dissatisfaction with the market which were common to most of the villages in the area. A basket tax had to be paid by all those who entered the market carrying a basket. Those who crossed the river to reach the market had to use a ferry provided, at a price, by the Tangs. Moreover, the owners of the market claimed as their right the first choice of all produce sold there . . .
>
> The solution that had long been proposed was the establishment of another market, which would operate in competition with the old one . . .
>
> It is said that the magistrate first sent a representative to see how near the proposed new market would be to the old one. This representative was taken from the site of the new market to the old one by the most indirect route it was possible to devise. It was, in fact, a veritable garden path, for he returned to report that another market would not be damaging to the interests of the established one.[6]

Competition between lineages for prestige (Face) in society was fiercest between neighbours. Leaders of the two lineages involved in that struggle for Tai Po market once competed to lay the longer line of silver dollars along a path. Doubtless something of prestige was also involved in the absurd case of two families who were caught up in an expensive law suit which had dragged on for:

> several years without reaching a decision. The two families therefore agreed to settle the matter out of court by throwing silver into the river. The family that threw in the most silver would win. The Chang family threw in pewter, but the Lo family threw in a great deal of silver. After that both families were poor . . .[7]

Conspicuous displays of wealth, such as carrying past a rival's village large quantities of expensive offerings to graveside ceremonies of ancestor worship, were frequently indulged in. Lineages would take the opportunity to parade in great strength, and if possible have their gentry members included, rejoicing in the added splendour of ceremonial honours boards and impressive sedan chairs. In 1964 I saw the Liao lineage spend thousands of dollars to erect a ceremonial arch across the main street of the market town. 100 yards down the street lineage C was doing exactly the same.

Another form of hostility lay in what was known as 'feng shui fighting'. We saw in Chapter 4 that the good fortune of families could be attributed to their tapping influences latent in the landscape in which they lived and buried their dead. But the corollaries of this belief were that failure to hit upon a good geomantic site could result in no good fortune or, worse, in positively bad fortune. A feng shui site to be effective had to be exactly positioned with reference to a compass direction and in relation to surrounding scenic features. It followed that any adjustment or change in the environment could upset the delicate balance of forces on which a site's efficacy relied. A landslide, the falling down of a tree, the dislodging of a brick, the erection of a building, the cutting of a road, could all spoil a feng shui site. Sometimes artificial improvement to a site was necessary to remedy defects:

Half a mile to the north-west of the village a low concrete
platform stands in the middle of the fields. It is six-sided and
hollow-centred, the remains of a pagoda. It is said to have been
built '300 or 400 years ago' by the lineage in an effort to
counteract the effect on the *feng shui* of the village of the rock
formation called Eagle Head Hill, which faces the village from
a distance of about a mile and a half. It was thought that the
open mouth of the eagle was swallowing some of the good
fortune of the Liaos, so that male children and examination
successes in particular were being denied the lineage, and a
geomancer suggested that between the village and the eagle a
feng-shui pagoda should be built to represent a bird table, thus
protecting the Liaos from the bird's appetite. Unfortunately
the pagoda was not built on the correct site, and other villages
to the west benefited instead, gaining unprecedented successes
in examinations. The lineage tore down the pagoda . . .[8]

But if a site could be artificially improved, it could also be ruined
by manipulation. The deliberate interference with a rival group's
feng shui sites was one of the weapons in a lineage's armoury.
Defacing grave-stones, chopping down trees and diverting
streams were common ploys, and there are reports of whole
villages full of people working for days to remove hillocks or large
rocks which were considered beneficial to the *feng shui* site of a
rival. An account of a prolonged *feng shui* war can be found in
Appendix II.

Most serious was the actual warfare carried on between
lineages. The possibility of battle was ever present in a lineage
dominated area, and a permanent state of preparedness was
maintained. The village watches, which existed in many villages
to guard against theft of crops and property, in lineage villages
were also the first line defence corps in case of inter-lineage strife.
The walls round lineage villages were high and strong—
sometimes built of better brick than much of the housing. They
were provided with ledges inside for the defenders to stand on,
and there were loop-holes to fire through. Entrance was gained
through a single doorway barely wide enough for one man to
pass, and that doorway could be closed by iron-mail gates and
stout wooden or iron bars. Watch-towers stood at intervals along
the walls, and the defences were completed by a broad moat.

Lineage armouries contained spears, bows and arrows, hand guns, swords, armour and cannon; and scythes, hoes, clubs and anything else that came to hand would be used if necessary.

It was not always the whole lineage which became involved in fighting; sometimes it was merely individuals or small groups. But even when the beginnings of fighting were trivial, the resulting conflict was potentially serious:

> Where the hostile parties live within a short distance, and carry on their labors and pursuits, each under the eyes of the other, occasions cannot long be wanting to call forth their cherished hatred. If one turns away the water-course from his enemy's little field to his own, and is too strong or obstinate to make reparation or be compelled to do justice, then not unfrequently [sic] the signal-gong sounds, the two parties marshal their hostile forces, and the whole of two villages are arrayed against each other in conflict.[9]

Fighting over water rights, over territorial boundaries, over personal insults, over business transactions in the market, over ritual benefits, over attempts to exploit or to throw off exploitation, over almost anything, could break out suddenly or could take place sporadically between long periods of smouldering distrust.

> The *Mans* of San Tin were numerous but poor, and for many years (up until the Japanese occupation in fact) they resorted to terrorism in the neighbourhood, running a 'protection racket', whereby in return for payment of an annual fee from the weaker villages they guaranteed that the villages would be patrolled and guarded against attack from bandits and thieves. The *Hau* village of Ping Kong had been paying this fee, but at one stage felt strong enough to dispense with the 'protection'. They sent the *Man* fee-collectors away empty-handed, knowing that there would be a battle. The *Mans* raised a large army from their village and descended on Ping Kong under their leader, a notorious fighter with an un-savoury nickname. The *Haus* of Ping Kong's sister village, Kam Tsin, had sent reinforcements for the defence of the walled village. On arrival outside the walls, the *Mans* had the

misfortune to see their leader shot dead, and immediately lost heart for the battle. They contented themselves with destroying Ping Kong's ancestral hall, which was several hundred yards from the village . . . the *Haus* have not paid protection money to the *Mans* since that day.[10]

For members who took part in the fighting in a full-scale lineage battle, a lineage provided incentives and rewards. The men would often be feasted before taking the field and on return if successful. If they fell on the battle-field their widows and families would be cared for by the lineage, and their sacrifice would be immortalised by the inclusion of their ancestor tablets on a special 'heroes' altar' in the main ancestral hall. The lineage would, of course, provide the arms and ammunition and whatever other logistic support was required. A household levy might be made if lineage funds were not sufficient for the purpose.

Battles did not last long but could be bloody, and damage to crops and property could on occasion be serious. The efforts of mediators, however, often brought hostilities to an end after only a short while.

A *Liu* and a *Hau* farmer quarrelled over an irrigation matter (a very common cause of trouble), came to blows, and within a short time were backed up by the entire *Liu* lineage on one side and the entire *Hau* clan on the other. No armies were sent out, but the *Lius* locked themselves inside their walled village, and the *Haus* installed cannon in three of their villages and bombarded Sheung Shui. At the same time one of their *literati* with contacts in Nam Tau, the district capital, arranged for the Imperial troops stationed there to be brought in on the side of the *Hau* Clan. The *Lius* got to hear of this, and used their contacts in the provincial capital to have the troops stopped. It is said that on being told of this *Liu* countermove the leader of the *Haus* 'spat out blood and died of rage'. The dispute was settled eventually by arbitration.[11]

Sometimes the fortunes of battle decided an issue very quickly:

an irrigation dispute arose with the Changs of Wong Pui Ling. A pitched battle was fought at Man Kam To (on the Sham

Chun river, roughly midway between the two villages), from which the Liaos retreated to Sheung Shui, where at Red Bridge they had a position prepared complete with cannon loaded with grape-shot. The Changs, however, were by then reinforced by their kinsmen of Heung Sai and Wu Pui, and the Liaos judged it expedient to retire into the walled hamlet without further fighting. This retirement constituted recognition of defeat, the Changs withdrew immediately, and the irrigation dispute was accordingly considered to have been resolved in their favour.[12]

LINEAGE AND STATE

What has been said so far of this system where the countryside was covered by a network of lineages has ignored the role of the Chinese government. Indeed, we ought to ask whether the government had any role to play at all in strong lineage areas. After all, lineages have been seen to have had their own internal control, regulated by written and unwritten law and custom, overseen by lineage leaders and enforced by village 'militia' under the control of those leaders. Externally the lineages achieved a comparatively stable society through a complex balance of power which exploited the volatile relationships between the component elements, and which resolved conflict through force of arms and/or through the mediator's tongue. The lineage system thus appears to have been a self-sufficient one, a free-enterprise system of kinship-organised petty states which paid scant attention to the authority of the central government.

What was the state doing about the situation? An interested observer in the 19th century said of one such area:

it is under the government of the Mandarin of Fuk-wing, who, by-the-by, though he is supposed to rule over 200 villages, confided to me, in a conversation that I had with him, that he had nothing to do but to eat, to drink, and to smoke . . .

The mandarins in the Sanon district have very little power. The people pay the taxes, but do not allow the mandarins to interfere with their own local government. Law-suits, differences, and offences are very seldom brought before the mandarins. The mandarin from whom I learnt the preceding facts had not, as far as I know, during a period of several years, more than one case brought before him for decision; in this instance he was both plaintiff and judge,—the criminal being a youth who was caught stealing fruit in his garden.[13]

But what of the military? One part of the district concerned boasted a force of 995 government troops under 13 officers:

> This force is employed in garrisoning the district town and three forts—one of which is in the neighbourhood of Sanon, and the other two occupy the promontories of the bay of Chikwan. It has also to supply men for twenty-four guard stations. The three forts above mentioned are ordered to have a garrison of twenty men, and to mount six guns each. I have visited these three places, but found neither guns nor soldiers, and the places themselves showed no signs of fortification, save a dilapidated wall.
>
> The guard stations should be furnished with from two to six soldiers each; they are scattered over the whole western part of the country, and are intended to serve as a check against the frequent highway robberies. I never found one of these stations occupied by soldiers. . . .
>
> The Mandarin at Fuk-wing has one war-junk at his disposal, but his revenue not being enough to support the expense, he was in the habit of letting out the vessel for hire for mercantile purposes. The hirers however converted it into a pirate boat, and it was seized by the Chi-yuen, and the Fuk-wing mandarin had to bribe his superior officer to avoid further punishment and degradation.[14]

The state was clearly not making a serious attempt to control the area in question, and this leads us back to a problem raised in an earlier chapter—why were lineages strong in the southern parts of China but less so elsewhere? Several answers were offered. We might now consider another aspect. China proper was geographically divided up from west to east by mountain ranges and by major rivers (of which the Yellow River and the Yangtze were the most important). Her political centre was in the north, only rarely moving even as far south as Nanking, and her political enemies were traditionally also in the north—the 'barbarian nomads' of Mongolia and the northwest. The military were therefore of prime importance in the north whence, until the incursions of the sea-borne West, attacks on China had always come. Large armies kept in the south would not only not have been required to repulse possible invasions, but also they might at that distance have been breeding grounds for rebellion. Political forces thus worked to keep the north as the major focus of government attention while, with the geographical difficulties of communication across the lie of the land and over vast distances, government power was less and less certain as it stretched southward. The strength of self-government in the south (one form of which was lineage organization) was no doubt related to this weakness of central political and military control.

While the throne was strong the central government was powerful and could cope with problems nationwide. But when dynastic fortunes were on the wane, central government lost much of its power, and this loss would have been felt most severely in the areas furthest away from the capital. To fill the partial power vacuum in these areas various forms of de-centralised, locally engendered self-government would emerge. Lineage organization being already strong would wax stronger as central government power declined. It happens, not un-naturally, that we know most about lineages as they were in the 19th and early 20th centuries, but this period was one when the Qing dynasty was ailing and dying, and when its hold on the state was deteriorating rapidly, so that the picture we have of lineage organization is probably of it at its strongest. We can surmise that it must have been strong ever since the Sung dynasty, let us say for the last 800 or 900 years; but probably never could it have been at such a level of development as in the late 19th century.

Confirmation of this growth in lineage power comes by inference from the Qing *Laws and Statutes*. The 1842 edition included for the first time a series of statutes aimed specifically at controlling the lineages of South China. The provinces involved were those of Kwangtung, Fukien, Kwangsi, Kiangsi, Hunan and Chekiang, with Kwangtung and Fukien receiving special mention, and Kwangtung being singled out from all. A comparison of Maps 2 and 3 shows how geographic isolation from the political centre of the north can be correlated with the areas where lineages were considered a particular problem. (The relevant law and statutes are translated in Appendix III.) That the central government should seek to control the lineages at that time seems to me significant: it was probably also a vain attempt, the situation having arisen precisely because the government was by then incapable of controlling it. Lin Tse-hsü (Commissioner Lin) was not the man to shy at difficult administrative problems, but even he found the lineages daunting:

> In Hui-chou and Ch'ao-chou there are clans [lineages] who made their fortunes through banditry; in such cases, the fact that their accomplices are numerous prevents [the government] from laying hands on them, since no one dares inform against them and no official dares arrest them. Sometimes entire clans or entire villages are bandits. Any attempt to arrest them may cause disturbances. . . . This is the reason that it is difficult to check the rampancy of banditry.[15]

Lineages were strong in inverse ratio to the power of the central government, but even when the state was at its weakest it was still not entirely without authority in lineage areas. On an

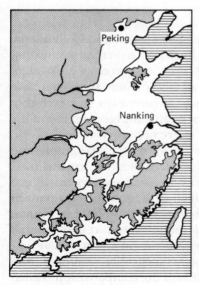

Map 2. China (physical)   Map 3. China (political)

ideological level, lineages drew much of their inspiration from Confucian doctrine. But Confucianism was also the guiding philosophy of the state and, despite its patent failure to operate efficiently as a universal political principle, it did give a powerful impetus to a cultural universality which transcended localism. Lineages were thus fundamentally conservative in nature and took their strength by operating illegally from within the framework of the law. They were not rebellious, still less revolutionary, and so in the final analysis had to recognize the state's authority.

On the practical level, the state had various cards up its sleeve. However reluctantly, it could if necessary call on its military to suppress any too powerful lineage. For this reason lineages must have had to gauge carefully the extent of government toleration of their activities, taking into account such variables as the character and standing of their local officials, the current commitments of government troops elsewhere, and the influence in high places of their own gentry members. Thus, at one extreme there are accounts of cases where the corpses of those slain in lineage battles were burned or thrown into water lest the magistrate should find the evidence of slaughter and take official action, and:

> In each of the villages in the vicinity of Canton and Whampoa, where these feuds are so common, a curious provision has obtained by custom to meet such exigencies. 'A band of devoted men' is there found, and a list of them kept, who have voluntarily offered themselves to assume such crimes and to take their chance for life. When complaint is made, therefore, so many of the first on this list as are necessary come forward, confess themselves the perpetrators of the slaughter, and surrender to the government. It then belongs to them and their friends to employ lawyers and bring witnesses to prove it a justifiable homicide, or one which calls for mitigated punishment. Notwithstanding, they sometimes suffer the capital penalty, but more frequently it is softened to transportation or a fine. In a recent instance, within the past year, when four men fell in an affray, all of the accused were acquitted, and returned again to their homes. The compensation which tempts to the formation of the devoted band, is security for the

maintenance of their families in case of suffering capital punishment, and a reward in lands or money, sometimes to the amount of $300.[16]

At the other extreme of the scale of indifference to state control were cases where recognition of government right to interfere approached lip-service only:

> There are two villages respectively named Sha-tsing, and Pak-tau-king, which carried on a war for five years; with each of these villages smaller hamlets were in league. The mandarins tried in vain to restore peace. At last the district magistrate himself repaired to Sha-tsing with a force of 1,000 men, but the inhabitants threatened to take up arms against him also, if he should show himself inimical to their party. The mandarin was at a loss what to do, till the people of San-keaou, who were not engaged in the quarrel, offered themselves as meditators [sic] between the mandarin and the inhabitants of Sha-tsing. Through their influence the magistrate was allowed to enter Sha-tsing with an unarmed body of his followers, and to pull down two old houses which belonged to the ringleaders in the quarrel. This was only to save the dignity of the mandarin, and had no influence at all upon the dispute, fighting being carried on afterwards just as before.[17]

This last account goes on to indicate another way in which the state could exercise a degree of control:

> The only way in which the government endeavours to put a stop to these disturbances, is by not allowing the fighting clans to send up their graduates for examination at Canton,—a severe punishment, which not only deprives the graduates of the titles and honours they might gain, but hurts the pride of the clans, who are wont to boast of the number of successful candidates for literary honours which they have produced.

A further element of practical government control stemmed direct from the basic idea of the kinship unit as a mutual responsibility group. The state felt justified in punishing a member of a recalcitrant lineage regardless of whether he was in fact the guilty party. In particular it held the lineage head and the elders responsible for the whole group, and could punish them for their failure to restrain those under them.

More important than their option to block preferment through the examination system was the role of the local magistrates as representatives of the state in keeping the land records. Since lineages were essentially land-based organizations, the titles to their land were vital to them. The government was well aware of this, and in its special statutes provided for the confiscation and redistribution of ancestral trust lands, a procedure which would undoubtedly have been effective in reducing lineage unity and power. It is not easy to assess the real situation with regard to land. Recent research points to consistent heavy under-registration, which would certainly have taken the edge off registration as a weapon for control. The government at one time actually issued instructions that no punishment should be imposed on people who failed to report newly-cultivated acreage immediately:

> while the imperial government at Peking showed no interest in pushing the registered acreage beyond the 1600 level, provincial and local officials saw in those instructions unmistakable enunciation of imperial benevolence towards the people. They felt that it was their moral responsibility not to surpass that level when reached. Conformity then took precedence over actuality. Reporting land acreage and land tax became a mere formality. Hence, what had been termed the original quota of land acreage at the beginning of the dynasty was by the middle of the eighteenth century transformed into a practically permanent quota. Although minor changes occurred in official land acreage from one year to another, they were by nature fictional.[18]

At the same time land transactions always seem to have been accompanied by at least a customary deed of sale and mortgage:

> These deeds are known as white deeds as in Ching times and had not been put through the formal process of registration in the District Office which would turn them into legal docu-

ments; or, as formerly in Ching days, in the Magistrate's yamen when they became red deeds. They were common until the Pacific war . . .[19]

To be unable to produce some kind of deed to land claimed could have embarrassed a lineage as much as an individual, and would have made it liable to costly government intervention. We might say that the existence of the land records in government hands meant that it was made difficult for a lineage to wage a war of territorial acquisition, and this in itself constituted a form of political control.

The lineages, then, were not fighting for outright territorial gain. Nor were they fighting in order to exterminate their rivals—such a course would almost certainly have brought massive retaliation from the government, even if the delicately maintained balance of power had permitted it. They were fighting from often trivial economic, agricultural, irrigational and inter-personal causes, and by so doing they endeavoured to maintain their prestige and their rough status quo in society. Above all they were concerned to keep the sovereignty of their territory and the independence from intimidation of their members. Sometimes there seems to have been no cause for fighting, it was merely a reflex antagonism towards all other groups. Since in general nothing momentous was to be gained from inter-lineage feuding, the form it took was not unlike a game—a kind of deadly charade—where men were killed, maimed and injured, but not too many of them; where property and crops might be damaged, but seldom on an extensive scale; where the game was played hard, but not for too long (there could always be a return match); and where at the end of the game the two teams totted up the score and sometimes, through the good offices of a mediator, evened it up by paying compensation to the side which had suffered more heavily.

* * *

Lineages developed for a variety of reasons, of which availability of land, high productivity of soil and distance from the centre of government were probably the most important adjuncts to the basic family-biased ideology. They flourished as units in a system of strong local government where the state was not ready or able to exert full authority. Though the state might be opposed to too great a usurpation of its powers, and from time to time might take fright at lineage independence, there were compensating advantages.

First, the lineages often acted as tax lords for the government, making the collection of taxes easier, and shifting responsibility (and blame in the case of default) onto the small number of lineage heads rather than to the large number of households which constituted the lineage and perhaps its subservient tenants and clients. We may note how well such a system agrees with the Confucian thinking on the simplification of government through exploitation of the family unit.

Second, competition and conflict between lineages was a way of life and inevitably led to bloodshed and civil disturbance. But the violence was on the whole self-regulating and limited by the inter-lineage balance of power, so that the state did not *need* to be as concerned with local order in lineage areas as it was elsewhere. We may contrast this with the government's attitude to armed struggle by religious groups or quasi-religious secret societies:

> The T'ai-p'ing rebellion, broken with foreign help and smothered in streams of blood, had again proved as clearly as possible to the minds of Chinese statesmen how dangerous to the reigning dynasty the religions were, and that therefore political wisdom required them to be exterminated with more determination than was ever displayed before. The restoration of Imperial authority resolved itself chiefly into a merciless destruction of human lives in all the provinces where the rebellion raged; who shall estimate the number of heretics that perished by this bloody work, continued for many years?[20]

Inter-lineage civil strife was by definition fragmented, not united in opposition to the government.

This does not mean that hostile lineages were incapable of uniting in the face of a common enemy. One goad to widespread co-operation was the threat posed by a single lineage so powerful that only an alliance of a number of lineages could meet it— inter-lineage conflict was by no means confined to one-against-one situations. The market-control conflict at Tai Po referred to above was primarily between two neighbouring lineages, but the victorious one had created an alliance of some 60 villages in order to pack more punch. And the Chinese countryside abounded in areas with names like 'The Eight Villages' and 'The Pact of Fourteen', where long-standing agreements bound lineages together in defensive alliances.

Another spur to co-operation was intrusion from outside. In 1899 the major lineages of the New Territories of Hong Kong, all of them normally involved in strife, fielded an army of over 2,000 men under joint leadership in order to oppose the assumption of rule there by Britain. But when the short-lived war was over, the lineages reverted to their accustomed mutual hostility. Not that the situation would ever be exactly the same again—government now was close at hand and would not have tolerated armed warfare within its domain. Weapons were confiscated, village gates torn down, and the expression of hostility in open warfare gradually became a thing of the past.

Lineage organization provided the most efficient form of village government, was little threat to the security of the state, subscribed to the government-sanctioned ideology, and was much concerned with prowess in the civil service examinations and orthodox bureaucratic careers. It might even have been a very positive advantage from the Chinese government's viewpoint were it not that the state needed to be strong in order to harness the benefits of conservative loyalty, steady tax generation and disciplined manpower which lineage organization could provide.

7

Non-kin as Kin

The pervasive influence of the family in Chinese society did not stop at the boundaries of physical kinship. The Chinese applied kinship terms to people who were unrelated to them, and they also had a penchant for organizing non-kin institutions along kinship lines. Perhaps we could say quite simply that, since it was for the Chinese a dominant element in thought, kinship organization manifested itself as a model in various other areas of social life.

TERMS OF ADDRESS

Within the family those superior to the speaker (that is, those older or senior in generation) were always addressed by the appropriate kinship term, while those younger and junior were usually called by their personal names. Needless to say, such a system constantly reinforced the superior-inferior hierarchy of relationships.

Outside the family the use of kin terms was very common:

So overwhelming was the importance of the family in 'traditional' China, and is even today for that matter, that the relations between friends came to be phrased in kinship terms. A friend of roughly the same age was generally called 'brother'. A friend of considerably older age was called 'uncle' or even 'father'. Here again the relative age question entered, and the honorific prefix *lao* (old) was used. If one were not very well acquainted with a friend, then one referred to him as *lao-hsiung*, 'old older brother', because one gave one's acquaintance honor by addressing him not only as *lao* but by

emphasizing that he was in the position of older brother to one
and hence in the position of leadership, honor, and so on.[1]

An older man would be addressed as 'father's younger brother',
while a much older (or much superior) man would be called
'father's elder brother'. A similar distinction according to age
and respect could be shown by using either 'elder brother's wife'
or 'father's younger brother's wife' to a woman, while 'father's
older sister' could also be used as a polite way of addressing a
female stranger.

The use of kinship terms between friends might well result in
their respective families being addressed accordingly; and the
trappings of a genuine kin relationship might appear:

> From the end of the first millenium A.D. to the present, not
> only have inter-generation marriages been rigorously for-
> bidden by law, but popular sentiment against them runs so
> high that even a teacher marrying his or her pupil, or a person
> marrying a friend's daughter or son, is condemned.[2]

Using these terms was not merely a politeness: their use carried
the expectation of commensurate respectful treatment. The
hereditary servants of lineages were addressed by kinship terms
deliberately lower than their age should have commanded, and
this was reflected in the contempt with which they were often
treated.

I once witnessed an interesting verbal battle at a lineage
meeting when a leader who wanted to bring a particularly
obstreperous opponent round to his point of view tried to do so by
addressing him over-humbly as 'uncle' instead of as 'elder
brother', which would have been the correct term given their
relationship. His opponent was not to be soft-soaped and publicly
rebuked the leader twice for not knowing his relationships
properly. Here was an instance of the deliberate manipulation of
kinship terminology to suit a specific purpose. In much the same
way the calling of a non-family member by a kinship term of
respect could on occasion be done in an attempt to benefit from
the flattered response of the addressee, but the ploy could not
have worked were it not that in most cases such terminology was
genuinely respectful.

QUASI-KINSHIP ORGANIZATIONS

The proven effectiveness of the family as an organizational force in Chinese society made the adoption of its values and institutions in non-kinship situations an attractive and obvious course of action. A family recruited its members primarily through birth and marriage: other institutions substituted swearing-in ceremonies of various kinds.

Probably the most famous brotherhood was that sworn by the heroes of *The Popular History of the Three Kingdoms*, a novel based on the official histories of China in the period after the collapse of the Han dynasty:

> Chang Fei said: 'Behind my cottage is a peach garden, the peach blossom fully out. There tomorrow let the three of us swear before Heaven and Earth to join in brotherhood, to be united in mind and action, and so thereafter to do great deeds.' Liu Pei and Kuan Yü with one accord replied, 'Excellent!' On the following day in the peach garden they made ready a black bull, a white horse and other ritual paraphernalia, and then lighting incense they made worship, swearing: 'Though we, Liu Pei, Kuan Yü and Chang Fei, are of different surnames, we now unite as brothers to act as one and to bear each other up through hardship and danger, to avenge our kingdom and to bring peace to its people. We sought not to be born at the same time, but we desire to die together at the same moment. May Heaven and Earth witness our intention, and may Heaven and Man combine to slay any of us who should forget his duty!' After the oath Liu Pei was made eldest brother, Kuan Yü second and Chang Fei youngest.

This brotherhood has been much looked up to by secret societies since, with Kuan Yü being worshipped as their patron god and the peach tree figuring large in initiation rituals. A number of different Triad (secret society) swearing-in ceremonies have been recorded. Inter-mingling of blood was a common feature:

> The Incense Master . . . pricks the middle finger of the left

hand of the recruit until blood appears. He then dips the finger into the bowl of wine carried by his assistant and then bends the hand backwards, palm facing up, and places the finger in the mouth of the recruit. After licking his finger, the recruit says 'It is sweet'. He then stands up and waits until the Incense Master has repeated this performance with all recruits.

After the finger pricking incident, the recruits again kneel on both knees and the Incense Master's assistant gives each a small bowl of wine, cock's blood, cinnabar, sugar, ashes from the 36 oaths, and mixed blood of the candidates. . . . Each recruit then drinks a small portion of the mixture.[3]

In addition to the blood-letting a series of oaths had to be sworn, usually 36 of them, of which some seem to have been designed to replace original true kinship relationships with the new sworn ones:

After entering, you swear, if you are a father, not to reveal the laws of the Brotherhood to your son, if an elder brother not to reveal them to your younger brother, nor to disclose them to your relations or friends: if you do, may you die under the sword.

After entering, you swear that if your own brother be fighting with a brother of the Association, you will exhort them to stop, but will not secretly assist your own brother: if you do, may you vomit blood and die.

But the primary emphasis was on reinforcing the kin-like nature of the recruit's new relationships. Thus:

After entering, you swear not to debauch a brother's wife, daughter, or sister: if you do, may you perish under the knife.

After entering, you swear to regard the parents of a brother as your own father or mother, and if a brother place his wife, or deliver his son into your charge, you will regard them as your own sister-in-law or your own nephew: if you do not, may Heaven destroy you.[4]

Clearly then, blood brothers were expected to act in some ways like true brothers, and although the treatment of a blood brother's kin as one's own was not carried to any great lengths, some of the proscriptions were severely sanctioned:

> The peculiarly binding nature of the Hung oath of Blood Brotherhood is attested by the rule that if a brother die no member of the Hung Society may marry his widow. The penalty attached for the breach of this is exceedingly severe, as will be seen from Oath 17, which runs as follows:
> 'If a Brother dies and leave behind him a wife and she desires to marry again, a Brother may not take her as his wife. Thus the brethren must be very careful in making enquiries before they marry. If any be so daring as to disobey this law, may he be blasted by five lightnings and his body be scattered here and there for ever.'[5]

Blood brothers were sometimes required by their oaths even to observe mourning for each other. The aim of solidarity akin to that of the family seems on the whole to have been well served by these oaths. Certainly secret societies have been strong enough to cause great problems not only to the Chinese government, but to those governments of Southeast Asia and elsewhere where Chinese have settled in large numbers. It was heavy secret society backing that sustained Sun Yat-sen's anti-Manchu revolutionary effort which eventually brought about the collapse of the Chinese empire in the early years of this century. The secret societies were mainly concerned with rebellion, but developed into criminal organizations in overseas territories and later on in China too.

In talking of ancestor worship we saw that nuns and other unattached women found hope of after-life care in artificial descent lines which provided them with substitute descendants. At the same time such women were of course finding a substitute family life with their 'sisters' and other 'kin' in convents or in Vegetarian Halls. In parts of Kwangtung province where silk making had since the early nineteenth century given considerable economic independence to the women workers who were its mainstay, numbers of women:

> either refused to marry or, having married, refused to live with

their husbands. Their resistance to marriage took regular forms. Typically they organized themselves into sisterhoods. The women remaining spinsters took vows before a deity, in front of witnesses, never to wed. Their vows were preceded by a hairdressing ritual resembling the one traditionally performed before marriage to signal a girl's arrival at social maturity. This earned them the title 'women who dress their own hair', *tzu-shu nü*. The others, who were formally married but did not live with their husbands, were known as *pu lo-chia*, 'women who do not go down to the family', i.e., women who refuse to join their husband's family. Such women took herbal medicines to suppress micturition and set off for their wedding ceremonies with strips of cloth wrapped, mummy fashion, under their bridal gown to prevent consummation. Three days after the wedding ceremonies they returned to their natal villages for the traditional home visit, which they prolonged for several years.[6]

Sisterhoods of this kind, nuns, prostitutes, monks, secret societies, close friends, all could find models for strengthening solidarity in the family system, and many of them borrowed too the reinforcement of ancestor worship.

THE STATE AS A FAMILY

The modern Chinese term for state or nation is *guo-jia*, which literally translated means 'the state family'. The derivation of the term does not allow that this was the original meaning, but it is probably not fanciful to say that over the centuries it has taken on something of the idea of 'the family of the state'. We have referred to the *wu-lun*, the five human relationships, on more than one occasion already. Only the first of the relationships, that between Ruler and Minister, really dealt with society outside the narrow circle of kin and friends. Its inclusion in the set implied that the relationship was to be treated as one of the same type as that between Father and Son (the next relationship of the five). A subject should, therefore, have brought the same qualities of respect and obedience to his relationship with the state as he was expected to bring to that with his father. Looked at in this way the emperor can indeed be considered a kind of symbolic father to the subject. Like a true father the emperor had authority of life and death over him. Like a true father the emperor worshipped on behalf of his family on special occasions, most notably in his exclusive worship of Heaven. Every year he ploughed a cere-monial furrow imparting fertility to the national soil for the benefit of his 'family' of subjects, much as a farming father tilled to support his family. But if the emperor were father to each of his subjects it follows that they must all have been brothers to each other, a belief supported at least in the world of fiction and proverb—'Within the four seas all men are brothers'. In theory, then, the question raised in Chapter 5—how were a man's dealings with strangers to be regulated?—could be answered with reference to the Elder brother/Younger brother relation-ship. In practice we have already discounted this attempt by the state to extend family values for its own purposes.

There was a more obvious way in which the state used kinship imagery in an endeavour to reinforce its authority. Its lower-level officials were known as 'father and mother officials'.

As Yuan Shou-ting put it, 'The district magistrate must see himself as a father and mother and the people as children. He must not look on himself as an official and the people as people.' Moreover, said Yuan, he should look on the people as if they were his own children, and administer them as if they were his own family. He should protect them 'as if he were protecting his infants'.

What did being the people's father and mother mean in practice? . . . In effect, the 'father and mother' role was a political rather than administrative role, in which the official must show that his concern was genuine. If he did, the benefit would accrue to both the people and himself. The magistrate who laboured over strengthening his character and promoting good government would provide the people with 'the blessing' of a father and mother. The people would see that his intentions were on their account, and none 'would not treat him as a father and mother and respect him as a sage'.[7]

The analogy was not inappropriate in that the local official and the typical Chinese father were both stern, unapproachable figures whose authority was paramount over the range of activities within their respective spheres. But it would hardly be in order to suggest that the district magistrate really cared for his charges after the manner of a father.

KINSHIP AND THE OVERSEAS CHINESE

During the Ming dynasty China had established strong contacts with Southeast Asia, and by the mid-eighteenth century had begun to export a considerable number of people to the various countries of the area. The motivating force was population pressure working from the north southwards, and so spilling people off the southern coast. One very distinctive feature of the emigration was the lack of female participation. Thus in the Philippines:

> In the Chinese community the sex ratio remained quite unbalanced during the nineteenth century. In 1870 official records showed 193 women in a Chinese population of about 23,000, a ratio of eight females per 1,000 males. Sixteen years later, official statistics registered 194 women (191 of them in Manila) in a Chinese population officially set at (in round numbers) 66,000. Thus, the ratio became 3 females per 1,000 males for the Philippines as a whole, and for Manila, where the Chinese population was close to 50,000, 4 females per 1,000 males.[8]

Under such circumstances the emigrants were cut off from their customary methods of organization along kinship lines—there could be no normal families, no lineages and no clans.

Kinship proper did play a part in the pattern of emigration in that there was a strong tendency for an established emigrant to act as a magnet for others of his kin, who would come to his area of settlement in the hope of emulating his success. It was not unusual to find a predominance of only a few surnames in an Overseas Chinese community, owing to this pattern. But it was not whole lineages or whole segments of lineages or whole families which emigrated in this way: rather it was random individuals from within these groups, so that they did not form an organized group in the overseas territory. Yet the Chinese were well convinced of the value of kinship as an organizational principle, and looked to kinship models as they institutionalized their lives abroad.

One important form of mock kinship organization for the Overseas Chinese was the secret society. These societies in the homeland were agglomerations of (mostly) males unrelated to each other but swearing blood brotherhood and combining against the state. Overseas the Chinese were almost all males, were as a body unrelated to each other, and were faced with native states and populations which were often hostile to them. To combine into secret societies through blood brotherhood seems to have been one of their earliest reactions:

> In 1828 the number of Chinese miners on Sungai Ujong was nearly 1,000, divided into nine *kongsis* chiefly of the Thian Ti Hui, or Heaven and Earth League (or Society). Each was under its respective *towkay*, or chief. . . . Jealousy of their fast-increasing power and numbers, or some alleged offence, but more probably the treasure amassed by the brotherhood of the Thian Ti Hui (whose property was in common), led in 1828 to their massacre by the Malays . . .
>
> We see, then, that wherever the Chinese went they took their secret societies with them. Indeed, these supplied practically the only social organization possessed by the community.[9]

Another response to moving to a non-kin environment was to organize along surname lines. We have seen that in China there was a common assumption that all people with the same surname were descended from the same ancestor, however far back. Although it was easy to prove in some cases that there was no common ancestry at all, still the feeling of kinship was strong enough that people of the same surname were forbidden to intermarry. Because of this special relationship it was always possible for a claim on the help, generosity or attention of another of one's own surname to be made, though the claim was so weak that it must often have been repudiated.

Among the Overseas Chinese, deprived of their accustomed family, lineage and clan support, the bond of common surname assumed an importance far greater than in the homeland. The Surname Association, sometimes called the Clan Association, became a feature of nearly all such communities from Taiwan to Southeast Asia, and from the United States to (more recently) the emigrant areas of Western Europe. It could not attempt to replace the family or the lineage, but it did form an organizational nub for some of the functions performed in China by those groups. In Thailand, for example:

> these surname associations often maintain a large common burial site or memorial at a Chinese cemetery in Bangkok for burial of members too poor to afford an individual grave, and where memorial services are held on certain Chinese festival days, normally Ch'ing-ming and Chung-yüan. The association also extends help to any indigent persons of the same surname and dialect group, even though they may not actually belong to the association. It collects money from members to support various Chinese community activities—schools, hospitals and temples. When called upon the association officers will mediate in disputes between association members or between member families and outsiders.[10]

Since members of a Surname Association could not in most cases prove their common origin and relationship, they obviously could not have leaders selected on the basis of generation/age precedences as could the lineage. Furthermore, the Associations flourished in urban environments overseas, not in the countryside as did lineages in China. Thus in financial and leadership matters an Association was organized on very different principles:

> each member subscribes to the funds of the Kongsi [Association] according to his means. In each a certain number of members are annually elected trustees, who collect subscriptions and the rents of houses that may belong to them, and pay the expenses of the Kongsi.
>
> One member is elected annually as chief or chairman of the society to whom the trustees account for the money collected by them; he is called the Loo-choo. On that day of election the members of the Kongsi meet at their house and each man's name is written on a separate piece of paper, which is rolled up tightly and placed in a box. A pair of lots is thrown up before the idol, if they fall with one flat side and one convex side

uppermost three times successively, one of the papers is unrolled and the man whose name is written on it becomes the Loo-choo for the ensuing year. In the same manner are the trustees chosen.[11]

It has often been assumed that the organizations of the Overseas Chinese were inspired by those of urban China, and it would therefore follow that Surname Associations were to be found in the cities of the South, the area from which the majority of emigrants came. Yet there is little evidence to bear this out. Some clan halls in China seem to have allowed anyone of their surname to worship in their ancestral halls, regardless of whether or not they were members of component lineages, but this is hardly the same thing as an Association organized solely on the basis of common surname. In fact, even the Overseas Chinese sometimes seem to have been dilatory in using mere common surname as an organizing principle. In Cambodia there have been strong Chinese communities for many centuries, but:

> Clan associations have developed among the Teochiu since 1959, when the municipal government of Phnom-Penh ordered the removal of four Chinese cemeteries to make way for urban expansion. Dissatisfaction with the plans of the Teochiu cemetery committee to dispose of unclaimed bones in a communal grave led groups of merchants sharing the same surname to build clan graves. Support for this operation was formalised into continuing clan associations, of which there were eight in 1963, representing the most frequent surnames among the Chinese in Phnom-Penh.[12]

Surname Associations through fictive kinship provided non-kin (or, at best, kin of doubtful provenance) with possibilities of organization for strength vis-a-vis societies which could overwhelm the unsupported individual. The most far-stretched use of kinship as an organizational feature was the Multiple Surname Association, of which a few have existed. These associations united men of more than one surname on the basis of some known link between their names. The most notable of them was the Lung Kong Association, comprising the surnames of four of the heroes of the Three Kingdoms (the Peach Garden oath of three of them has been quoted above). The culture which could make mock-kinship groups out of mock-kinship elements in this way was a culture which was committed indeed to kinship!

KINSHIP AND DISTANCE

Chinese kinship organization operated most effectively within a given small area of countryside (and doubtless the same would be true of most kinhip systems). The family was most stable when linked with land, and land of course does not move. Similarly, the lineage was tied to its land and its limited territory.

Land, constant in space and time, was the 'anchor against the wind' which gave permanence to the kinship group even while its members came and went over generations. Chinese people still ask each other 'Where is your native land?' as a matter of importance to mutual understanding. In many cases the answer which is given may appear false in that the person concerned may never have been there in his life, but it is the place from which his father or even grandfather came, the place of his ancestral lands, and even if he no longer has a direct claim on those lands he has a deeply felt loyalty to them.

But to be tied to locality had disadvantages, not least being the constraints on expansion due to limited availability of land. Indeed, any increase in family numbers tended to bring more pressure to bear on the land and so to depress standards of living for the family.

Unless he migrates to the city, a man of humble origins in the country has almost ceased to have any chance to climb, which explains why a permanent or temporary city dwelling becomes an inevitable step in climbing the social ladder. . . . The average farm in China was only a few acres. (In Yunnan a good-sized farm was only about one acre.) Small farming made accumulation of capital impossible. Villagers put it neatly, 'Land breeds no land'. In a community in which industry and commerce were not developed, in which land had already done its best, and in which pressure from the increasing population was felt, ambitious people had to seek their fortunes not through ordinary economic enterprises but through acquiring power, either legally or illegally. They had to leave their villages for good. When they obtained wealth, they might come back to their villages to acquire land, but if they retired to live in the villages, the pressure of population would bear down on them and soon wear them out—and after a few generations the big house would break up into a number of small holdings again. It was therefore essential for the rich to keep away from the villages. The place where they could maintain their power and wealth was the town.[13]

Kinship and its links with locality may be seen as working against the advancement of the individual, who none the less craved the security and stability of kinship organization. When the individual tore himself away from land and kin and ventured into the urban or overseas arena of opportunity he, paradoxically, sought a measure of stability through the creation of kinship-type organizations. It is probably true to say that these 'artificial' groupings were weaker and less permanent than the 'real' ones because they were not bolstered by localistic ties; that is to say, the principle of kinship alone was insufficient foundation for effective social organization, despite its universal acceptance. The successful man in an urban environment was often the man who was able to free himself from the bonds of kinship—but successful men were few. A huge majority was wedded to the ideals of the family, and looked to those ideals for succour even in circumstances inappropriate to their application.

8

Kinship in the 20th Century

The bulk of this book has dealt with the 'traditional' Chinese kinship system, and has mostly presented it as though it was unchanging and permanent. Of course such a presentation is a distortion in that kinship like all other social institutions was not static but bound up with the ongoing development of the culture. The universal keeping of written genealogies, for instance, did not begin until some 900 years ago in the Sung dynasty, and was associated with neo-Confucian trends. Ancestral halls apparently did not become common until the 16th century during the Ming dynasty. Nevertheless, the composite picture of 'traditional' kinship probably is largely true for the China of the 19th century and does serve as a convenient base from which to examine the contemporary situation.

Traditionally the individual (male or female) had been subordinated to the family. While he lived it was the family which controlled his marriage, his finances, even the names of his children. In death it was the family which preserved his memory and which gave succour to his soul through ancestor worship. We must assume that for the majority this subordination was not queried for, if the family were demanding, it did at least have advantages in its corporate strength vis-à-vis the rest of society. The fate of the 'loners' was seldom to be envied.

The 20th century has seen cataclysmic changes in all aspects of Chinese life, and the kinship system was bound to change too. Successive governments and political ideologies have busied themselves clipping the wings of kinship, a process both contributing to and resulting from an increasing emphasis on the importance of the individual on the one hand and the state on the other. If the kinship system has been weakened, then we must ask what other institutions have usurped its functions for the individual. In this chapter some of the major landmarks in the process of change will be pointed out, and an attempt will be made to draw a general picture of the contemporary family within the same frame as that of the traditional family.

MILESTONES OF CHANGE

In the mid-19th century the Qing dynasty was challenged and very nearly overthrown by the Taiping Rebellion. The Taipings had a programme of reforms which, had they been fully carried out, would have revolutionized Chinese society and culture. The reforms included the equality of the sexes, with both men and women being eligible to take state examinations and to hold civil or military office. To bolster the new position of women, prostitution, concubinage and foot-binding were all to be banned. Marriage was to be based on personal choice through love, and arranged marriage and bride-price were forbidden. Ancestor worship was condemned, along with other elements of the Chinese religious system, and ancestor tablets were destroyed: the Taipings' own brand of Christianity was to be substituted as the popular religion. There was to be a vast programme of land reform, with all land and property being held in common, each family taking only its needs and the surplus going to public granaries and banks. Out of the common funds were to be paid the costs of all ceremonies, including those of greatest importance to the family, such as Full Month Feasts, weddings and funerals. In short, the Taipings planned a thoroughgoing upheaval of the social system, and clearly saw traditional family organization as an obstacle to change.

The reasons for the failure of the revolt were complex and included such diverse factors as the siding of Western forces with the Qing government and the reluctance of the Taiping leaders to submit to the same austere regime as they were promoting for society at large. The measures to weaken the family and to destroy ancestor worship (the religion of the family) doubtless contributed to the failure, for China was unused to *revolutionary* ideas despite a hallowed tradition of *rebellion*. Not only the educated elite, but many of the peasantry were unsympathetic to the sweeping away of these basic principles by which society and life were governed. The country may have been ready for a change of dynasty, but the traditional system itself had not lost credibility.

Perhaps because of the failure of the Taipings, but probably more because of gentry-elite leadership, later 19th-century attempts at reform were more conservative in nature and neither dared nor desired anything so radical as an attack on the kinship system. The immediate reaction to the Taiping collapse was a Confucianist revival—what is usually called the 'T'ung Chih Restoration':

> In Prince Kung's words, which might have been those of any member of the Sino-Manchu governing class, the foundations of the state were secure when moral authority proceeded from above and was accepted from below. Conversely, confusion between superior and inferior was the basic cause of all unrest. . . . The first task of the Restoration statesmen was to reassert the principles of Confucian society and to make certain of their acceptance by both the literati and the common people. The ideological heresies of the Taiping doctrine had little appeal to the educated when contrasted with the still tremendous attractive powers of the revived Confucian doctrine.[1]

The family was of course both a part of and a model for the superior/inferior hierarchy.

By the 1890s the inability of Confucianism to cope with foreign aggression and constant internal disaffection was obvious to many Chinese. The Emperor's reform movement of 1898 (the Hundred Days Reform) attempted to tackle problems of education, production, finance and military modernization, but family reforms seem to have been limited to some strengthening of anti-footbinding sentiments.

Secret society risings too were essentially conservative in nature: we have seen how the societies looked to the family for organizational principles, so that no revolution within the kinship sphere was likely to have resulted from their success. At the turn of the century the Boxer movement began by being both anti-Manchu and anti-West. As such it contained the seeds of 20th-century Chinese nationalism, but it was not otherwise revolutionary in ideology and turned ultimately to support the

Manchus against the West. The Christian missionaries and their converts were the prime targets of and principal sufferers from Boxer aggression, perhaps not least because of their interference with the family and with local custom. They forbade concubinage, for example, and would tolerate no other religious observances such as ancestor worship:

> A case of almost everyday occurrence was one in which (in the missionary version) 'a native who is very devoted to his Church is persecuted because he refuses to give contributions towards expenses connected with idolatrous worship'. Yet it did not require very much acquaintance with the customs of the Chinese to know that 'joining in idolatrous worship' was a pure invention of the native Christians. It was in fact a remarkably successful ruse for evading the payment of one's just liabilities as a member of the village community (for communal entertainment, upkeep of the temple as a village meeting-place, etc.).[2]

The kind of social reform envisaged by the Taipings was not advocated again by any major group until the second decade of the 20th century. By then imperial China had collapsed and government and society were in a state of chaos. One thing which was clear to many intellectuals of the time was the inadequacy of the traditional social organization in the face of modern conditions. The May Fourth Movement* gave forceful expression to this feeling. Thus, according to Ch'en Tu-hsiu, one of its cultural leaders:

> Modern society was composed of individuals acting as independent units, and its laws and ethics tended to protect individual freedom and rights. Confucianism was based on a feudal society composed of family and clan units. The individual was regarded only as a member of the family, and not as an independent unit in the society and state. Confucian ethics imposed on the individual filial piety to the family and loyal duty to the ruler, without providing him with individual

* Named after a day of student protest, May 4th 1919, when public indignation at international treaties humiliating to China was expressed in the burning of the house of the Minister of Communications.

rights. All these ethical principles of the feudal ages were highly inappropriate to modern individualistic society.[3]

From this it followed that under Confucianism democratic principles could not be applied, nor could women be as useful members of society as they ought, nor was there the financial independence of the individual necessary for modern economic advance, nor the encouragement of a sense of individual purpose and strength. The May Fourth Movement did not itself achieve reform in these fields, but it marked the turning point from which thorough social reform was not again obscured:

> After the May Fourth Incident, girls started to join the student movement and its attendant social and political activities. Co-education was established. Before the incident there had been very few girls' schools of higher learning. In 1922, however, twenty-eight universities and colleges had girl students. They were taught to be independent citizens instead of dependent beings in the family. After the incident, women were allowed to teach in boys' schools. Professional opportunities for women increased. Free marriage was practiced more often. Morality concerning the sexes started to change and the concept of birth control was introduced.[4]

A milestone on the path of good intentions was the Civil Code of the Republic of China, promulgated in 1931. The Chairman of the Civil Codification Commission wrote:

> In order to turn China into a real State, in the modern sense of the word, Dr. Sun Yat Sen thought it necessary to substitute for the primitive notion of unity of clan or family, the notion of unity of the population formed by these clans or families. The particular interest of the isolated groups had to yield to the general interest of the nation. To put into practice this new ideal and to enable the citizens to make use of their personal abilities to the best interest of their country, it was imperative that the excessive grip of the old family ties over the individuals should be loosened.[5]

To achieve this loosening the new laws swept away most of the supports which formerly the state had given to the patrilineal family. With regard to marriage, it was laid down that the male and female individuals should make an agreement to marry of their own accord. Betrothal could not take place until a man was 17 and a woman 15, and marriage could not be concluded for a further year after those ages. The taking of more than one spouse was expressly forbidden. Divorce was made available either by mutual consent or to either male or female on the grounds of adultery, bigamy, maltreatment, desertion, incurable physical or mental illness, attempted murder of the spouse, etc. Surname exogamy disappeared, though there was still a wider spread of ineligible patrilineal kin than of those on the mother's side; that is to say, the *wu-fu* group remained the exogamous unit. Male and female heirs were to inherit equally. The right of the individual to make a will was recognized, but some safeguards were built in so that those who might normally expect to inherit could not be dispossessed entirely through the whim of the testator. The status of 'married-in son-in-law' (*chui-fu*) was recognized. The requirement to mourn for particular kin was done away with. Emphasis on the patrilineal family remained in that custody of the children of a divorced couple was to be given to the father.

This fine-sounding legislation had little hope of universal implementation. None of the governments of the pre-1949 era was in complete agreement with the 'New Thought', and none had sufficient power to implement the reforms even had full conviction been there. Late 19th- and early 20th-century industrialization had begun to attract to the cities of China the wealthy and the intellectuals, creating a gulf between city and countryside such as had not previously existed. These new urban intellectuals did not represent majority Chinese thinking, and what they advocated and put into practice was not necessarily either followed by or even transmitted to the mass of the people:

> The actual social impact of the codes in question was of the slightest. The overwhelming mass of the population, even in the territories administered directly from Nanking, continued to be regulated in day-to-day transactions by the traditional customary law, which lacked little of its former binding force throughout the peasantry in spite of the disappearance of the old Chinese state. . . . One hears it said quite often by those

who ought to know better that concubinage was 'abolished' by the Nationalist Civil Code. . . . It is true that in sophisticated and intellectual circles old-fashioned concubinage was becoming infrequent in the twenties and thirties, but the reason for this had nothing to do with any legal policy, being simply a consequence of the westernization of those particular classes of society. Among the more conservative elements, concubinage was still common whenever financial circumstances allowed, and it was rare for a wife to resent it to the point of suing for divorce.[6]

Changes in the attitudes to the family and especially in the position of women did take place in the cities and to some extent in their rural hinterlands:

> The progress of eliminating footbinding in an area as vast and diverse as China was uneven and varied. A Japanese encyclopedia article published in 1932 remarked that women in the large cities had all let their feet out, with resistance confined to the villages. But the writer added that women in the Honan city of Loyang had recently reverted to the custom of binding feet and admiring them for their beauty. Gotō Asatarō, a less objective Japanese student of Chinese customs, in 1938 . . . stated that an observer who restricted himself to Shanghai and Peking might conclude that footbinding had ended, but asserted that eighty to ninety per cent of the women in the rural areas still practised it.[7]

But even in the cities change was slow and patchy. Research undertaken in 1935–37 led to the following report:

> We investigated 360 marriages in 170 families in the villages of North China, of Fukien and Kiangsu. In only one case did the parents ask the consent of the young man (a college student). Out of 170 rural inhabitants interviewed only 3 women admitted ever having heard of 'modern marriages'. . . .
>
> Even among the workers and lower middle class of Peiping the old ways have continued. In only 3 out of 112 marriages in 81 families did the bridegroom show an awareness of modern trends . . .

Yet parents in the cities are less conservative than in the country. Thus 6 out of 16 Peiping workers over 35 years of age who were interviewed on marriage declared that they would permit their children to choose their mates. 'But this is unlikely to happen', said several Peiping coolies, 'this new idea is something for the rich people, like modern dress and automobiles'.

In the cities three deviations from the old pattern appear: (1) parents arrange matches and ask their children's consent; (2) children choose their mates and ask their parents' approval; (3) children marry without asking their parents' approval. The first two deviations are compromises. The third often involves a complete break with the parents and is rather uncommon.[8]

In the greater part of the countryside so little effect of the modernization trend was felt that we have been able to discover much of what we know of traditional kinship organization from research done in the field in the 1930s and 1940s. The rural areas were largely unspoiled reserves of pre-modern culture and social organization.

Writing in 1927, six years after the founding of the Chinese Communist Party, Mao Tse-Tung said:

The abolition of the clan system, of superstitions, and of inequality between men and women will follow as a natural consequence of the victory in political and economic struggles. If we crudely and arbitrarily devote excessive efforts to the abolition of such things, we shall give the local bullies and bad gentry a pretext for undermining the peasant movement by raising such slogans of counter-revolutionary propaganda as 'The peasant association does not show piety towards ancestors', 'The peasant association abuses the gods and destroys religion', and 'The peasant association advocates the community of women'. . . . The idols were set up by the peasants, and in time they will pull down the idols with their own hands; there is no need for anybody else to throw away prematurely the idols for them.[9]

Once political control had been established the Communist

Party wasted little time in making sure that the cultural changes did come about, and especially was this so with regard to the position of women. The Kiangsi Soviet came into precarious life in 1928, and in 1931 the 'Marriage Regulations of the Chinese Soviet Republic' was published. In general the regulations were similar to the Nationalist Civil Code of the same year, though the age of marriage for both males and females was made higher, and there was no distinction in the exogamous group between patrilineal and other kin.

Forced out of Kiangsi by the Nationalists' extermination campaigns, in 1934 the Communists trekked north to Yenan where again they published marriage regulations which held to the basic principles of monogamy, equality of the sexes and individual freedom to marry and divorce. By the time that the whole of mainland China was theirs in 1949 they had considerable experience in applying their revolutionary social programme.

'The Marriage Law of the People's Republic of China' was promulgated in 1950 and has remained substantially unchanged since then. Its first two articles are clear statements of general principles:

> ARTICLE 1. The feudal marriage system based on arbitrary and compulsory arrangements and the supremacy of man over woman, and in disregard of the interests of the children, is abolished.
>
> The New-Democratic marriage system, which is based on the free choice of partners, on monogamy, on equal rights for both sexes, and on the protection of the lawful interests of women and children, is put into effect.
>
> ARTICLE 2. Bigamy, concubinage, child betrothal, interference in the re-marriage of widows, and the exaction of money or gifts in connection with marriages, are prohibited.[10]

Under the law a man has to be 20 years old and a woman 18 before being allowed to contract a marriage. The group within which marriage is forbidden is to consist of direct lineal blood relatives only, but allowance for customary prohibitions beyond that is made. The marriage is to be registered at a local government office, upon which a marriage certificate will be issued. Husband and wife have equal status, have equal rights in the possession and management of family property, and have the right to inherit each other's property. They have a duty to love, respect and look after each other, and to work jointly for the welfare of the family. As parents they have a duty to rear and educate their children, and the children in turn have a duty to support and assist their parents. Infanticide is forbidden. Parents and children have the right to inherit one another's property. Divorce by mutual consent is available on registering with the local government office. If only one party wants the divorce there is a required procedure for attempted reconciliation, but if it fails then a court should give a decision on the case.

On the one hand the law does away with features which placed the individual in subjection to and bolstered the traditional family; on the other hand it is a clear statement of the importance of the simple family, both to husband and wife, as the correct environment in which to bring up children. It is in no way a law aimed at the destruction of the family.

At almost exactly the same time as the Marriage Law came the Land Reform Law. Under land reform:

> Well over a hundred million acres of farmland were taken from four million landlords and given to fifty million previously landless tenant cultivators, within the first three years of the Communist administration. To each village came a team of Communist-led enthusiasts who investigated the land ownership, spread propaganda about its inequity, promoted discussion and organized those peasants who were most responsive—the 'positive elements'—into a task force. To break the power image in the peasants' minds, the cadres held meetings, iconoclastic events at which increasingly articulate and voluble poor peasants 'spoke bitterness' and 'settled accounts' for the past misdeeds of the petty tyrants of the village.[11]

Not only were large private holdings of land broken up in this way; large corporate holdings were also redistributed. At a stroke the economic base of large-scale family organization and of lineages was destroyed, reinforcing the Marriage Law in its attack on the traditional power of the family over the individual:

Land reform had a direct effect on the internal structure of the family. Since land was redistributed not to the family as a whole but to each member on an equal-share basis regardless of age and sex, land reform gave the young and the women an unprecedented sense of importance in contrast to the traditional system of family property ownership, in which the head of the family had sole right to dispose of the family property and female descendants enjoyed no inheritance rights. Moreover, the land reform regulations stipulated that each member of the family might take his or her share of the family land out of the family, for instance in case of a divorce, an egalitarian arrangement of roles of the members and the economic leverage that clearly strengthened the position of the young and the women.[12]

However, land was still in private ownership, albeit on a more equitable basis, and it would have been only a matter of time before differential holdings again developed. The inept, the lazy, the reckless and the unfortunate would inevitably lose their land little by little to the diligent, the hard-headed and the lucky. That this should not happen was ensured by an accelerating process of public ownership. Within three years of the Land Reform Law families were being encouraged to co-operate with each other in 'Mutual Aid Teams', sharing tools, labour and land in order to farm in a more economical way. By 1955 the movement was towards 'Co-operatives', land being pooled and farmed co-operatively as one unit, though original title to ownership was retained. The co-operatives in turn gave way, and by 1957 land had become the property of the 'Collective', the members receiving income in proportion to their work-hours without reference to previous private ownership. Finally in 1958 appeared the 'Communes', huge property-owning units:

There are about 74,000 people's communes in China. They are divided into three 'levels of organization', the commune, the brigade and the team. The commune is responsible for big projects like tractor stations, irrigation works, farm machinery repair shops, secondary schools. A typical commune might have a population of 20,000 to 50,000 people, some as little as 10,000. The brigade is responsible for smaller projects including small reservoirs, primary schools and health clinics. There may be twenty or so brigades in an average-size commune, or as few as ten. The team is about the size of a small village with one or two hundred inhabitants. This is the main level of organization. The team keeps its own accounts and registers the 'work-points' earned by each household. At the year's end it has a 'share-out' of its income. . . . Households usually have small 'private plots' where they can raise poultry or grow vegetables.[13]

The family has in this way come to be landless, the small private plots being assigned to individuals to work, but not made over to them as property. Family property is confined now to housing and personal possessions, and for a time during the formation of the communes there were those who advocated bringing even these into public ownership. The movement towards communes was in fact the time of greatest danger to the Chinese family, zealots wanting to break away many of its functions. Mess halls were set up so that no food needed to be prepared at home, for instance; and nurseries and kindergartens took over much of the family's child-rearing function:

A French newspaperman returning to the West after two years in China reported what may well be the new philosophy of family life, painted on the wall of an urban commune mess hall and supposedly composed by a woman worker:
      The machine is my husband,
      The factory is my family,
      The fruits of my labour are my children,
      The Party is my father and my mother.[14]

Extreme measures were by no means universally carried out, and the solidarity of conjugal family life has not again been seriously challenged.

Since 1949 the Chinese government has flirted with birth control measures. In 1956 and 1957 there was a birth control campaign advocating not only contraception and late marriage but also the sterilization of both men and women. Perhaps to make the campaign more palatable to the rural masses there was some emphasis on traditional methods of abortion and contraception. One much quoted technique propounded by a herbalist doctor involved a woman's swallowing doses of live tadpoles, this allegedly giving protection from pregnancy for five years. However, the campaign did not last long:

> 1958 was a year of unbounded optimism in China. . . . In keeping with this optimism the birth control campaign was dropped and China's vast population came to be regarded as an asset rather than a hindrance to the tremendous expansion of the economy projected by the Chinese. 'People in the past (have worried often) about our 'over-population'. . . . But the idea has been overturned. . . . The question is not so much over-population, as shortage of man-power'.[15]

In 1962 a second birth control campaign got under way, and with varying degrees of emphasis has continued up to the present. Late marriage was still an important element of the programme:

> The health of mothers and children was said to be a prime consideration of the Party and Chairman Mao. For health reasons, women were advised not to get married and begin childbearing too early. Until the age of twenty-five, their bones were not fully calcified and their reproductive organs were not 'mature'. The physical burden of the 'ten months' of gestation, the pain and loss of blood at delivery, and the drain of nutrients from the mother's body during lactation were described in harrowing detail, along with a host of special problems for the too-young mother, including ovarian disorders, menstrual irregularities, difficult labor, and cancer of the cervix. Young men who married too early were also in grave danger. . . . Besides all this, the children of early marriages were weak, sickly, and difficult to nurse and did not develop satisfactorily, and the marriages themselves were beset by emotional upsets, mental anguish, and quarrels, and likely to end in divorce. All of these terrors of early marriage and early prolixity could be avoided by marrying after the age of thirty and using birth control religiously.[16]

There has been a considerable scientific effort involved, and:

contraceptives such as condoms, pills, foams, jellies, dia-
phragms and especially intra-uterine devices were made more
readily available throughout the countryside in the 1960s.
Perhaps of special significance was the increased use of IUDs
which have apparently become progressively more acceptable
from the point of view of the woman and of the medical
personnel.[17]

The bare-foot doctors, medical front-line personnel with limited
training, are competent to give advice on birth control and are
equipped with supplies of contraceptives. Their ubiquitous
presence means that scientific contraception has become available throughout the countryside as well as in the cities.

The Cultural Revolution of the late 1960s was a period of
some uncertainty for the family:

> In the initial stages of the Cultural Revolution, youth turned
> against old customs and on their rampages destroyed objects
> such as ancestral plaques which supported the traditional
> family. However, as the Cultural Revolution became pro-
> gressively more violent, many youths became frightened and
> returned to the safety of their homes for a period of intensive
> togetherness. The result may have been that the Cultural
> Revolution eventually did as much to strengthen the family as
> it did to weaken it.[18]

After the Cultural Revolution came one more attack on the
family. It took the form of a demand for the abolition of the
'family head system' and was at its height in the 1969–70 period:

> Family study of Mao's works was used to challenge excessive
> parental authoritarianism. During this family interaction
> process, young children and daughters-in-law were en-
> couraged to examine their family relationships and to criticize
> those in authority in the family for any excessive use of power.
> Youths reported beatings by parents; mothers-in-law were
> criticized for ordering and demanding compliance, husbands
> for dinnertime demands. The youths challenged parents for
> being house-proud: cleaning up the community was to come
> first. . . . How much were family relationships and solidarity

weakened because of this ideological approach? . . . The vast majority of families may not even have participated in the process of examining their authority structure.[19]

THE COMPOSITION OF THE CONTEMPORARY FAMILY

The ideal family of traditional times no longer holds attraction for the Chinese rulers, and every effort has been made through law and exhortation to eradicate Big Family mentality and its supporting institutions. More now than ever in the past the simple and stem families are the norm. The stem family has the dual advantage of providing care for the elderly and baby-sitters for the young: there is no sign that it is considered anything other than desirable. One recent visitor to China reports on a four-generation stem family:

> A family we visited on a new housing estate in Shanghai consisted of grandmother, grandfather, the wife and husband (he was away except for five days a month at a staff job at a May 7th Cadre School), daughter, son, daughter-in-law and their two children. They have two rooms and shared a kitchen and bathroom.[20]

There has been much emphasis on limiting the number of children born to a family, two or at the most three if economic circumstances permit are generally cited as the optimum: yet there is apparently a difference between rural and urban attitudes, and in the countryside families of four or five children are common. The national average number of members per family, then, is probably quite high, especially when stem families are taken into account. Startlingly, as late as 24th October 1958 the *Shan-xi Ri-bao*, a newspaper from Shansi Province, carried the headline 'Large Family of Twenty-four Members', followed by an approving account of the family, which was under the strong leadership of an old woman, and comprised her younger brother, her four sons and their wives, and her fourteen grandchildren. Their harmonious relationships were said to be the result of the old woman's equitable and careful apportionment of work, plus their individual willingness to place family above self in economic and other matters. Old preferences die hard.

Birth is, of course, the normal form of recruitment to the family, but adoption has not been abolished:

Adoption is a useful solution to the problem of ensuring that a large number of orphans and unwanted children are taken care of. A rule for the form of adoption is found in a decision of the Supreme Court, bearing no date, which states that there should be an agreement between the parents of the child and its adoptive parents. It is not necessary that such an agreement should be in writing. The adoption may be annulled by order of the court on account of ill-treatment or abandonment of the child by the adoptive parents or at the request of the parents. . . . The adoption of a son for the purpose of continuation of the ancestral cult is naturally an anathema.[21]

Methods of family size limitation have been modernized, but are not in essence much changed from earlier times.

Contraception is free, and so is abortion. Abortions, available on the request of the woman alone, are encouraged after the birth of two children and are generally performed only during the first three to three and a half months of pregnancy. . . . When the abortion is performed within fifty days of conception, the woman has ten days off from work. When it is done from fifty to a hundred and twenty days of pregnancy— something which is not usual—she has a month off from work. The emphasis, however, is on 'planned birth' and the use of contraceptives rather than abortion.[22]

Infanticide has been outlawed, though occasional reports of its occurrence are made. Late marriage used to be a result of poverty, and contributed to the battery of family limitation factors. In the contemporary situation everyone is being urged to postpone marriage. The legal minimum age of marriage is 20 for a man and 18 for a woman, but:

I asked a final year university English language class if anyone were engaged; they smiled and shook their heads. When I asked if any were married, there was a chorus of denials! The best marriage age for a boy, they told me, was twenty-eight to

thirty and for a girl twenty-six to twenty-eight. . . . Young
people have first to work hard, to get a good training and help
their country and their parents. They have to learn more of life
and of themselves before entering a lifelong partnership. Of
course, late marriage is also one of the ways of keeping down
the birthrate.[23]

Some of the patrilineal bias of the family remains. Surname is
still taken from the father. Though the ban on marrying someone
with the same surname has vanished, the Marriage Law allows
that the question of prohibiting marriage between collateral
relatives by blood is to be determined by custom, leaving the way
clear for the observance of the old *wu-fu* system of imbalance, and
so for the time being helping to preserve patrilineal bias. More
important, the normal residence pattern is still for a wife to go to
live in her husband's family or village. The *chui-fu* (married-in
son-in-law) is still not favoured, and in the countryside at least
couples do not often set up on their own.

Marriage is still normally patrilocal, and the bride has often to
move to another village. This is unfavourable to the unmarried
woman because the probability of her joining another work
team (that of her husband) upon marriage makes her own
work team reluctant to send her to courses for cadre training or
special agricultural skills. Once married, a girl is still less likely
to be put forward as a candidate by her new team because she
must first win the confidence of her teammates. By the time she
has established a local reputation, she may be involved in
child-bearing and -rearing.[24]

The family remains an economic unit and profits by having as
many wage-earners as possible. It follows that sons who will not
move away on marriage are in the long run of greater usefulness
to the family than daughters who will. In due course the parents
will be too old to earn a significant wage, and the presence of
married sons then ensures that they are cared for.

The importance of household ownership for the family is that it
makes grown children more dependent on their parents. When
a son decides to marry, he cannot just request a house from the

collective. He may request a small plot of land on which to build a new house, but the building expense must come out of his own or his family's pocket. Houses are not cheap. . . . The result of both the expense of building and the occasional shortage of building materials is that most sons must live close to their parents. By the time he is ready to marry in his early twenties, a man will not have been able to save enough money to build a new house. He must therefore either simply stay within his own parents' house, take money from the combined family savings to build a new wing onto the old house, or take even more savings to build a more complete house elsewhere in the village. . . . The most common practice seems to be either to remain with the parents after marriage or to build an additional room or set of rooms very close by. If parents control the sum of money being used for building it is reasonable to assume that they might see to it that children did not move too far away.[25]

Both sons and daughters are equally eligible to inherit under the law, but it seems unlikely that married-out daughters can expect to inherit a share of the house, especially as there appears to be a legal reluctance to allow inheritance rights from both sides of a family. Thus the family's patrilineal principles have by no means been completely cast aside.

THE INDIVIDUAL AND THE CONTEMPORARY FAMILY

The Marriage Law was designed to abolish the hold of the family over the individual, giving him the power to take independent decisions, but it did not attempt to destroy the family as such, and built in protection for the institution. Article 8 reads:

Husband and wife are in duty bound to love, respect, assist and look after each other, to live in harmony, to engage in productive work, to care for their children and to strive jointly for the welfare of the family and for the building up of the new society.

Article 13 says:

. . . ve the duty to rear and to educate their children; the children have the duty to support and to assist their parents. Neither the parents nor the children shall maltreat or desert one another.

The law also makes clear the equality of male and female. However, we have seen that there remain inbuilt preferences for sons over daughters, and this preference probably has an effect on the birth rate, particularly in the conservative countryside, parents wanting at least one son regardless of how many daughters have been born to them.

In the cities it seems to be normal for babies to be delivered in hospitals, but in the countryside most children are born at home. In either case improvements in medical facilities, increased pre- and post-natal care, plus entitlement to maternity leave have doubtless had an effect on infant and maternal survival. Child immunization programmes have also been implemented. Registration of births seems not to have been systematically practised since 1949. This will possibly ultimately raise problems over the right to inherit and duty to support, especially in areas such as cities where the population is comparatively mobile and family circumstances not so well known to neighbours. In traditional times the Full Month Feast acted as a kind of social registration by advertising the birth to kin and neighbourhood. Perhaps because of the lack of an alternative, the holding of such feasts seems not always to have been discontinued despite attempts to remove it from custom as a wasteful and unnecessary luxury. On 17th October, 1964 the following not untypical article appeared in the Peking publication *Zhong-guo Qing-nian Bao* (*China Youth*):

The Full Month Ceremony is an old and widespread popular custom of Huai Pei Village in Anhui Province. . . . On the 18th June this year Yang Su-ying had a son. When her family got to hear of it, they wanted to send some presents over right away. Her older brother, Yang Shou-lüeh, suggested sending 30 catties of dough fritters, four chickens, four fish, 200 eggs, two yards four feet of cloth, and 40 yuan 'greeting money'. When Su-ying heard this, she took the initiative in arranging a meeting with her brother and mother, and told them, 'I appreciate your kind intentions in giving full-month presents, but it is too prodigal to spend so much money on buying so many things, you'd do better to save it'. 'No', said her mother, 'it is not just our family which has this rule. In this place it has always been that the mother's family send gifts when she gives birth to a child'. 'That's just so', agreed her brother. Yang Su-ying patiently argued: 'The reason why other people act like this is because they also think like you, so the custom can't be done away with . . .'

The question of how to go about naming the child has become a little difficult. In the past, one element in a personal name often was chosen with astrological factors in mind. In particular there was a tendency to use characters associated with the Five Elements (Water, Fire, Wood, Metal, Earth) to compensate for elemental weaknesses connected with planetary influences at the time of birth. Superstitious naming systems of this kind cannot be applied where the ritual specialists and reference works by which they were fixed are no longer available. *China Youth* on 26th October, 1963 gave clear guidance on naming procedures in an article headed 'Do we still need to update genealogies and differentiate between generations?'. A reader from Chekiang Province, confused by contradictory arguments at home, mentioned that in the past generation-names had been given in his family according to the sequence of words in a poem in the genealogy. Now the poem had been used up and the genealogy was not being kept up to date. As a result children were being given names at random—such as Little Bright or Little Light for a boy, and Little Swallow or Little Red for a girl—and it was feared that in a few years no-one would be clear about generation distinctions any more. Was he correct in saying that the genealogy should not be updated?

You are right, genealogies belong to feudal society and we should not nowadays keep them . . .

As for generation names . . . that business you mention of using a poem or set of characters to differentiate between generations, that began to be popular in the Ming and Qing 'ynasties. The object of it was to define more clearly and to 'd more tightly the blood ties between clansmen as they 'ferated and spread, so as to promote control by clan authority. Today, of course, we have no need to distinguish rigorously between collateral branches and different generations, or to be clear about whether people of the same surname whom we do not know are related to us or not. . . . Of course, if close relatives wish to select names for their children based on an identical character or a meaningful phrase, that is quite alright. It is entirely a matter for the parents and children themselves, and should not be confused with genealogy revision or generation demarcation.

In traditional times education was in family hands under a system of private tutors, but this began to change in the early years of this century. In China now primary education is free and universally available, and many children receive some secondary schooling as well. Traditional education was deeply rooted in Confucian philosophy—the contemporary philosophy of Chinese Communism is no less heavily involved with modern education. Thus there has been a change of political bias, a removal of control over education from family to state, and the opportunity to educate the young in social rather than family consciousness. This is especially so with the introduction of creches and kindergartens, which cater for a high percentage of children in the 3 to 7 years old range in the city at least. Paradoxically perhaps, since many mothers are out at work, those young children not at kindergarten are commonly looked after by grandparents, the very people most likely to be out of sympathy with the state's anti-clannism drive.

Foot-binding had died out long before the Communists came to power. Prostitution, along with venereal disease, has been eliminated, it is claimed. Children can no longer be betrothed, nor can child brides be taken into the groom's home. Concubinage is forbidden. Ghost marriage must surely have died out. But what of betrothal practices?

Lao Man and Ta Sao had been married in the old style. Thirty years earlier they had been chosen for each other by their parents and had never seen each other until the wedding w~ over. . . . But now the people's law would only recognize register 'free-choice marriages', so their son Ching would be married in the new way. In Upper F~

means that the tentative choice of a partner for son or daughter and the initial arrangements for betrothal and marriage are made by the parents. Then the two prospective partners meet each other. If they agree, the betrothal takes place to be followed almost certainly by the wedding. There have been local cases of the prospective bride breaking the engagement. There was even one notorious case, not in our hamlet, where a girl had broken two engagements. But no one could recall an instance where a young man had backed out of his commitment. This would have been so scandalous that it would have been difficult to find a wife for him afterwards.[26]

As late even as 1970, by this account, betrothal was not the matter of free choice which the Marriage Law was insisting upon. Probably there is still wide variation, with the practice in urban areas more nearly coinciding with the ideal, and rural areas being to a greater or lesser extent laggardly. This same recent source says:

Because of the delicate nature of such marriage arrangements, the services of a go-between are nearly always required. And there is another peculiar circumstance: In these Honan hamlets many families have the same surname. Thus most families in Upper Felicity are named Man and so presumably are related, therefore marriages cannot be contracted between them. That means that spouses have to be found in other hamlets and how is one to know who there will make a suitable spouse? Short of parents themselves going out to make inquiries, they must use the services of a go-between to learn of possible spouses for their children. The go-betweens thus obviate a lot of possible embarrassments.[27]

Such a first-hand report contrasts strongly with the consciousness-raising accounts of the horror of old marriage forms d the stark simplicity of new with which the Chinese press
the _s its readership. A 1st March, 1957 article in *Xin Guan-cha*
   _wpoint *Fortnightly*) bears the headline 'Do away with
witnes_
      iage customs' and tells of some visitors' distress at
         vedding where:

the groom's family were terribly happy, and busied themselves looking after the guests, the groom himself being overjoyed. But although the bride was beautifully made up, her face was not a happy one, and this led us to wonder whether she could be dissatisfied with the match. But when we asked our neighbours they said the couple were very fond of each other, so it all seemed very odd.

In the evening the ceremony began. The bride was led out by a middle-aged woman. First she worshipped the ancestors, then she stood facing the door of the house. A 50 year old man was pushed forward from the crowd. He stripped off his shirt and bared his chest. Then he drank several cups of wine and began to prance around with his eyes on the bride. He was chanting and singing, and the other people joined in, with gongs and drums beginning to beat too. He smacked himself on the legs and body, and then gave the bride a sharp box on the ears with his right hand, followed by his left, at which the crowd burst out laughing. As soon as a man got tired the next would take his place, and this went on for an hour. The bride's face was beaten till it was red and swollen, and her eyes were brimming with tears, but she didn't dare to cry out . . .

This was a special custom of the area. It had apparently been said for many years that the beating was to ensure wealth, the so-called 'beating for wealth, the more you are beaten the wealthier you get, without a beating you don't get wealthy'.

An article in *China Youth* on 28th March, 1958 refers to the old custom of 'disturbing the bridal chamber', also known as 'teasing the bride', where the groom's friends do their best to embarrass the newly-wed pair and to delay consummation of the marriage until late into the night:

In our region from the first to the fourth night after a wedding people come to 'disturb the bridal chamber'. Recently after a young couple were wed, a crowd of young people went to do so after the bride and groom were already asleep, kicking in the door and bursting in. They picked up the bride 'to give her a plane ride', then threw her down again, crushing her shoulder. When she begged for mercy, they made her perform a number of indecent acts and say some coarse words.

All such customs were to be eschewed under the new order:

> Couples intending to get married come before the Communist
> official in charge of marriage registration for the locality. He
> asks the couple whether the intended marriage is taking place
> with the consent of both parties, whether duress from any third
> party has been exerted, whether polygamy or concubinage is
> involved. If the answers agree with the legal provisions, and if
> the results of an investigation check with the answers, a
> marriage certificate is issued and the couple is legally mar-
> ried.[28]

Not only is the marriage ceremony itself simple, but also there is
to be no wasteful expenditure on feasting, entertainment or
wedding gifts. (Bride-price is banned under the Marriage Law.)
Under the banner 'A wedding for only 15 yuan' the *People's Daily*
on 24th January, 1958 reported a ceremony attended by:

> all manner of people from this and other villages, by cadres
> working in the area, and by the head of the village work section
> of the County Party Committee. In the middle of the hall was
> hung a portrait of Chairman Mao, simple and unadorned. To
> entertain the guests there were only a few sweets, cigarettes
> and home-roasted peanuts. In the past the bride would have
> ridden in a bridal sedan-chair to the accompaniment of music
> and gongs, and the groom's family would have had to lay on
> feasting for three days. Everyone was conscious of how
> refreshing the simplicity of this young couple's wedding was. A
> 40 year old guest said: 'This is an excellent way to conduct a
> wedding—it saves money and it's great fun . . .'

It must be doubted whether the 40 year old guest is typical of the
Chinese citizen even now. However, the pressure to change
customs continues, and recently there has been a drive for the
periodic registration of marriages with 'revolutionized collective
wedding ceremonies'.

An unhappy marriage may now be terminated by either party,
though arrangements for mediation are built into the divorce
procedure in order to prevent frivolous use of the institution. The
rash of divorce cases in the years immediately following the 1950

Marriage Law was only to be expected, but since then things have settled down and divorce is apparently not common. There probably remains some difficulty for a woman who is divorced in that having lived in her husband's village she has no obvious place to move to; moreover, social attitudes have not kept pace with legal, so that the divorcee may not feel as guiltless as the law allows that he or she should. There is no bar to remarriage of either the divorcee or the widow/er:

> It's the custom for people to marry. Women marry, even if they are over forty. They can even be fifty when they marry. After all, a woman can't live alone. If a middle-aged woman wants to marry, people will have no objection. Tu Fang-lan was known to be wanting to marry. She wanted to get hold of a man. She needed a man.
>
> She married Ching Chung-wan. He is eight years younger than she is. . . . As I said, people remarry a lot here in Liu Ling. As soon as the husband or wife has died, the survivor tries to remarry. 'People should not live alone, and if a woman can remarry, she should do so. Who is going to carry water for her otherwise?'[29]

In the past the family head was given great power by the state and by custom over the individuals in the family. In answer to a reader's query ('What was the family head system?'), the *Gong-ren Ri-bao* (*Workers' Daily*) replied on 31st January, 1959:

> The so-called family head system was quite simply the occupying by the family head of the place of mastery in the household, holding the overall authority over the economy of the entire family, deciding and doing as he pleased, and making himself the centre of all activity. The majority of members of the family because of either complete or partial lack of ability to operate independently in society was unable to achieve economic independence. So this resulted in wives being dependent on husbands, and children on the family head. The family head treated his wife and children as his own personal property to dispose of as he wished . . .

The legal equality of man and woman, the alienation from

landed property, and the removal of state support for the role of family head have all combined to weaken the traditional form of family control. The post-Cultural Revolution concern with the family resulted in a call to replace the 'feudal family head system' with the 'political family head system'. The *wu-lun* were to give way to Mao thought, and the person in the family who best understood that thought was to run the group, regardless of standing in the Generation–Age–Sex hierarchy. Yet an older person of strong personality must still in many cases override those younger and weaker and, where grown and married children live with their parents through inability to afford separate accommodation, parental authority must often be heavy.

The old constitute a special problem. On the one hand excessive concern for them smacks of traditional subordination to age, while on the other the state is in no position to take over the full burden of care of the aged if families were to have insufficient concern. Something of this knife-edge can be appreciated in the following answer to a reader's letter asking whether it was necessary to kowtow to elders (*China Youth*, 22nd January, 1956):

Kowtowing is a ritual legacy of feudal society, and seen with today's eyes it is not good. In the kowtow, one man gets down on both knees and knocks the ground with his forehead, while the other man sits comfortably in receipt of the honour—this reflects the inequality between people in the old society.

At New Year each year, it is good to greet the older generation and to show respect to them, but it is not necessary to show respect by kowtowing. The people deeply love and respect Chairman Mao, but when the people see Chairman Mao they certainly don't kowtow to him—to show their respect they cheer, they present flowers, they shake hands and so on . . .

In line with other attempts to cut down on family ceremonial, there has been criticism of the holding of birthday feasts for the old. For instance, the *Workers' Daily* on 14th September, 1964 carried a headline 'Don't hold the birthday feast' and went into some detail of the case of an old woman called Liao Hai-fang whose 70th birthday was approaching. Four of her five sons wanted to hold a feast for her, but the fifth held out against it, until the old woman herself was convinced, and finally said:

He's right. Under the old society I suffered to bring you up so that I should not starve in my old age. These last two years I have often attended political study sessions on the family, and I've come to understand many of the reasons behind it, and my thinking has altered. Provided you obey the Party and Chairman Mao and strive hard to build socialism this will make me much happier than giving me a birthday feast or feeding me with fish and meat every day.

For this old woman there was clearly no problem of neglect, but there are old people whose children fail to support them, and the state is then forced to step in:

To show that they mean business, the courts have been taking a sterner attitude toward dereliction of duty toward old parents. Cases received considerable publicity. One such affair occurred in Harbin, Manchuria, where two brothers and their wives were convicted of mistreating their old step-mother. The sentences of the culprits varied from six months' to two years' imprisonment but suspension was ordered to give the guilty a chance to rectify the situation.[30]

Old people who have no children to support them come under the 'Five Guaranteed Households' system, in which local administrations guarantee food, housing, clothing and a funeral to the aged, the weak, the orphaned, the widowed and the disabled. In places there are Homes for the Aged provided, often under commune administration. More difficult is the situation where the old have daughters but no sons:

The most common solution is for the production team to assume that old people with daughters are no better off than people with no children at all, and thus, to give them five-guarantee support. In the village of Willow Grove, visited by Jan Myrdal for a second time in 1969, for example, one elderly man with a daughter was to receive five-guarantee support. However, information gathered from the press and interviews with expatriates reveal other villages which only grudgingly give aid to old parents with daughters. In one Kwangtung village the production team supported an aged mother from 1958 to 1971, and then, after thirteen years, tried to get her daughter living in another village to take over her support. They proposed that if the daughter would pay for the grain her mother had consumed in the past thirteen years, the daughter could claim her mother's house on her death.[31]

Ceremonies for the dead like those for the living are now much curtailed:

The funeral procedure now being popularised in cities is simple. The arrangements are carried out by funeral parlours, which insist that they should be frugal. A parlour is provided for the necessary period, where the friends and associates come to pay their last respects and bring or send wreaths and flowers. The mourners are recommended to wear black armbands, but not the traditional white robes, hats and shoes of sackcloth, and there is neither traditional music nor professional wailers. A eulogy may be delivered by one or several persons, after which the mourners file past the body. There are no public processions and no funeral feasts.[32]

In the cities cremation appears to have become the norm, but in the countryside, where cremation facilities are rare, burial in the ground remains common. However, burial has been under attack for some years as being wasteful. The Peking *Guang-ming Ri-bao* (*Light Daily*) published a long article on the advisability of cremation on 8th January, 1957:

There are many advantages to cremation over burial. From the economic point of view it saves money and trouble, there is no need for shrouds or coffins, and it saves land. . . . If someone dies away from home it can save the bother of transporting the coffin back to his native place. But the greatest advantage is its benefit to public hygiene: if a corpse is cremated, regardless of what kind of disease the man has died of, all the microbes will be destroyed, and no one else can be infected. The only disadvantage of cremation is that forensic evidence is destroyed . . .

A family's graves scattered about its fields or overlooking them from surrounding hills were visual reminders of permanence, of links with the land, of the continuity of the group over past, present and future, and the place of the individual in it. The land no longer belongs to the family and the individual is not encouraged to have the same kind of loyalty to the family. The removal of graves to release land for agriculture is also a physical sign of the break with the past.

In all aspects of the individual's life in the family men and women have legal and theoretical equality. They may expect to receive similar education, to have the same job opportunities, and to have an equal say in choice of marriage partner. By law both husband and wife have the right to free choice of occupation and free participation in work or in social activities. They have equal rights in the possession and management of family property. If both are out at work, then according to the *Guang-zhou Ri-bao* (*Kwangchow Daily*) of 20th February, 1967:

> Domestic duties should be the joint responsibility of husband and wife . . .

> I have two children who are looked after by their grand-mother, but as she is over 70 many household chores have to be done by us, so we divide them up between us. Things like washing clothes, wiping the floor and cleaning communal areas are done by whichever of us is free to do them at the time, or else we do them together on Sundays. On Sundays while I wash the clothes, he wipes the floor and sweeps and tidies up the furnishings. Afterwards I buy food and cook the meal, and by the time his jobs are done I have the meal ready. We eat together and then can both take it easy, perhaps going out to the cinema or to stroll in the park.

(There have been many other reports of couples who were not quite so egalitarian as this one, however.) Husband and wife call each other by the same term, *ai-ren* ('darling'), unlike husband and wife in the past who had different ways of referring to and addressing each other, ways which emphasised the superiority of the husband. Legally the wife is entitled to use her own family name rather than her husband's if she so wishes. They each have the same power to seek divorce and the same freedom to remarry.

Yet in practice there are still inequalities. Women do not always get equal pay for equal work with men, giving them an inferior position as a wage earner in the family. Women tend to do most of the domestic chores, and are thus prevented from taking an active part in social and political life or have to work doubly hard in order to be able to do so. Moreover, as residence remains virilocal, the woman is at a disadvantage in the midst of her husband's family.

THE FATE OF THE LINEAGE

Lineages derived their power from control over trust land and its income. This income financed education, welfare, public works, ancestral ceremonies, community defence and public relations. Out of these came advantages for the lineage membership in terms of freedom from outside interference, improved irrigation and communication, a higher level of schooling than elsewhere, a bigger and better ceremonial life, and an expectation of at least a minimum standard of living. The lineage leadership on the one hand exploited weaker members for its own purposes, but on the other attempted to exploit the outside world for the benefit of the lineage as a whole.

Land reform cut away lineage power at a stroke by removing the land base. Almost immediately lineages collapsed. Ceremonial life could not be sustained without funds, and in any case religious observances were frowned on by the state. Centralised government institutions took over community leadership, education, welfare, entertainment, and law and order. The lineage had no function to perform in a non-particularist social environment. Nevertheless, the state felt it necessary, as in non-lineage areas, to overthrow the traditionalist leadership completely, lest it batten on to the new institutions. The discrediting of lineage leaders went on simultaneously with land reform:

> In villages with several lineages it was easier to take advantage of cleavages between families to stir up criticism against village

leaders. Members of a small disadvantaged lineage, for example, would be very cooperative with the Communist cadre who gave official encouragement and support for their criticism of the head of the largest lineage in the village. In villages where everyone belonged to the same lineage, however, the common tie made it more difficult for outsiders to rouse the poorer lineage members to 'struggle against' their richer relatives . . .

To be sure there were often rivalries between sub-lineages of a large lineage which the land reform team could try to exploit, but pressure from outsiders might easily lead to the strengthening of lineage ties rather than their collapse.[33]

Periodic attacks on 'clannism' have been made in the Chinese press since that time, partly no doubt as a prophylactic, but partly in response to a continuing tendency to favour kin. Many rural areas still have heavy concentrations of kin living close together, and the danger of resuscitated lineage unity is therefore ever present. On 13th July, 1963, long after lineage power had been broken, *China Youth* gave a reminder of the danger of one lineage feature in an article headed 'What is a genealogy?' Labelling it 'one of the ropes of peasant bondage', it went on:

Recorded in a genealogy were the names of generation after generation of lineage members, together with their dates of birth and death, their places of residence and the location of their graves. Every so often the genealogy was brought up to date under the lead of the lineage head. It was kept in the ancestral hall. But you wouldn't find the names and exploits of the leaders of peasant revolts there, for revolutionary ancestors and descendants were rejected for inclusion in the genealogy. On the contrary, the main purpose of the genealogy was to trumpet the deeds of officials and landlords. Ordinary people just had their names recorded: officials qualified for a biographical entry. Those who had risen to senior officialdom had not only a biography but often a portrait too, and this was considered to be for the 'glory' of the whole lineage.

For the most part women were only included as the appendages of men, with only their surnames recorded; but the sacrificial victims of feudalist morality—the 'chaste virgins', 'exemplary women' and 'celibate widows'—these were praised and shown off . . .

If we compare what the genealogies were opposed to (peasant revolts etc.) with what they promoted (feudal loyalty, filial piety, chastity, righteousness, etc.), it is easy to see that their function was to exalt feudal virtues and preserve the feudal order, to make the peasantry obey and not oppose the landlord class.

On the same lines a *People's Daily* issue of 19th February, 1964 devoted a lot of space to a report of an investigation into the Wang lineage ancestral hall in a place in Hupeh Province. The report drew attention to the exploiting nature of lineage leadership, the anti-woman philosophy of the lineage, the economic drain on the peasantry of supporting a hall and ceremonies from which few of them benefited, the anti-revolutionary activities carried on in the hall, and so on. It also emphasised recent improvements, with part of the hall being used as a dormitory for commune workers and the rest as a school for children from the commune.

In short, the state continues to be aware of the potential problem posed by communities of kin. Yet the actual danger is not great. The support which the individual required of his lineage is now given to a large degree by the state; and at the same time the buttressing institutions which gave the lineage added strength have also been weakened. If the lineage is shattered it goes without saying that lineage feuding has little likelihood of flaring up and probably barely smoulders. The clan no longer exists.

ANCESTOR WORSHIP IN CONTEMPORARY CHINA

The Chinese state is avowedly atheistic and since 1949 has discouraged all religious practices. Before the excesses of the Cultural Revolution there was a certain amount of latitude for religious worship, and some Christian churches, Buddhist monasteries and Taoist retreats continued in modest operation. Many of them were damaged in the late 1960s, and their practices condemned and interfered with. Private religious worship has also been severely curtailed, and such supporting paraphernalia as incense sticks, paper spirit money and ritual candles are now said to be banned from manufacture and sale. As an article in the *Nan-fang Ri-bao* (*Southern Daily*) put it on 1st February, 1970:

> We materialists just do not believe in any of this stuff. In this world there are no gods and there are no ghosts. So-called gods and ghosts and geomancy and so on were just spiritual shackles employed by the exploiting classes to fool, control and enslave the people.

Worship of the gods which were associated with the community—gods such as temple gods, tree gods and earth gods (*tu-di gong*)—has been more or less eliminated, partly because the temples and images have been destroyed or converted to secular use, partly because publicly conducted worship was easiest to spot and most dangerous to the state's aims since it emphasised localism. But worship of home-based gods has been less easy to prevent, both because it was nearest to the hearts of the people and because its perceived support for the family institution did not necessarily run counter to the state's social policies, so that attack on its practice was not a matter of such great urgency.

The main gods of the home were the ancestors and the kitchen god. The kitchen god was sent down annually by the Emperor of Heaven to be the resident inspector of the household, and once a year he returned to heaven to report. In 1956 a unique visit to the Chekiang Province village studied by Fei Hsiao-tung twenty years earlier elicited the following:

> In every house which I visited, except one, I found that a representation of the kitchen god was still kept in the proper place above the stove. Even people who had earlier declared that they had completely abandoned the old religious beliefs and practices, admitted, when asked specifically about the kitchen god, that they kept his paper symbol. They all told me that they no longer made offerings to him. This was probably an overstatement. Almost certainly there must have been some ceremony when the old paper inscription was destroyed and replaced by a new one at the end of the year. It would be truer, probably, to say that the kitchen god has lost status, but that he still remains as a vague censor of household activities.[34]

Quite probably a visitor now, a further twenty years later, would not be able to find kitchen gods.

But ancestor worship above all was central to the Chinese ritual system. To have attempted a frontal attack on it might have cost the state the very peasant support which had been its strength. True, ancestor worship at the lineage level could not be tolerated:

> Ceremonial occasions such as spring and autumn sacrifices to the ancestors were reduced to simple affairs performed only by a small number of older clansmen who also privately contributed toward the sacrificial expense which was formerly financed by the income from the now confiscated clan property. To the Communist cadres, ancestor worship was a superstition like other forms of supernatural worship, and they would do nothing to remedy the situation. Most of the ancestral halls in the village were transformed into classrooms for literacy and political training and offices for the new organizations; they no longer served as places of religious inspiration for the perpetuation and development of the clan.[35]

But at home and family level the attack was slow to develop. In 1962 a North China village which had been under Communist control since long before 1949 showed little evidence of decline in ancestor worship or, indeed, other family-centred ceremonial:

> We butcher our pig and goats for the New Year festival. Then we make millet cakes and 'Chinese bean pudding'. We eat dumplings filled with pork and lots of other things. Then we go visiting, and our neighbours come to see us, and, on New Year's Day, everyone eats until you can't squeeze another bit of food down. We drink home-made wine and spirits from the shop. We paste paper cut-outs on the paper windows of the cave. My sister does that. She is clever at that sort of thing. We fix up verses beside the door, but I can't read those, because I can't read.
>
> Then comes the mid-spring festival. We go to our ancestors' graves then to make offerings. We take food and wine with us and offer a little at the graves, pouring out a little wine in front

of them. I and my husband and the children all go together. Everyone in the whole village goes to their ancestors' graves on that day. No, there isn't anyone who neglects to do so.[36]

Religious practices in general had been branded 'superstitions' and subjected to heavy derision, but ancestor worship specifically was for long not included. The *Workers' Daily* on 27th January, 1957 published a long article on 'Ritual avoidances and superstition', which said:

> If we hang up portraits of our ancestors at New Year or at festival time, that is a good thing as it indicates that we have not forgotten our kin even though it is a festival. And if at these times we tell our children of the hardships of the previous generation, of how hard they laboured, of how they were oppressed and exploited, and of how they fought with the reactionaries to win for us our present happy life, so as to arouse the coming generation to greater love for the new society, that would be even better. But if we don't hang up ancestral portraits, and instead worship gods and heaven, burning paper spirit-money and making offerings, that is meaningless, for in fact there are no such things as 'gods' and 'heaven', so why fool ourselves?

Of course, the removal of ritual goods from the market, the cessation of geomantic practice, and the systematic attack on all supernatural beliefs were in fact cutting away the peripheral support for ancestor worship, and sniping at some of the more vulnerable aspects of it was fair game. On 5th September, 1964 a *Workers' Daily* report said:

> Not long ago I suddenly received a telegram from home saying that my mother was acutely ill and telling me to hurry back there. I immediately requested leave and hurried home by train the same day. Would you believe it, when I got across the threshold there was my mother busily cooking, no sign of illness. Only then did I discover that the day after next was the third anniversary of my grandmother's death, and my father had decided to hold the 'Full Three Years' ceremony. Fearing that I would be unwilling to come home he had dashed off his mendacious telegram.

The writer had then proceeded to argue his parents out of holding the ceremony on the grounds that it was actually a device of the former landlord class to put the peasantry into debt and so keep them under control.

In 1965 the Qing Ming festival, the traditional time for sweeping and worshipping the ancestral graves, was renamed 'Memorial Day for Revolutionary Martyrs', this giving socialist respectability to what was taking place out of tradition, and at the same time paving the way for change to new forms of grave ritual. At one cemetery in Shanghai:

> Entrance was by ticket and those who had no real business to come in were not admitted. There were constantly coming in school children and delegations of workers, in marching order, carrying wreaths and flowers, who proceeded to the several graves of the revolutionary martyrs and those who lost their lives in fighting for the liberation of Shanghai. They performed a simple ceremony of wreath laying, standing in silence and bowing . . .
>
> Those who had visited the country cemeteries said that elderly country folks performed most of the rituals associated with Ching Ming Festival, including the burning of joss sticks and eating a family meal at the graveside.[37]

Again there is evidence of rural-urban differences, with the city being ahead of the countryside in the process of change.

On 8th March, 1966 the Hong Kong *Xing-dao Ri-bao* carried the headline 'Chinese Communists forbid ancestor worship: Mao's portrait replaces ancestor tablets. Large and small cities of Kwangtung already carrying this out: rural ancestors may stay for the time being'. The cult of Mao Tse-Tung gained momentum. A description of a house in a small village in 1970:

> The large room is the center of family life. The big portrait of Chairman Mao is over the long altar table where the ancestral tablets were once kept. And usually around the portrait are photographs of members of the family, particularly absent ones.[38]

The cult later lost some of its intensity, but it was surely in line with a consistent policy that a socialistically acceptable alternative to ancestor tablets should be found—just as with the renaming of Qing Ming. Probably ancestor worship is still very much alive in China, but it is the ancestor worship of the family and not of the lineage, and it is practised for the most part out of the public eye.

THE FAMILY IN CONTEMPORARY SOCIETY

The family remains the basic unit of village society. The relationships between family members are still very close; parents are responsible for the upbringing of their children, and children in turn are responsible for their aged parents. The fact that peasants' annual incomes are computed in terms of households provides further evidence that the family remains a recognized and cohesive unit. The commune system has not undermined the family institution; on the contrary, I found it has helped strengthen the family and made it a more efficient unit for socialist construction.[39]

State support for the family has changed greatly from traditional times, however. Where the *wu-lun* and the law used to back the authority of the family head and of the Generation–Age–Sex hierarchy, now the Marriage Law is much concerned with the obligations owed by parents to children, and with protection of weaker family members who might suffer because of divorce or incapacity. The *wu-fu* exists only where local custom wishes it to do so, and then only as a limiter of marriage choice: there is no distinction between crimes against *wu-fu* relations and crimes against others. That is, the state is no longer interested in buttressing any kinship institution larger than the stem family.

Furthermore, state backing even for the family is not as high in degree as it was. Divorce has been made easier. Many very young children, particularly in the cities, are removed from the home for long periods:

When our daughter was one and a half years old, we put her in the full-time nursery, that is, she lived there all week and came home to us for Saturday night and Sunday. We could go and visit her any time we wanted. In this way I needed to worry even less about the child . . .

All three of my daughters grew up in the nursery. Beginning collective life at a very early stage, they have developed good habits and are all in good health. While they were in the nursery I did not have to be bothered when they had light illnesses, as these were attended to by the nursery health worker.[40]

Married couples are separated for years when one spouse is posted elsewhere and the other is unable to transfer. In 1956 there was a spate of agonised letters to the newspapers complaining of long separations. Many likened their case to the traditional (willow-pattern) story of the weaving maiden and the cowherd, condemned forever to live apart and allowed to meet only one day a year when the magpies fly up to heaven to form a bridge over the Silver River (Milky Way) for them. Accompanying cartoons featured uncaring bureaucrats sitting unmoved on the bridge with the despairing lovers one at each end. 'Is it backwardness of thought to want to be together?' a railway worker four years separated from his wife plaintively asked the *People's Daily* on 2nd August, 1956. 'Married for three years, but husband and wife for only one night' ran a *Ji-lin Ri-bao* (*Kirin Daily*) headline of 4th September the same year. Ironically, in traditional times such separations were commonplace and unremarked—perhaps the Marriage Law's insistence that 'Husband and wife are companions living together' gave rise to new expectations?

'Dear are our parents, but dearer still is Chairman Mao' go the words of a popular Chinese song. Accusations to the state against senior family members were punishable in Qing law, but the movement after the Cultural Revolution to politicize the family was to have worked in precisely the opposite way: the young were encouraged to lay bare the misdeeds or deviant thought of their parents. An alarmist headline in the Hong Kong newspaper *Ming Bao* on 19th June, 1969 ran: 'The countryside has become a world of divulged secrets: father can't trust son, husband can't trust wife. Man gets five years for one remark after wife informs on him'. The weight of the evidence shows that such extreme damage to the family was not commonly attempted. Nevertheless, that it could and did happen is an indication of the degree to which the state has strengthened its grip on the family. And people do not to the same extent need the family solidarity of former times: it is no longer so difficult to survive as an unsupported individual in the new society.

But still the family has its relationships with other families. Affinal ties can still create problems. 'Wooden gates matching with wooden gates' is a continuing problem albeit in a new guise. For instance the following dilemma which occurred in 1970:

> One proposal concerned a young woman from a former rich peasant family. She was an able housewife and fieldworker and good-looking as well. But should a red-flag poor peasant get allied in marriage with a former rich peasant family? It wasn't only the two young people who had to be taken into account.[41]

However, it is likely that affines have become less rather than more important, if only because the necessity for particularist relationships has been reduced.

Neighbours have remained important, and in both city and countryside organization by street or hamlet has featured strongly since 1949. Newspaper reports have lauded the advantages of neighbourly co-operation, often falling back on family metaphor to describe it. A 13th February, 1957 report in the *Nan-Jing Ri-bao* (*Nanking Daily*), for instance, was headlined 'Eight households united like a single family'. In essence, associations of neighbours are similar to the old *bao-jia* organizations, but the environment today is considerably more propitious for their successful operation.

THE FAMILY OF THE STATE

On 3rd December, 1961, long before the Cultural Revolution, *China Youth* published some stories under the title 'There are kin everywhere in our homeland':

> In the past when people went away from home they always had the idea that '1000 days at home is easy, one hour away is hard'. But now no matter where you go in the country, no matter what difficulties you encounter, you can always meet

with kin-like concern and assistance. The following stories give a small side-light on the great warm-hearted family of our land . . .

But these universal kin do not use kinship terminology. It is all right to speak in general of all men being 'brothers', but in practice, the term of address and reference is 'comrade', a word which has neither sex nor age difference connotations.

On 4th September, 1963 a letter to the *Workers' Daily* asked, 'Is it right to swear brotherhood?':

> In our section there are four workers who have sworn brotherhood and who stand up for each other in everything they do they are so tight-knit . . .

The answer was lengthy and emphatic:

> The swearing of brotherhood was a product of the old society. In those days, when friends wanted to be brothers they swore an oath to heaven, and some of them even 'cut their fingers and drank the blood' as a mutual show of 'loyalty'. In fact sworn brotherhood was for nothing more than individual gain and mutual exploitation. Landlords, despots, warlords and officials formed brotherhoods as a means of oppressing the people more cruelly. There were brotherhoods formed by workers too for the purpose of mutual support, mutual aid, and alleviating oppression and bullying . . .
> But since 1949 the character of our society has radically changed . . . the people are united like one flesh and blood . . . so brotherhoods have become unnecessary.

Beyond the home the all-embracing family of the state replaces, in theory at least, the family of kin; and in the same way it makes redundant any other form of organization of a kinship or quasi-kinship nature. So, nepotism should disappear and social conscience be born. It seems that there has indeed been some progress in this direction.

Of course not all Chinese live within the People's Republic, and those who do not are not members of that 'state family'. In Hong Kong live some 4 million Chinese whose family life has not suffered from the same kind of politically prescribed change, but where social conditions have since the late 1940s been of a unique order. Many of these people were refugees from the mainland who fled without family. Others came with family but without money or contacts in Hong Kong. Longer established residents range from those in rural areas with histories of ancestral settlement going back over 1,000 years, to city dwellers of three, four or five generations. As a result it is still possible to find there a full variation of family type, from the simple family to the full-scale lineage village of several thousand members, to a higher-order lineage with numbers probably in the ten thousands, and to surname associations operating from the cities. At the one extreme are large numbers (perhaps the majority) of urban families which are Christian, atheist or apathetic and do not worship ancestors. At the other are the vast majority of rural families, still worshipping a wide range of gods and spirits including ancestors, while the lineages spend huge sums annually on colourful and impressive ancestral ceremonies. On the one hand are the townspeople marrying in registry offices and being buried in public cemeteries. On the other the country people marrying home-to-home with sedan chairs, ancestor worship and full custom, and being buried in individually selected, geomantically auspicious sites in the hills. But tradition is comparatively fragile, and despite the absence of direct interference with custom, there is little doubt that other factors—pressure on land and resources, urbanization, westernization, a stable political situation under strong government, and the comparative ease with which the individual can make his own way without family help—are bringing about rapid change even in the most entrenched and conservative of lineages. As in China it is the rural areas, where there is permanence of settlement and an attachment to the land, which stand up to change most firmly.

Some 16 million more Chinese live in Taiwan. There can be found a different set of complexities. Again many people were refugees from the mainland of China, but the 'indigenous' Chinese had been under Japanese rule from 1895 to 1945. Again there exists a wide range of family types, from simple family to lineage and surname association; but land reforms both under the Japanese and under the Nationalist government (especially the 1953 Land-to-the-Tiller Act) have had an effect on the larger groups which makes them different from their equivalents in Hong Kong or the pre-Communist mainland.

Overseas Chinese communities in Southeast Asia and elsewhere are increasingly being forced to adapt to the ways of their host cultures as a necessary survival technique. Family development among them seems likely to diverge from the Chinese model in different directions.

*   *   *

Imperial Chinese governments were for long periods either non-existent or too weak to exert the strong centralised authority they ideally possessed. At such times local self-government swelled in importance, and power was fragmented between self-interest groups. Even at their most powerful governments allowed a considerable degree of authority to remain vested in kinship groups, authority which when misused worked against the interests of the state, and which remained ever prepared to exploit any weakening of central control.

In the mid-19th century the Taipings could see the dangers of latent localism and attempted to break down the power of the family. They were premature. When the Emperor later attempted to revive a traditional strong central government, he was too late. The early Republic of China had learned the lesson of the Taipings, but it lacked the power to enforce its reforms. It was not until 1949 that the military conquest of the whole of China put into the hands of the Chinese People's Republic the powers necessary for any effective attack on particularism.

The Chinese Communists have always seen the family—the traditional social unit in China, based on the Confucian principles of filial piety and brotherly love—as a major obstacle to the thoroughgoing establishment of communism in China. The efforts to redirect loyalties from family to the leadership in Peking have proceeded primarily on three fronts. First, through the promulgation of the Marriage Law and the 'emancipation' of women; second, through the indoctrination and education of children and youth; and third, through the collectivization and subsequent communization of agriculture.[42]

They can be seen to have concentrated on destroying the traditional power of the family over the individual. Late marriage, so that the couple would be less likely to be under the sway of their parents; the forbidding of bride-price and concubinage; the comparative ease of divorce; the registering of marriage with the state representatives and not with kin and the ancestors (the family representatives); the alienation of family-owned land; these and other factors struck at the roots of family dominance. In its stead have been advocated the freedom and independence of the individual within the conjugal or stem family, units of limited size and functions; while other loyalties are directed to a hierarchy of non-kin institutions at the top of which is the state.

It is not easy to judge to what extent these measures have succeeded. In the past the picture of kinship in action was certainly not the one drawn by state law, though that law was doubtless responsible for the broad outlines, custom filling in the detail. Equally clearly the Marriage Law of 1950 is not observed to the letter, and recent accounts show there is still much deviation in practice even with fundamental tenets such as bride-price and arranged marriage. Comparison with Hong Kong would indicate that there too kinship is being reduced in importance as a vehicle for social organization, though not in as traumatic a fashion. In any event it seems that the family is to survive in China and to continue to play its role in the reproductive, emotional and welfare aspects of the new society.

Appendix I

1. Do your utmost to be filial and brotherly so as to give proper importance to the human relationships
2. Be sincere with your kin so that harmony may be apparent
3. Be at peace with neighbours and community so as to put an end to dispute and litigation
4. Give priority to agriculture and sericulture so that there may be enough food and clothing
5. Esteem economy and frugality so that you take care of your resources
6. Make excellent the halls of learning so as to make correct the practices of the scholars
7. Reject heterodoxies so as to exalt the true learning
8. Expound the laws so as to warn against stupidity
9. Let good manners and deference shine forth so that customs may be worthy
10. Work hard at your trade so as to make constant the will of the people
11. Admonish your sons and younger brothers so as to make wrong-doing impossible
12. Put an end to false accusations so as to make safe the innocent
13. Do not conceal fugitives lest you become an accessory to crime
14. Pay your taxes in full so as to obviate being pressed for payment
15. Organize into *bao-jia* to do away with thieves and bandits
16. Resolve hostilities so as to value human life.

Appendix II

FENG-SHUI FIGHTING

Translated from Qi Tong-ye, *Feng-shui ling-qian guai-tan* (*Strange Tales of Divination by Geomancy*), 1963, Vol. 1, Hong Kong, pp. 22–30.

In Wen Zhou in Chekiang there was an old grave belonging to the Mi family: it was called 'The Mi Family Grave', and used to be a good *feng-shui* grave. It is said that on the opposite hillside there was already a grave belonging to the Yao family before the Mi grave was built, and the geomancers called this a 'Double prosperity—sons and wealth' site. The descendants of the Yao family all prospered. In every generation at least four sons were born to each branch of the family, while each branch became wealthy. So the Mi family requested their geomancer to select a site like the Yao one. Originally he found them a site above and to the left of the Yao grave. The land was owned by a man surnamed Pang, and the Mis bought it.

It was said that if a grave were built on this site its *feng-shui* would be superior to that of the Yao grave. When the Yaos heard this news they hired a geomancer to go and have a look. He reported that if a grave were to be built on the site then the *feng-shui* of the Yao grave would be suppressed. When the Yaos heard this they bought a plot of hill land from Pang, the plot being immediately above the plot bought by the Mis for their grave; and there they planted five large trees and dug out a cess-pit. It was said that this could ruin the good *feng-shui* of the grave site.

And indeed, the next year when a geomancer went to align the Mi grave in preparation for work on it to start, he discovered that someone had planted trees and made a cess-pit right above the site, and realised that the *feng-shui* had been poisoned and ruined. According to him the proposed site was a 'green frog location', and the grave-site was just on the belly of the frog. The place where the trees and cess-pit were was right on the frog's spine, and so the *feng-shui* of the belly was completely drained away and destroyed.

At first the Mis thought that someone who knew about *feng-shui* had deliberately arranged this in the certainty that the Mis would be willing to pay a high price to buy the land when they wanted to build their grave, and thus could make themselves a tidy sum on the deal. So they went to discuss with Pang the purchase of this additional plot. But Pang said the land had been sold to the Yaos the year before, and that he had heard that they had planted the trees and dug the pit because of the *feng-shui* of their grave. When they heard this the Mis knew that there was no hope of buying the land back from them.

Sure enough, after several earnest pleas to the Yaos had been courteously rejected, the Mis had to accept the misfortune. It was bad enough that they should lose a grave site, but to lose such a superlative one was insufferable, and they nursed a desire for revenge. They took counsel with the geomancer on how to accomplish this. Naturally he also was angry. Spurred on by their ire they hunted for all they were worth for 'dragon's veins' around the Yao grave, always hoping to find a grave site even better than the Yao's. Before long they did in fact find an excellent dragon halfway up the hill opposite the Yao grave.

Strangely enough the Yaos didn't wake up until eight years after the building of the Mi grave to the fact that from the year after its building the population of all their branches had begun to suffer. Practically every year there had been infant deaths. They had five branches, and the business of one family in each branch had collapsed. They began to suspect that perhaps the *feng-shui* of their ancestral grave had been damaged by the Mi family grave. As the Mi village was ten *li* away from the Yao settlement, they didn't normally meet each other, but the Yaos made enquiries everywhere and found that according to neighbours of the Mi village, the Mis had become prosperous in both progeny and wealth since the building of their new grave. Hearing this the Yaos naturally enough went to seek the advice of their geomancer.

At first, despite the geomancer's going to the Mi grave to look around, he was unable to spot anything which could be harming the Yao grave. But there was one point which made him suspicious, namely that in his judgement the Mi site was a very ordinary one, and he could not understand how it could produce riches and sons for the Mis.

The geomancer could not but seek answers to the doubts which inspecting the Mi grave had produced, for in his estimation of the dragon veins, the Mi grave *feng-shui* was undistinguished and should not have given rise to 'double prosperity' conditions. But since such conditions actually existed, there had to be a reason for them. Only two reasons would explain things: first, that the people buried in the Mi grave must have been of great virtue while alive; second, that secretly they had stolen someone else's *feng-shui*. As far as was known, the persons buried in the grave had not been especially virtuous; so they must be relying on stolen *feng-shui*. If that were so, then it was beyond question the Yao grave's *feng-shui* they were stealing, because it had originally been good *feng-shui*, with double prosperity always: but since the building of the Mi grave the Yaos had lost both sons and wealth, and this was an undeniable fact.

After more than a year of research by three geomancers the conclusion was that the Mi grave was stealing the Yao grave's *feng-shui* in that there were problems with a stream in the low-lying land between the two hills on which the two graves faced each other. According to their findings, the stream was originally the property of the Tang family, but had been bought by the Mis from the Tangs when they built their grave, and they had then diverted the water course to its present bed. It was beyond doubt that the diversion of a stream would have an effect on *feng-shui*, and this one was right in between the two grave hills and so would undoubtedly affect the *feng-shui* of both graves. In fact, after the diversion of the stream the double prosperity of the Yaos had gone to the Mis, and this proved that the Mi grave was using the stream to steal the Yao grave's *feng-shui*.

But the three geomancers did not know why it should be so, even though they were certain that it was so. This was because the three of them were all southern hill-geomancers: they understood the geomancy of mountain dragons, but were strangers to the *feng-shui* of the water dragons of the plains. Then the Yaos asked a northern friend to find a geomancer experienced in the *feng-shui* of plains to come to help them. In fact in the south here we stress the mountain veins, that is the so-called mountain dragons, but in the north there are mainly plains and no hills, so their grave *feng-shui* stresses water courses, that is, the water dragons.

Oddly enough, as soon as the northern geomancer had looked at the Yao grave, he spotted the defect: the diverting of the stream for the Mi grave was called 'bending the bow to embrace the grave', and the 'bent bow' water dragon had 'bent' the good *feng-shui* of the Yao grave. Of course this also meant that there was an element of 'a secret arrow to injure others'.

After this judgement by the water dragon geomancer, there was nothing for it but to move the Yao grave. If it were not moved, then in twenty years it would have become a 'single strand' site, that is, where only one son per generation could be produced. As the water course belonged to the Mis there was no way to alter it, so there was no way but to move the grave.

Although the Yaos realised that this was in revenge for their previous ruining of the Mi *feng-shui*, they could hardly avoid natural anger at this action of the Mis. In order not to let the Mis know of the moving of their grave, they took the bones from the ancestral grave secretly and reburied them elsewhere, meanwhile preserving the original grave, and retaining their reputation among the surrounding villages for having the good *feng-shui* of the Yao Family Grave.

It is wonderful how *feng-shui* is both indescribably marvellous and at the same time terribly fascinating! After the building of the Mi Family Grave the Mis were doubly prosperous and all were delighted. After ten years all was well on both counts, but in the eleventh year came an unhappy event, a newly born child bore signs of leprosy.

Leprosy! How fearful! Having survived for two years and undergone unsuccessful treatment by many doctors, the dread disease of leprosy was definitely confirmed, and they reluctantly buried him alive. This was in the 13th year after the building of the Mi grave. Then in the 15th year another one was born, and in the 17th yet another, and in every odd year the Mis gave birth to one leprous child. This terrified the Mis. Every two years they had to bury a child alive—how heartbreaking and cruel!

In such circumstances country people always think in terms of *feng-shui*. *Feng-shui* has only two types—*Yang* and *Yin*. The Mi settlement consisted of Ming dynasty houses and no changes had occurred either inside or outside them, so there was no suspicion of change in their *feng-shui*, and thus what was doubtful was the grave. As the senior generations of the Mis all knew that their good *feng-shui* had been stolen from the Yao grave, and as 'the thief always feels guilty', having stolen someone else's *feng-shui* they quickly realised that perhaps this had been discovered by the opposition and secretly wrecked by them.

A famous geomancer was invited to the Mi village. First, he inspected the *Yang feng-shui*, but there was nothing wrong with the old houses at all. Then he looked at the *Yin*—the Mi and Yao graves faced each other on their respective hills as before, and neither the mountain dragon nor the water dragon had changed. The geomancer who had built the grave for the Mis had died, and although his son had succeeded to his father's profession, they did not at first call him in because of his youth and inexperience. Afterwards, as successive geomancers recommended that the best thing would be to ask the man who had aligned the grave whether there were any other stratagems which could be used to reveal the inner secrets, they did call in the original geomancer's son.

Although this young geomancer was only just over twenty years of age, he was deeply versed in and wise about sudden changes in the *feng-shui* of both *Yang* and *Yin* types, because his father had specialised in the *feng-shui* of 'alteration'. After he had inspected the two graves, he went back home and looked up his father's notebooks, discovering that the Mi grave *feng-shui* was stolen from the Yao grave through a water dragon 'bending the bow to embrace the grave' ploy.

Naturally he couldn't tell this secret to his fellow geomancers. He merely said that from his privately inherited knowledge the sudden defect in the Mi grave *feng-shui* was caused by the Yao grave, and that they would have to find a way to open up the Yao grave and get inside to inspect it.

Here was a great problem. Not only the Mi elders but all the other geomancers as well realised that this was something that could not be done, because no-one would be willing to open up his ancestral grave without reason to allow a stranger to inspect its *feng-shui*. Especially in the case of the older Mis, they knew that there was a *feng-shui* feud on with the Yaos and that it would be next to impossible. But if this were not done there would be no way to solve their problem.

What could they do? To resolve it, the Mis thought up a plan. They hired two grave-diggers, booked the geomancers, and taking advantage of a day when there was a heavy mist, went up to the Yao grave and got ready to open it up.

It was the first time any of the Mis had been to the Yao grave. They had imagined it to be a splendid and superior old grave, but when they got there they got a surprise, because it was like one abandoned for many years.

As country *feng-shui* lovers all know, any good *feng-shui* grave must be worshipped, swept, repaired and cleaned every year by the descendants, making the mortar take on a deep gray glow; but the mortar on the Yao grave now had discoloured till it was like a heap of raw soil!

The Yao grave was a large one of eight chambers. According to the date on the grave-stone it could hardly be considered an ancient grave yet: the more junior generations had probably not yet been all buried, so why should it look as though no-one had been there to worship for a long while? Why was it like an abandoned tomb? While the Mis were wondering, the two labourers opened up the grave, and lighting a lantern crawled inside.

'Ai ya!' the second man shouted as he saw the one in front fall soundless to the floor, his lantern going out; and he retreated, pulling his fallen companion with him. When he got out they set about reviving the man straight away. At first they all thought that there was a ghost in there, but on investigation they decided that as when they went in they could smell a stench of excrement, it was merely the effect of the marsh gas in the tomb, not possession by a spirit.

They had brought with them a bundle of incense sticks in case they were unable to light lanterns in the tomb. So they cut down a branch of bamboo from beside the grave and tied the bundle of burning incense to it. Then they waved it around inside the tomb to see what things were like in there. At first glance they were staggered: there was nothing at all in the tomb, the coffins had all gone.

'Why?' marvelled one of the geomancers.

'Ah, yes! I know!' replied the young geomancer. 'They knew the *feng-shui* had been stolen from them, so they removed the coffins.'

'In that case, there must be something else in there, or it wouldn't have spoiled the Mi grave *feng-shui* and caused them to suffer the leprosy evil', said another geomancer shrewdly.

'That's right. There must be, but I don't know what', said the young geomancer.

Now that they knew that the Yaos had abandoned the grave, they were not afraid for having opened it up. So they piled up dead wood and old leaves from the hillside in the tomb and set fire to it. Then they left the doors open and decided to go in there again the next day after the fresh air had blown in for a day.

Sure enough, when they went back, they found that after the Yaos had removed the coffins they had dug out a cess-pit in the main chamber of the grave, and poured in ten or more gallons of excrement. At the time the Yaos had done this strange thing to the grave in great anger, knowing that their *feng-shui* had been stolen and that it was the Mis who had stolen it using the water course dragon vein as a 'bent bow embracing the grave'. Their idea had been merely to make their enemies steal the stink as well, they hadn't at first realised that doing this would cause the birth of a leprositic child on alternate years in the Mi family.

In principle once the defect had been pinpointed it should have been possible to redress the *feng-shui*; but first, the grave-site belonged to the Yao and could not be bought so as to change it, and second, because the great quantity of manure had been there for so long it had soaked deep into the soil and probably could not be remedied. So the Mis had to copy the Yaos and move their own grave elsewhere in order to escape from the leprosy evil. To this day the two old graves sit facing each other on the barren hills, the weirdest conversation pieces in local *feng-shui* lore.

Appendix III

Translated from the *Da-Qing lü-li zeng-xiu tong-zuan ji-cheng* (*Qing Laws and Statutes*), 1842, juan 26.

The Law. Fighting and Killing with Intent.

Anyone who kills in the course of an affray, regardless of whether it is done with the hand, foot, any other weapon or knife, shall be sentenced to strangulation subject to revision. For killing with intent the sentence is decapitation subject to revision. If more than one plot together to attack someone and death results, then the one who caused the most serious injury leading to death shall be sentenced to strangulation subject to revision. The instigator (regardless of whether or not he took part in the attack) shall receive 100 strokes of the *zhang* and be permanently exiled 3000 *li*. Any other persons (not dealing the fatal blow nor instigating) shall each receive 100 strokes of the *zhang* (whether numbers involved were large or small and the injuries received heavy or light).

The relevant Statutes.

1. In cases of mob fighting in Kwangtung, Fukien, Kwangsi, Kiangsi, Hunan and Chekiang—except cases of ordinary affray or planned affray where, in spite of large numbers being involved, fighting with weapons is not resorted to, and except for fighting with weapons in Taiwan, all of which should be dealt with under the old statutes—if examination reveals preparation, amassing of money, and fixing of a date for fighting with weapons and killing in feud, then, if more than ten or twenty men have been assembled and they kill four or more of the other party, the major offender and the instigator of the mob fight are punishable by immediate strangulation. If there are thirty or more men in the group and they kill four or more of the other party, or

226

if there are less than thirty in the group but they kill ten or more of the other party, the major offender is punishable by immediate decapitation. If there are forty men or more in the group and they kill ten or more of the other party, or if there are less than forty in the group but they kill twenty or more of the other party, then the major offender is punishable by immediate decapitation with exposure of the head. If, despite the assembly of large numbers, only one of the other party is killed, the major offender is banished to military servitude on the near frontiers. If two are killed, then it is military servitude on the far frontiers. If three, then military servitude on the farthest frontiers at a full 4000 *li*. If two or three in one family of the other party are killed, then the sentence for the instigator and the major offender, should be decided under other statutes. Immediate decapitation or strangulation, according to the severity [of the crime], should be dealt to those whose blows result in injury causing death. Those who resist [such attacks] are to be dealt with under the pertinent law and statutes, and those who in resisting cause injury and those who do not should be judged separately each under the relevant law and statutes. As for the other party [the attacked] who hurriedly ask others to [help them] resist, they by no means have any prior intention of fighting with weapons, and should be judged under the appropriate statute on affray. If the magistrate does not discover who are the instigator and major offender and punish them, and intends to screen them and protect them by treating the one fighting with weapons case as different cases, the Governor or Governor General shall peremptorily impeach him under the statute on officials involved in the crimes of others, and the Board will judge his crime.

Entered in 1825 and revised in 1830.

2. In cases of armed fighting in the two provinces of Kwangtung and Fukien, after careful investigation, if the income from ancestral land has been used to hire mercenaries and a quarrel picked in order to engage in armed fighting, apart from severe judgement on the crime of the instigator who hired the ruffians, there should be penetrating examination of the property of the lineage; several tens of *mu* of ancestral

land should be retained to cover ritual expenses, and the rest of the land and remaining funds should be distributed among the branches of the lineage. If the lineage headman and *xiang-yue* cannot point out the person who collected money and hired the ruffians, then the lineage headman shall be dealt with under the instigator of affray statute and suffer beating and permanent banishment in accordance with the numbers killed, the punishment being one degree worse for each life, to a maximum of exile in military servitude to the most distant malarial regions; and the *xiang-yue* shall receive sixty strokes and banishment for one year, to which shall be added one degree of punishment for each life, to a maximum of one hundred strokes and three years banishment.
Entered in 1825 and revised in 1830.

3. In cases in Kwangtung province where a group has been assembled, a fight planned and death has resulted, the instigator should receive punishment according to the numbers of dead of the other party, as laid down in the statute. Even if some of those who were assembled were killed by the other party, regardless of how many dead there were and whether or not the other party had made a plan to provoke this party, those who were assembled should be punished with beating and banishment as laid down in the statute for major offenders carrying weapons, rioting and fighting along the streams and shores, 100 strokes and permanent banishment 3000 *li*.
Entered 1825.

Notes

CHAPTER 1. THE COMPOSITION OF THE FAMILY

1 Spencer and Barrett, 1948, pp. 464–5.
2 Buck, 1937, p. 369.
3 Leong and Tao, 1915, p. 8.
4 Hsiao, 1961, p. 380.
5 Buck, 1937, p. 463.
6 *Ibid.*, p. 392.
7 Hsu, 1971, p. 109.
8 Ho, 1959, p. 60.
9 Couling, 1917, p. 249.
10 Ball, 1904, pp. 349–50.
11 Ho, 1959, p. 61.
12 Douglas, 1894, p. 347.
13 League of Nations, 1933, p. 40.
14 Fei, 1939, p. 52.
15 Myers, 1970, pp. 90–1.
16 Hayes, 1962, p. 80 and p. 97.
17 Cohen, 1970, pp. 29–30.
18 Cohen, 1976, p. 78.
19 Martin C. Yang, 1948, pp. 57–8.
20 Cohen, 1976, pp. 210–11.
21 Lin Yueh-hwa, 1948, p. 128.
22 Freedman, 1966, pp. 66–7.
23 Freedman, 1958, p. 30.

CHAPTER 2. THE INDIVIDUAL AND THE FAMILY

1 Pruitt, 1967, p. 239.
2 Granet, 1975, pp. 88–9.
3 Gernet, 1962, p. 204.
4 Doré, 1914, vol. I, p. 11.
5 Eberhard, 1972, p. 32.
6 Burkhardt, 1958, vol. III, p. 7.
7 Martin C. Yang, 1948, pp. 239–40.
8 Osgood, 1963, pp. 276–7.
9 Gray, 1878, vol. I, p. 205.
10 Osgood, 1975, vol. I, p. 108.
11 Chiu, 1966, p. 82.

12 Fried, 1969, pp. 42–3.
13 Jamieson, 1921, pp. 2–3.
14 *Ibid.*, p. 29.
15 Martin C. Yang, 1948, p. 57.
16 Myers, 1970, p. 96.
17 Kulp, 1925, p. 197.
18 De Groot, 1892–1910, vol. III, p. 1391.
19 Howard S. Levy, 1966, pp. 30–1.
20 Ball, 1904, pp. 419–20.
21 Osgood, 1963, p. 276.
22 Martin C. Yang, 1948, p. 58.
23 Margery Wolf, 1972, pp. 178–9.
24 Lau, 1970, p. 127.
25 Van der Valk, 1956, p. 60.
26 Ch'ü, 1965, p. 118.

CHAPTER 3. THE LINEAGE AND THE CLAN

1 For all references to the Liaos of Sheung Shui see Baker, 1968.
2 C. K. Yang, 1959b, pp. 93–4.
3 Liu, 1959, p. 38.
4 Chen Ta, 1939, p. 129.
5 Nelson, 1974, pp. 252–3.
6 C. K. Yang, 1959b, p. 81.
7 Pasternak, 1972, p. 146.
8 Freedman, 1966, p. 21.

CHAPTER 4. ANCESTOR WORSHIP

1 Creel, 1937, p. 175.
2 De Groot, 1892–1910, vol. II, p. 769.
3 Addison, 1925, p. 48.
4 Ahern, 1973, p. 201.
5 Smith, 1900, p. 184.
6 De Bary, 1960, pp. 543–4.
7 Werner, 1932, p. 601.
8 De Groot, 1892–1910, vol. I, p. 51.
9 Graham, 1961, p. 123.
10 C. K. Yang, 1961, p. 47.
11 Stent, 1877, p. 158.
12 Ahern, 1973, p. 125.
13 Jordan, 1972, pp. 140–41.
14 Topley and Hayes, 1968, p. 136.
15 Chong, 1968, pp. 640–41.
16 Humana and Wang, 1971, p. 141.
17 Jamieson, 1921, pp. 13–14.
18 Doolittle, 1865, vol. I, p. 197.
19 *Ibid.*, p. 198.

20 Baker, 1965, p. 37.
21 Doolittle, 1865, vol. I, pp. 207–8.
22 Lin Yutang, 1936, p. 181.
23 Hu, 1948, p. 36.
24 De Groot, 1892–1910, vol. IV, pp. 154–5.
25 Addison, 1925, p. 54.
26 Freedman, 1966, p. 141.
27 Hsu, 1971, p. 47.
28 Gray, 1878, vol. I, p. 83.
29 Ch'ü, 1965, p. 88.
30 De Bary, 1960, p. 117.
31 Addison, 1925, p. 55.

CHAPTER 5. THE FAMILY IN STATE AND SOCIETY

1 De Groot, 1892–1910, vol. II, p. 568.
2 Bodde and Morris, 1967, p. 37.
3 Ch'ü, 1965, p. 56.
4 Bodde and Morris, 1967, p. 38.
5 Arthur P. Wolf, 1970, p. 189.
6 Ch'ü, 1972, p. 26.
7 Bodde and Morris, 1967, p. 92.
8 Ch'ü, 1965, pp. 28–9.
9 Ibid., p. 55.
10 Ibid., pp. 99–100.
11 Hsiao, 1961, p. 45.
12 Chang, 1955, p. 15.
13 De Groot, 1892–1910, vol. II, pp. 771–5.
14 Hummel, 1943, p. 511.
15 Hsü, 1971, pp. 230–31.
16 Freedman, 1967, pp. 11–12.
17 Fei, 1939, pp. 41–2.
18 Ibid., pp. 86–7.
19 Gallin, 1966, p. 177.
20 Gamble, 1968, p. 302.
21 M. C. Yang, 1948, p. 132.
22 Fei and Chang, 1949, p. 82.
23 Fukutake, 1967, p. 86.
24 Twitchett, 1959, p. 130.
25 Chow, 1966, pp. 242–3.
26 Hsü, 1971, p. 307.

CHAPTER 6. THE LINEAGE IN SOCIETY AND STATE

1 Chen Han-seng, 1936, pp. 37 and 35.
2 Smith, 1899, pp. 21–2.
3 Potter, 1968, p. 20.
4 Hu, 1948, p. 92.

5 Watson, 1975, pp. 78–9.
6 Groves, 1965, p. 18.
7 Graham, 1961, p. 115.
8 Baker, 1968, pp. 87–8.
9 'Clanship among the Chinese', 1836, pp. 412–13.
10 Baker, 1966, p. 40.
11 *Ibid.*, pp. 40–1.
12 Baker, 1968, pp. 188–9.
13 Krone, 1967, pp. 107 and 125.
14 *Ibid.*, pp. 117–18.
15 Hsiao, 1961, p. 369, translating from one of Lin's memorials.
16 'Clanship among the Chinese', 1836, p. 413.
17 Krone, 1967, pp. 125–6.
18 Wang, 1973, p. 30.
19 Hayes, 1962, p. 96.
20 De Groot, 1903–4, vol. II, p. 559.

CHAPTER 7. NON-KIN AS KIN

1 Marion J. Levy, 1949, p. 135.
2 Feng, 1948, pp. 25–7.
3 Morgan, 1960, p. 259.
4 Chesneaux, 1971, pp. 23–7.
5 Ward, 1926, p. 66.
6 Topley, 1975, p. 67.
7 Watt, 1972, p. 85.
8 Wickberg, 1965, p. 174.
9 Purcell, 1965, p. 261.
10 Coughlin, 1960, p. 39.
11 Vaughan, 1971, p. 102.
12 Willmott, 1967, p. 86.
13 Chow, 1966, pp. 238–9.

CHAPTER 8. KINSHIP IN THE TWENTIETH CENTURY

1 Wright, 1962, p. 62.
2 Purcell, 1963, p. 135.
3 Chow, 1960, p. 302.
4 *Ibid.*, p. 258.
5 Hsia, 1931, p. vii.
6 McAleavy, 1968, pp. 267–8.
7 Howard S. Levy, 1966, p. 93.
8 Lang, 1946, p. 123.
9 Mao, 1953, pp. 44–5.
10 The Marriage Law . . ., 1950, p. 1.
11 Wilson, 1966, p. 7.
12 C. K. Yang, 1959b, pp. 178–9.
13 Gittings, 1973, p. 208.

14 Coughlin, 1962, p. 398.
15 Freeberne, 1965, p. 4.
16 Aird, 1973, pp. 458-9.
17 Orleans, 1972, p. 47.
18 Parish, 1975, p. 629.
19 Salaff, 1971, p. 321.
20 O'Sullivan, 1975, p. 24.
21 Meijer, 1971, p. 206.
22 Sidel, 1972, pp. 58-9.
23 Roper, 1971, p. 93.
24 Davin, 1975, p. 271.
25 Parish, 1975, p. 621.
26 Jack Chen, 1973, p. 73.
27 Ibid., pp. 73-4.
28 C. K. Yang, 1959a, p. 32.
29 Myrdal, 1965, p. 210.
30 Fried, 1959, pp. 158-9.
31 Parish, 1975, p. 624.
32 Far East Economic Review, 28.4.66, p. 183.
33 Vogel, 1971, pp. 103-04.
34 Geddes, 1963, p. 49.
35 C. K. Yang, 1959b, p. 180.
36 Myrdal, 1965, pp. 232-3.
37 South China Morning Post, 19.4.65.
38 Jack Chen, 1973, p. 7.
39 Wu, 1974, p. 8.
40 Croll, 1974, pp. 76-7.
41 Jack Chen, 1973, p. 74.
42 Orleans, 1972, p. 45.

List of Works Cited

ADDISON, J. T., *Chinese Ancestor Worship*, Shanghai, 1925.

AHERN, Emily M., *The Cult of the Dead in a Chinese Village*, Stanford, 1973.

AIRD, John S., 'Population Problems, Theories, and Policies', in WU Yuan-li (ed.), *China: a Handbook*, Newton Abbot, 1973.

BAKER, Hugh D. R., 'Burial, Geomancy and Ancestor Worship', in Marjorie TOPLEY (ed.), *Aspects of Social Organization in the New Territories*, Hong Kong Branch of the Royal Asiatic Society, 1965.

BAKER, Hugh D. R., 'The Five Great Clans of the New Territories', *Journal of the Hong Kong Branch of the Royal Asiatic Society*, Vol. vi, Hong Kong, 1966.

BAKER, Hugh D. R., *A Chinese Lineage Village: Sheung Shui*, London and Stanford, 1968.

BALL, J. Dyer, *Things Chinese: or Notes Connected with China*, London, 1904.

BODDE, Derk and MORRIS, Clarence, *Law in Imperial China*, Cambridge, Mass., 1967.

BUCK, John Lossing, *Land Utilization in China*, Nanking, 1937.

BURKHARDT, V. R., *Chinese Creeds and Customs*, 3 vols., Hong Kong, 1953–58.

CHANG Chung-li, *The Chinese Gentry*, Seattle, 1955.

CHEN Han-seng, *Landlord and Peasant in China*, New York, 1936.

CHEN, Jack, *A Year in Upper Felicity: Life in a Chinese Village During the Cultural Revolution*, London, 1973.

CHEN Ta, *Emigrant Communities in South China*, London, 1939.

CHESNAUX, Jean, *Secret Societies in China in the Nineteenth and Twentieth Centuries*, (translated from the French by Gillian Nettle), London, 1971.

CHIU, Vermier Y., *Marriage Laws and Customs of China*, Hong Kong, 1966.

CHONG Tong Mun, 'Epidemic Koro in Singapore', *British Medical Journal*, 9th March, 1968.

CHOW Tse-tsung, *The May Fourth Movement: Intellectual Revolution in Modern China*, Cambridge, Mass., 1960.

CHOW Yung-Teh, *Social Mobility in China*, New York, 1966.

CH'Ü T'ung-Tsu, *Law and Society in Traditional China*, Paris, 1965.

CH'Ü T'ung-Tsu, *Han Social Structure*, Seattle, 1972.

'Clanship among the Chinese', in *The Chinese Repository*, Vol. iv No 9, 1836.

COHEN, Myron L., 'Developmental Process in the Chinese Domestic Group', in Maurice FREEDMAN (ed.), *Family and Kinship in Chinese Society*, Stanford, 1970.

COHEN, Myron L., *House United, House Divided: the Chinese Family in Taiwan*, New York and London, 1976.

COUGHLIN, Richard J., *Double Identity: the Chinese in Modern Thailand*, Hong Kong, 1960.
COUGHLIN, Richard J., 'Population Controls in China', in Edward SZCZEPANIK (ed.), *Symposium on Economic and Social Problems of the Far East*, Hong Kong, 1962.
COULING, Samuel, *The Encyclopaedia Sinica*, Shanghai, 1917.
CREEL, H. G., *The Birth of China: a Study of the Formative Period of Chinese Civilization*, New York, 1937.
CROLL, Elisabeth, *The Women's Movement in China: a Selection of Readings, 1949–1973*, London, 1974.
DAVIN, Delia, 'Women in the Countryside of China', in Margery WOLF and Roxane WITKE (eds.), *Women in Chinese Society*, Stanford, 1975.
DE BARY, W. T. et al (eds.), *Sources of Chinese Tradition*, New York, 1960.
DE GROOT, J.J. M., *The Religious System of China*, 6 vols., Leyden, 1892–1910.
DE GROOT, J.J. M., *Sectarianism and Religious Persecution in China: a Page in the History of Religions*, 2 vols., Amsterdam, 1903–4.
DOOLITTLE, Rev. Justus, *Social Life of the Chinese*, 2 vols., New York, 1865.
DORÉ, Henry, (translated by M. Kennelly), *Researches into Chinese Superstitions*, Shanghai, 1914.
DOUGLAS, Robert K., *Society in China*, London, 1894.
EBERHARD, Wolfram, 'Chinese Genealogies as a Source for the Study of Chinese Society', in Spencer J. PALMER (ed.), *Studies in Asian Genealogy*, Utah, 1972.
Far Eastern Economic Review, Hong Kong, 28th April, 1966.
FEI Hsiao-tung, *Peasant Life in China: a Field Study of Country Life in the Yangtze Valley*, London, 1939.
FEI Hsiao-tung and CHANG Chih-i, *Earthbound China: a Study of Rural Economy in Yunnan*, London, 1949.
FENG Han-yi, *The Chinese Kinship System*, Cambridge, Mass., (Reprinted from the *Harvard Journal of Asiatic Studies*, vol. 2 No 2, July 1937), 1948.
FREEBERNE, Michael, 'Birth Control in China', in Francis HARPER (ed.), *This is China: Analyses of Mainland Trends and Events*, Hong Kong, 1965.
FREEDMAN, Maurice, *Lineage Organization in Southeastern China*, London, 1958.
FREEDMAN, Maurice, *Chinese Lineage and Society: Fukien and Kwangtung*, London, 1966.
FREEDMAN, Maurice, *Rites and Duties, or Chinese Marriage: an Inaugural Lecture*, London School of Economics and Political Science, London, 1967.
FRIED, Morton H., 'The Family in China: the People's Republic', in R. N. ASHEN (ed.), *The Family: its Functions and Destiny*, New York, 1959.
FRIED, Morton H., *Fabric of Chinese Society: a Study of the Social Life of a Chinese County Seat*, New York, (Reprint of 1953 edition), 1969.
FUKUTAKE, Tadashi, *Asian Rural Society: China, India, Japan*, Seattle and London, 1967.
GALLIN, Bernard, *Hsin Hsing, Taiwan: a Chinese Village in Change*, California, 1966.
GAMBLE, Sidney D., *Ting Hsien: a North China Rural Community*, Stanford, 1968.

GEDDES, W. R., *Peasant Life in Communist China*, New York, 1963.

GERNET, Jacques, *Daily Life in China on the Eve of the Mongol Invasion 1250–1276*, (translated by H. M. Wright), London, 1962.

GITTINGS, John, *A Chinese View of China*, London, 1973.

GRAHAM, D. C., *Folk Religion in Southwest China*, Washington, 1961.

GRANET, Marcel, (translated by Maurice Freedman), *The Religion of the Chinese People*, Oxford, 1975.

GRAY, J. H., *China: a History of the Laws, Manners, and Customs of the People*, 2 vols., London, 1878.

GROVES, Robert G., 'The Origins of Two Market Towns in the New Territories', in Marjorie TOPLEY (ed.), *Aspects of Social Organization in the New Territories*, Hong Kong Branch of the Royal Asiatic Society, 1965.

HAYES, J. W., 'The Pattern of Life in the New Territories in 1898', *Journal of the Hong Kong Branch of the Royal Asiatic Society*, vol. 2, 1962.

HO Ping-ti, *Studies on the Population of China, 1368–1953*, Cambridge, Mass., 1959.

HSIA Ching-lin et al (trans.), *The Civil Code of the Republic of China*, Books IV and V, Shanghai, 1931.

HSIAO Kung-chuan, *Rural China: Imperial Control in the Nineteenth Century*, Seattle, 1961.

HSU, Francis L. K., *Under the Ancestors' Shadow: Kinship, Personality and Social Mobility in China*, Stanford, 1971.

HU Hsien Chin, *The Common Descent Group in China and its Functions*, New York, 1948.

HUMANA, Charles and WANG Wu, *The Ying-Yang: the Chinese Way of Love*, London, 1971.

HUMMEL, Arthur W. (ed.), *Eminent Chinese of the Ch'ing Period (1644–1912)*, Washington, 1943.

JAMIESON, G., *Chinese Family and Commercial Law*, Shanghai, 1921.

JORDAN, D. K., *Gods, Ghosts, and Ancestors: the Folk Religion of a Taiwanese Village*, California, 1972.

KRONE, Rev. Mr., 'A Notice of the Sanon District', *Transactions of the China Branch of the Royal Asiatic Society*, vol. VI, 1859, reprinted in *Journal of the Hong Kong Branch of the Royal Asiatic Society*, vol. VII, 1967.

KULP, Daniel H., *Country Life in South China: the Sociology of Familism*, New York, 1925.

LANG, Olga, *Chinese Family and Society*, New Haven, 1946.

LAU, D. C., *Mencius*, London, 1970.

LEAGUE OF NATIONS, *Commission of Enquiry into Traffic in Women and Children in the East: Report to the Council*, Geneva, 1933.

LEONG, Y. K. and TAO L. K., *Village and Town Life in China*, London, 1915.

LEVY, Howard S., *Chinese Footbinding: the History of a Curious Erotic Custom*, Tokyo, 1966.

LEVY, Marion J., *The Family Revolution in Modern China*, New York, 1949.

LIN Yueh-hwa, *The Golden Wing: a Sociological Study of Chinese Familism*, London, 1948.

LIN Yutang, *My Country and My People*, London, 1936.

LIU Wang Hui-chen, *The Traditional Chinese Clan Rules*, New York, 1959.

MAO Tse-Tung, *Report of an Investigation into the Peasant Movement in Hunan*, English translation, Peking, 1953.

Marriage Law of the People's Republic of China, English translation, Peking, 1950.

MEIJER, M. J., *Marriage Law and Policy in the Chinese People's Republic*, Hong Kong, 1971.

MORGAN, W. P., *Triad Societies in Hong Kong*, Hong Kong, 1960.

MYERS, Ramon H., *The Chinese Peasant Economy: Agricultural Development in Hopei and Shantung, 1890–1949*, Cambridge, Mass., 1970.

MYRDAL, Jan, *Report from a Chinese Village*, London, 1965.

McALEAVY, Henry, *The Modern History of China*, London, 1968.

NELSON, H. G. H., 'Ancestor Worship and Burial Practices', in Arthur P. WOLF (ed.), *Religion and Ritual in Chinese Society*, Stanford, 1974.

ORLEANS, Leo A., *Every Fifth Child: the Population of China*, London, 1972.

OSGOOD, Cornelius, *Village Life in Old China: a Community Study of Kao Yao, Yünnan*, New York, 1963.

OSGOOD, Cornelius, *The Chinese: a Study of a Hong Kong Community*, 3 vols., Arizona, 1975.

O'SULLIVAN, Sue, *The Moon for Dinner: Changing Relations . . . Women in China*, London, 1975.

PARISH, William L., 'Socialism and the Chinese Peasant Family', *Journal of Asian Studies*, vol. 34 No 3, 1975.

PASTERNAK, Burton, *Kinship and Community in Two Chinese Villages*, Stanford, 1972.

POTTER, Jack M., *Capitalism and the Chinese Peasant: Social and Economic Change in a Hong Kong Village*, California, 1968.

PRUITT, Ida, *A Daughter of Han: the Autobiography of a Chinese Working Woman*, Stanford (reprint of 1945 edition), 1967.

PURCELL, Victor, *The Boxer Uprising: a Background Study*, Cambridge, 1963.

PURCELL, Victor, *The Chinese in Southeast Asia*, Second edition, London, 1965.

ROPER, Myra, 'The Family', in J. A. JOHNSTONE and Maslyn WILLIAMS (eds.), *The New China*, Sydney, 1971.

SALAFF, Janet Weitzner, 'Urban Communities After the Cultural Revolution', in John Wilson LEWIS (ed.), *The City in Communist China*, Stanford, 1971.

SIDEL, Ruth, *Women and Child Care in China: a Firsthand Report*, New York, 1972.

SMITH, Arthur H., *Village Life in China*, New York, 1899.

SMITH, Arthur H., *Chinese Characteristics*, London and Edinburgh, 1900.

South China Morning Post, Hong Kong, 19th April, 1965.

SPENCER, R. F. and BARRETT, S. A., 'Notes on a Bachelor House in the South China Area', *American Anthropologist*, vol. 50, 1948.

STENT, G. Carter, 'Chinese Eunuchs', *Journal of the North China Branch of the Royal Asiatic Society*, new series, vol. XI, Shanghai, 1877.

TOPLEY, Marjorie, 'Marriage Resistance in Rural Kwangtung', in Margery WOLF and Roxane WITKE (eds.), *Women in Chinese Society*, Stanford, 1975.

TOPLEY, Marjorie and HAYES, James, 'Notes on Some Vegetarian Halls in Hong Kong belonging to the Sect of Hsien-T'ien Tao: (The Way of Former

Heaven)', *Journal of the Hong Kong Branch of the Royal Asiatic Society*, vol. 8, 1968, pp. 135–48.

TWITCHETT, Denis, 'The Fan Clan's Charitable Estate', in David S. NIVISON and Arthur F. WRIGHT (eds.), *Confucianism in Action*, Stanford, 1959

VAN DER VALK, M. H., *Conservatism in Modern Chinese Family Law*, Leiden, 1956.

VAUGHAN, J. D., *The Manners and Customs of the Chinese of the Straits Settlements*, Singapore, (Reprint of 1879 edition), 1971.

VOGEL, Ezra F., *Canton Under Communism: Programs and Politics in a Provincial Capital, 1949–1968*, New York and London, 1971.

WANG Yeh-chien, *Land Taxation in Imperial China, 1750–1911*, Cambridge, Mass., 1973.

WARD, J. S. M., *The Hung Society or the Society of Heaven and Earth*, vol. 3, London, 1926.

WATSON, James L., *Emigration and the Chinese Lineage: the Mans in Hong Kong and London*, California, 1975.

WATT, John R., *The District Magistrate in Late Imperial China*, New York and London, 1972.

WERNER, E. T. C., *A Dictionary of Chinese Mythology*, Shanghai, 1932.

WICKBERG, Edgar, *The Chinese in Philippine Life: 1850–1898*, New Haven and London, 1965.

WILLMOTT, William E., *The Chinese in Cambodia*, Vancouver, 1967.

WILSON, Dick, *A Quarter of Mankind: an Anatomy of China Today*, London, 1966.

WOLF, Arthur P., 'Chinese Kinship and Mourning Dress', in Maurice FREEDMAN (ed.), *Family and Kinship in Chinese Society*, Stanford, 1970.

WOLF, Margery, *Women and the Family in Rural Taiwan*, Stanford, 1972.

WRIGHT, Mary Clabaugh, *The Last Stand of Chinese Conservatism: the Tung-Chih Restoration, 1862–1874*, Stanford, 1962.

WU, Silas H. L., 'The Experience of My Native Village', *Eastern Horizon*, vol. XIII No 4, 1974.

YANG, C. K., *The Chinese Family in the Communist Revolution*, Cambridge, Mass., 1959a.

YANG C. K., *A Chinese Village in Early Communist Transition*, Cambridge, Mass., 1959b.

YANG C. K., *Religion in Chinese Society*, California, 1961.

YANG, Martin C., *A Chinese Village: Taitou, Shantung Province*, London, 1948.

Glossary

ai-ren	愛人	darling
ba-zi	八字	'Eight characters'
bai	拜	to worship, to pay respects to
bao-jia	保甲	household control system
chui-fu	贅夫	married-in son-in-law
feng-shui	風水	geomancy
guo-jia	國家	state, nation
jia	家	family, household, lineage
li	里	Chinese mile (approx. $\frac{1}{3}$ English mile).
mu	畝	Chinese acre (approx. $\frac{1}{6}$ English acre).
pai	牌	ten households
qi-lao	耆老	elders
qing-ming	清明	grave-sweeping festival
sui	歲	year of age
tu-di gong	土地公	earth god
wu-fu	五服	five mourning grades
wu-lun	五倫	five human relationships
xiao	孝	filial piety

xiang-yue	鄉約	popular lecture system, popular leadership
yang-yin	陰陽	the opposite and complementary dualistic principles of the universe

Index

241

$ 7.18